Ships from Scotland to America, 1628–1828

Volume II

Ships
from SCOTLAND
to AMERICA

1628 – 1828

Volume II

By David Dobson

INTRODUCTION

One of the more difficult tasks encountered by genealogists in North America is establishing how and when their immigrant ancestor arrived from Scotland. This is particularly true for the seventeenth and eighteenth centuries, periods for which records are far from comprehensive. If the vessel that the immigrant sailed on can be identified, then the ports of arrival and departure may also follow, and in turn this may indicate the locality from which the immigrant originated, thus narrowing the search. Information pertaining to the ship that brought one's immigrant ancestor is an essential feature of a comprehensive family history. What kind of ship was it? What was its tonnage? Where was it registered? Who was the skipper? All these questions are of interest to the family historian and are partially answered in this book.

This book is designed as an aid to the family historian by identifying ships from Scotland to what is now the United States and Canada for the period 1628 to 1828. Evidence of direct shipping between Scotland and the Americas can be established as early as 1600 when the <u>Grace of God</u> returned to Dundee from Newfoundland. Links with the West Indies date from 1611 and the voyage of the <u>Janet of Leith,</u> and with the Chesapeake with the <u>Golden Lion of Dundee</u>, which sailed via London in 1626. All these, however, are believed to have been trading voyages. Emigration to America from Scotland began with the attempt by Sir William Alexander to settle Nova Scotia in the 1620s. It is believed that although there were a number of vessels which could be described as "emigrant ships", the majority of emigrants during our period went on cargo ships. There seems to have been a continuous trickle of emigrants across the Atlantic from the mid-seventeenth century onwards, to staff the tobacco warehouses in Virginia, for example, or as felons banished to the Plantations. Economic forces generally determined emigrant routes from Scotland: ships sailed to Georgia and the Carolinas for cotton and rice, to the Chesapeake for tobacco, to the Canadian Maritimes for timber, and carried with them innumerable emigrants, many as indentured servants. The significant rise in emigration from Great Britain, especially from the Scottish Highlands that occurred in the decade before the American Revolution resulted in the British government maintaining a Register of Emigrants. This, albeit incomplete, covers the period 1773 to 1774 and identifies who emigrated, how they emigrated, why they emigrated, when they emigrated, plus their ports of departure and destination. The only similar large-scale emigration occurred in the years after the end of the Napoleonic Wars when thousands of Scots sailed from the Clyde bound for Canada. Apart from these two periods the picture is far from complete. Passenger arrival records in the United States and Canada are sometimes vague and identify the port of origin as "Scotland" or "North Britain". This is particularly true in the case of emigrant ships that sailed from remote bays or inlets in the Highlands and Islands where the catchment area for the emigrants was highly localized. By the early nineteenth century Greenock had become the major port for emigrants from all over Scotland, but ships did sail from other ports, and their passengers are highly likely to have come from their immediate neighborhoods.

This source book, Volume II of Ships from Scotland to America, 1628-1828 is largely based on the Exchequer records in the National Archives of Scotland which identify vessels, skippers, and cargoes on which duties or bounties were charged or given. Such records are almost complete from 1742, and though designed to record income raised for the government through customs duties they do on occasion refer to passengers.

Ships from Scotland carried a range of manufactured goods such as linen, woollens, clothing, leatherware, metal wares, tools, food and drink. When there was surplus capacity shipowners offered passage to emigrants, sometimes leaving the Clyde in ballast and arriving in North America with passengers, having picked up groups of emigrants from islands off the Scottish coast or Ireland.

Records, particularly newspapers, on both sides of the Atlantic have been scrutinised for reference to vessels arriving and departing from Scotland to augment the aforementioned Exchequer data.

David Dobsor
St Andrews, Scotlanc

REFERENCES

Archives

GAR	=	Glasgow Archives
NAS	=	National Archives of Scotland, Edinburgh
	AC =	Admiralty Court
	CE =	Customs and Excise
	CS =	Court of Session
	E =	Exchequer
	GD =	Gifts and Deposits
	NRAS=	Nat.Reg.Archives Scotland
	RD =	Register of Deeds
	RH =	Register House
NLS	=	National Library of Scotland, Edinburgh
NCSA	=	North Carolina State Archives, Raleigh
PAPEI	=	Public Archives, Prince Edward Island
PRO	=	Public Record Office, London
	CO =	Colonial Office
	HO =	Home Office
	PCC =	Prerogative Court of Canterbury
SCA	=	South Carolina Archives, Columbia
USNA	=	United States National Archives, Washington

Publications

ANY	=	Biographical Register of the St Andrews Society of New York
CCA	=	Clyde Commercial Advertiser, series
CG	=	City Gazette, series
CM	=	Caledonian Mercury, series
CNSHS	=	Collections of the Nova Scotia Historical Society
DCr	=	Dumfries Courier, series
DW	=	Dundee Advertiser, series
DWJ	=	Dumfries Weekly Journal, series
EA	=	Edinburgh Advertiser, series

EEC	=	Edinburgh Evening Courant, series
GA	=	Glasgow Advertiser, series
GaGaz	=	Georgia Gazette, series
GC	=	Glasgow Chronicle, series
GCr	=	Glasgow Courier, series
GJ	=	Glasgow Journal, series
GkAdv	=	Greenock Advertiser, series
GM	=	Glasgow Mercury, series
GSP	=	Glasgow Saturday Post, series
IJ	=	Inverness Journal, series
JCTP	=	Journal of the Commissioners for Trade and the Plantations, series
JLQ	=	Journal of a Lady of Quality, [Yale, 1922]
MdGaz	=	Maryland Gazette, series
MG	=	Montreal Gazette, series
NCGaz	=	NC Gazette & Wilmington Weekly Postboy, series
NE Wkly	=	New England Weekly Journal, series
pa	=	Passenger Arrivals at New York 1820-1829
PAB	=	Passenger arrivals at Boston 1715-1769
PAP	=	Passenger Arrivals at Philadelphia 1800-1819
PaGaz	=	Pennsylvania Gazette, series
PEIGaz	=	Prince Edward Island Gazette, series
PennMerc	=	Pennsylvania Mercury, series
PhilaGaz	=	Philadelphia Gazette, series
PIG	=	Philadelphia Independent Gazette, series
QueGaz	=	Quebec Gazette, series
RG	=	Royal Gazette, Charlottetown, series
RPCS	=	Register of the Privy Council of Scotland, series
SCGaz	=	South Carolina Gazette, series
SHR	=	Scottish Historical Review, series
SM	=	Scots Magazine, series
TGSI	=	Transactions of the Gaelic Society of Inverness, series
Times	=	Times, London, series
VG	=	Virginia Gazette, series
WSGA	=	Wilmington Sentinel & General Advertiser, series

LIST OF ABBREVIATIONS

FLA	=	Florida
GA	=	Georgia
GK	=	Greenock
MD	=	Maryland
NB	=	New Brunswick
NE	=	New England
NC	=	North Carolina
NFD	=	Newfoundland
NO	=	New Orleans
NS	=	Nova Scotia
NY	=	New York
PA	=	Pennsylvania
PEI	=	Prince Edward Island
QUE	=	Quebec
SC	=	South Carolina
VA	=	Virginia

SHIPS FROM SCOTLAND TO AMERICA
1628-1828
Volume II

ABIGAIL, a schooner, Hugh Davidson, arr. in New London *with passengers* fr. Scotland in 1820. [pa]

ACADIA OF GREENOCK, John Marshall, fr. GK to Quebec in Apr. 1784; fr. GK to Quebec in Apr. 1785 [E504.15.39/40/41]

ACHILLES, a snow, John Wilson, fr. GK to SC in Sept. 1762; arr. in Charleston on 23 Nov. 1762 fr. Glasgow. [E504.15.11][SCGaz#1480]

ACHSAH, a brig, John Hayward, arr. in MD in Sept. 1756 fr. Glasgow. [MdGaz#593]

ACORN, James Patterson, fr. GK to Montreal in Sept. 1791. [E504.15.60]

ACTIVE OF GLASGOW, William Miller, fr. Port Glasgow to Port North Potomac, MD, in June 1773; fr. Port Glasgow to VA in Mar.1774; Thomas Foster, fr. Port Glasgow to VA in Aug. 1774; Capt. Crawford, fr. the Clyde to Halifax on 23 Apr. 1780; Gavin Hamilton, fr. GK to Charleston, SC, in Aug. 1781. [E504.28.22/23/33][GM#III/134]

ACTIVE OF GREENOCK, 149 tons, Robert Reid, fr. GK *with 6 passengers* to Quebec in Apr. 1796. [E504.15.71/72]

ACTIVE OF GREENOCK, 102 tons, Archibald Kelso, fr. GK to NFD in Feb. 1796. [E504.15.71]

ACTIVE, a brigantine, John Stirling, fr. Fort William *with 36 passengers* to Pictou, NS, in June 1807. [E504.12.7]

ACTIVE OF GLASGOW, 209 tons, R. Barr, fr. GK to Montreal 22 March 1816. [E504.15.111]

ACTIVE, J. Walker, fr. Tobermory, Mull, *with 200 passengers* to Canada 27 July 1827. [E504.35.2]

ADAMENT OF DUXBURY, 157 tons, B.Smith jr., fr. GK *with 23 passengers* to Boston, 14 May 1812. [E504.15.96]

ADELPHI OF ABERDEEN, 122 tons, James Garie, fr. Aberdeen *with 2 passengers* to Philadelphia, 31 May 1816. [E504.1.26]

ADEONA OF QUEBEC, 142 tons, William Maxwell, fr. GK to Quebec 11 March 1815; fr. Dumfries *with 111 passengers* to NB on 8 Apr. 1820. [E504.15.107][Times#10916]

ADVANCE OF BOSTON, Cap. Boden, fr Dundee to Boston Nov.1822. [E504.11.22]

ADVENTURE OF GLASGOW, Thomas Rodgers, fr. GK to Boston in Apr. 1747; Walter Pollock, fr. GK to Boston in Jan. 1748; Archibald Yuill, arr. in Charleston, SC, in Sep. 1758 fr. Glasgow; fr. Port Glasgow *with passengers* to Boston in Aug. 1759. [E504.15.2] [GJ#931] [SCGaz.15.9.1758]

ADVENTURE OF ABERDEEN, 90 tons, James Melvin, fr. Aberdeen to VA in Mar. 1750. [E504.1.3]

ADVENTURE OF LONDON, Andrew Smith, fr. Kirkcaldy via Loch Erribol to Cape Fear, NC *with 200 passengers* in July 1772. [E504.20.8]

ADVENTURE, Capt. Lumsden, arr. in Charleston during Apr. 1787 fr. Leith. [Phila.Gaz.#242]

ADVENTURE, Robert Moore, fr. GK *with passengers* to Wilmington, NC, in June 1775; Robert Hunter, fr. GK to Quebec/Montreal in Apr. 1793. [CM#8356/8363] [GCr#249]

ADVENTURE, Capt. Rogers, fr. the Highlands to Quebec in 1793. [GC:27.7.1793]

ADVENTURE OF AYR, fr. Ayr to Quebec in Sept. 1802. [GkAd#81]

ADVENTURE OF TRURO, 246 tons, John Hardie, fr. GK to Halifax 9 Sep.1818; fr GK to Halifax 29 Feb.1820. [E504.15.122/128]

ADVICE OF GLASGOW, Alexander Wardrop, fr. GK to VA in Mar. 1750; fr. GK to VA in Oct. 1751 [E504.15.5]

AEOLUS, John Rankine, fr. Port Glasgow to MD in Sept. 1774; Thomas Edgar, fr Port Glasgow to St Augustine March 1779. [E504.28.23/30]

AGGY OF GREENOCK, Robert Shedden, fr GK to Halifax Apr.1778; Capt. Brown, fr. the Clyde to Savannah, GA, and Charleston, SC, on 30 May 1780, captured and taken to NC. [E504.15.29][SM#42.561][GM#III/174]

AGINCOURT OF LEITH, J. Matheson, fr. Leith *with 214 passengers* to Quebec 14 May 1817, arr., via Halifax, in Quebec on 8 Aug. 1817. [E504.22.77][MG]

AGNES, Robert Duthie, fr. GK to VA in May 1758, [E504.15.8]

AGNES, a brigantine, James Borland, fr. GK to Charleston, SC, and NY on 29 Aug. 1780; fr. the Clyde to NY on 16 Sept. 1781

when captured by the privateer <u>Franklyn</u> and taken to Boston.
[GM#III.224; IV.13] [SM#43.165]

AGNES, Capt. Allan, fr. the Clyde to MD on 10 Oct. 1786.
[GM#IX.459.334]

AGNES, a brigantine, John Anderson, fr. GK *with passengers* to
Wilmington, NC, in July 1792. [GC:21.6.1792] [GCr#128]

AGNES OF GREENOCK, 105 tons, Robert McEwan, fr. GK to
NFD 20 Sep.1815. [E504.15.109]

AGNES, Cap. Barclay, fr Dundee to NO Oct.1820. [E504.11.21]

AIMWELL, David Robertson, fr. GK to Savannah, Georgia, in
Nov. 1802. [GkAd#88]

AIMWELL OF ABERDEEN, 239 tons, John Morrison, fr.
Aberdeen *with 27 passengers* to Halifax, NS, 15 July 1816; fr.
Aberdeen *with 32 passengers* to Halifax, 27 Feb. 1817; fr
Aberdeen to Halifax 17 Feb.1819; fr Aberdeen to Miramachi 1
Aug.1820. [E504.1.26/28]

AIRDGOUR OF FORT WILLIAM, a brig, William Lillie, fr.
Fort William *with 108 passengers* to Quebec and Montreal on
28 June 1817, arr. at Quebec on 6 Aug. 1817. [E504.12.6][MG]

AJAX OF GREENOCK, a 100 ton brigantine, John Wallace,
fr.GK to NC in Mar.1772, *with passengers* ; fr GK to NC
Oct.1772; Robert Cunningham, to Wilmington 15 Jan. 1774;
arr. in NC fr. Glasgow on 23 May 1774; fr. the Clyde to NC in
June 1775; John Hunter, fr. the Clyde to Charleston on 15
Aug. 1780; fr. the Clyde to Charleston in 1781 when
captured; Thomas Workman, fr. GK to NFD in Apr. 1782,
[E504.15.21/23/36][GJ:12.3.1772; 10.3.1774][SM#43.109]
[NC Gaz#223] [NCSA.S8.112] [CM#7783/8362]
[GM#III.262]

AJAX OF GREENOCK, 402 tons, David Weir, fr. GK to
Philadelphia on 16 Apr. 1791. [E504.15.59]

AJAX OF ABERDEEN, 233 tons, William Mackie, fr Aberdeen to
Miramachi 9 May 1818. [E504.1.27]

ALBANY, a 160 ton snow, John Crawford, fr. Port Glasgow *with*
passengers to the James River, VA, in Apr. 1759; fr. Port
Glasgow *with passengers* to the James River, VA, on 20 Jan.
1760 [GJ#920/959]

ALBION OF GREENOCK, 244 tons, William Ambrose, fr. GK to
Quebec in Apr. 1787; fr. GK to NY on 11 Aug. 1788; John
Simmons, fr. GK to the Rappahannock, VA on 2 July 1789; fr.

GK *with passengers* to Rappahannock, VA on 5 July 1790; fr.
GK to VA 14 July 1791. [E504.15.44/ 45/48/51/56/60]
[GM#XII.596.174; 601.214; XIII.651.199]

ALBION R. Kidd, fr. Dundee *with 39 passengers* to Quebec in
1809. [QueGaz.6.7.1809]

ALBION OF WORKINGTON, 185 tons, John Faraqher, fr. GK to
Quebec 25 July 1814. [E504.15.105]

ALBION, a brig, fr. Aberdeen *with 3 cabin passengers* to Halifax,
NS, in July 1829. [GD316/15]

ALBUERA OF ABERDEEN, a 177 ton brigantine, Alex Jamieson,
fr. Inverness to Pictou, NS, 3 Sept. 1812. [E504.17.8]

ALERY OF ST JOHN, 183 tons, W. Dawson, fr. GK to St John,
NB, 11 Sep.1819. [E504.15.125]

ALERT, James McDougal, arr. in NY *with passengers* fr. Alloa on
22 Sep. 1821. [USNA#m237]

ALEXANDER OF INVERKEITHING, Thomas Thomson, to
Carolina 1686. [GD172.1585]

ALEXANDER, a snow, James Hamilton, arr. in MD during Feb.
1757 fr. Leith; Laurence Brown, fr. Leith to Philadelphia on 11
Sept. 1764, [E504.22.11] [MdGaz#615]

ALEXANDER OF GREENOCK, 300 tons, John Kirkwood, fr GK
to PEI, Mar.1772; William Kerr, fr. Port Glasgow to VA in
Jan. 1773; fr GK to Harbourgrace, NFD, Sept.1773; John
Dean, fr GK to NY Oct.1778; John McLean, fr. Glasgow *with*
passengers to NY or Charleston, SC, in Oct. 1780; fr. Port
Glasgow to NY in Feb. 1781; fr. the Clyde to NY on 20 May
1781. [E504.28.21//15.23][GM#III/336; IV/24/166]

ALEXANDER, Alexander Alexander, fr GK to St Augustine
Dec.1778. [E504.15.30]

ALEXANDER OF LEITH, Alexander Ritchie, fr. GK to
Philadelphia in Apr. 1785; fr. GK to Philadelphia in Oct. 1785;
fr. GK *with passengers* to Philadelphia on 9 June 1786; fr. GK
to Philadelphia in Apr. 1787; arr. in Philadelphia in June 1787
fr. Glasgow; fr. GK to Philadelphia in Apr. 1787.
[E504.15.41/42/43/44/45][Phila.Gaz.#256]
[GM#IX.424.49/190] [PennMerc#93]

ALEXANDER, Capt. Durham, fr. the Clyde to NFD on 10 Apr.
1802. [CM#12573]

ALEXANDER OF ST JOHNS, a 214 ton snow, William Swinall,
fr. GK to Halifax 10 Aug.1814. [E504.15.105]

ALEXANDER OF STRANRAER, 227 tons, William Hamilton, fr. GK to NFD 15 Aug.1814. [E504.15.105]

ALEXANDER OF GREENOCK, 247 tons, Robert McKie, fr. GK *with 8 passengers* to Philadelphia 25 March 1816; fr. GK *with 60 passengers* to N.B. 19 Apr.1817. [E504.15.111/115]

ALEXANDER, T. Henry, fr. Leith *with 44 passengers* to Quebec 28 May 1817, arr. there on 22 July 1817. [E504.22.77][MG]

ALEXANDER, John Young, fr. GK 21 Apr. 1820 *with 95 passengers* to Quebec, arr. there on 5 Jun 1820. [QueGaz, 8.6.1820]

ALEXANDER OF GLASGOW, 169 tons, R. Lyon, fr GK *with 181 passengers* to P.E.I. 15 Apr.1820. [E504.15.129] [PEIGaz.22.5.1820]

ALEXANDER OF DUNDEE, 249 tons, William Martin, fr. GK to New Orleans 20 Dec.1817; James Farmer, fr Dundee to NO 18 Nov.1818; fr Dundee to NO 19 Dec.1821 [E504.15.114; E504.11.21/22]

ALEXANDER OF ABERDEEN, 142 tons, John Hogg, fr Aberdeen to Halifax 25 Feb.1819. [E504.1.28]

ALEXANDER AND ANNE OF ABERDEEN, 130 tons, John Clark, fr. Aberdeen to VA in July 1749; fr. Aberdeen to MD in Aug. 1750. [E504.1.3]

ALEXANDRIA, John Crawford, fr. GK to VA in Jan. 1762; John Montgomery, fr. GK to VA in July 1763; fr. GK to Quebec in Mar. 1765; John Heasty, fr. GK to Quebec in Mar. 1767; fr. GK to Boston in Sept. 1767; fr. the Clyde to Casco Bay, NE, 26 Apr. 1768. [GC#57/67] [E504.15.10/11/12/14]

ALEXIS OF GREENOCK, a 154 ton brig, Dugald Livingstone, fr. the Clyde to Wilmington, NC, in July 1802; William Allison, fr. GK to Wilmington in Oct. 1804; arr. in Wilmington on 31 Dec. 1804 fr. GK; fr. GK *with passengers* to Wilmington 22 July 1805; fr. GK to Montreal in Apr. 1806; arr. at Wilmington fr. the Clyde 1807; James Bell, fr. GK to NFD 5 July 1815; fr. GK to N.O. 28 Aug.1816; William Cook, fr GK to Pictou 30 May 1821. [GkAdv#46/:26.2.1805;24.7.1805][GC:25.9.1804;24.2.1807] [E504.15.77108//113]

ALEXY OF ST JOHN, NB, Wm Dawson, fr GK to St John 26 June 1821; Thomas Corfield, fr GK to St John 21 Mar.1822. [E504.15.136/139]

ALFRED, Capt. Ferrie, fr. the Clyde to MD in Dec. 1791.
[GCr#48]

ALFRED OF ABERDEEN, 127 tons, Andrew Deary, fr Aberdeen to Pictou 7 Apr.1818. [E504.1.27]

ALLAN GRANT OF GLASGOW, 382 tons, fr GK to NO 20 Mar.1821. [E504.15.135]

ALLIANCE, a snow, George Fortune, arr. in MD during June 1753 fr. Leith. [MdGaz#422]

ALLISON OF ST JOHNS, 136 tons, John McLeod, fr. GK to St Johns, 7 Apr. 1814. [NAS.E504.15.104]

ALMIE OF GREENOCK, a 191 ton brigantine, William Hastie, fr. GK to NY in July 1784; arr. in Charleston, SC, in Feb. 1785 fr. Glasgow, *340 passengers disembarked, while 40 continued on* to NY; Daniel H. Braine, fr. GK to NY 6 Aug. 1791; fr. GK *with passengers* to NY in Jan. 1792; fr. GK *with passengers* to NY in July 1792; Michael Cutter, fr. GK *with passengers* to NY in Jan. 1793.[E504.15.39/60] [PaGaz#2857][GCr#42/119/195]

ALNOMAIK, US ship, Capt. Wheelwright, fr. GK to Charleston, SC, in 1797. [CM#11780, 4.3.1797]

ALPHA OF GREENOCK, 157 tons, Daniel McCormack, fr. GK to NFD 4 Oct.1814. [E504.15.105]

ALPHEUS OF PETERHEAD, 204 tons, Alexander Duncan, fr. Aberdeen to Quebec 18 Mar. 1817. [E504.1.26]

ALMIA, John Williamson, fr. GK to Charleston, SC, in Oct. 1785. [E504.15.42]

AMERICA, Capt. Ritchie, fr. Glasgow to America, seized by the Spanish between the Capes of VA in May 1741 [CM~3324]

AMERICA OF AYR/GLASGOW, 130 tons, John Francis, fr. GK to MD in Aug. 1747, arr. in MD during Jan. 1748; fr. GK to VA in Feb. 1749; James Gammell, fr. GK to Potomac, MD, in Apr. 1759; fr. GK via Guadaloupe to SC in Dec. 1759; Robert Park, fr. GK to VA in July 1767; fr. GK to Boston in Mar. 1769; George Ruddiman, fr. Ayr to Boston in July 1769; Robert Park, fr. Ayr to VA in May 1770; fr. Ayr via Dieppe to VA in Jan. 1771; James Moody, fr. GK *with 102 passengers* to Cape Fear 15 July 1773, arr. in Port Brunswick, NC.; John Dean, fr GK to Wilmington, NC, Oct.1774, arr. in Port Brunswick on 12 Dec. 1774, [GJ#925][NCSA.S8.112]

[E504.15.2/4/9/14/16/22/24;4.5][GJ:8.7.1773;19.8.1773]
[MdGaz#141] [Port Brunswick Ship Register, fo.2]

AMERICA OF GREENOCK, 400 tons, James McAlester, fr. GK
to Charleston and Wilmington *with passengers* on 20 Aug.
1784; ? William Jamieson, bound fr. GK to Charleston,
wrecked off Charleston 27 Dec. 1784.
[CM: 9.8.1784] [E504.15.39][SCGaz&Pub.Adv.#142]

AMERICA OF WILMINGTON, 108 tons, Erskine Brown, to
Wilmington, NC, on 19 May 1786; fr. GK to Wilmington on
26 Nov. 1787, [GM: 18.5.1786] [E504.15.46]

AMERICAN PLANTER OF LEITH, a 100 ton brigantine,
Robert Alexander, arr. in Charleston, SC, in July 1772, fr.
Leith; fr. Leith to Charleston in Feb. 1773.
[SCGaz:5.7.1772][EA#19/14][E504.22.18]

AMETHYST, 138 tons, Alexander Greig, fr. Aberdeen *with 36
passengers* to Halifax, NS, 6 Mar. 1816. [E504.1.26]

AMHERST, Alexander Marquish, fr. GK to NY in Apr. 1761.
[E504.15.10]

AMITY OF AYR, 70 tons, William Reid, fr. GK to VA in Sept.
1748; fr. GK to VA in June 1753. [E504.15.2/6]

AMITY OF GLASGOW, James Weir, fr. Port Glasgow to
Philadelphia in Dec. 1743, [E504.28.1]

AMITY OF GREENOCK, a 94 ton brigantine, Neil Campbell, fr.
GK *with passengers* to Wilmington, NC, in Aug. 1789, arr. in
Port Brunswick, NC, on 27 Oct. 1789. [NCSA.S8.112]
[E504.15.52][GM#XII.602.223]

AMITY OF NEWCASTLE, 261 tons, Richard Peacock, fr. Ayr to
Quebec 26 Aug. 1806. [E504.4.11]

AMITY, fr GK to Montreal May 1828. [E504.15.164]

AMPHION OF HARTFORD, 297 tons, Levi Goodrick, fr. GK to
Philadelphia 15 Oct.1817. [E504.15.118]

AMPHREDITE OF HALIFAX, David Izett, fr. GK *with 14
passengers* to Pictou in Apr. 1811. [E504.15.92]

AMSTERDAM PACKET OF NEW YORK, a 177 ton US ship,
Archibald McLachlan, fr. GK *with 76 passengers* to NY in
July 1795; Charles Henderson, fr. GK *with 100 passengers* to
NY in Mar. 1796; fr. GK *with 80 passengers* to NY in Aug.
1796; Henry Green, fr. GK *with passengers* to NY 3 Feb.
1802; fr. the Clyde to NY on 20 Apr. 1802. [E504.15.69/71/73]
[GkAd#16][CM#12578]

ANDERSON OF GLASGOW, 160 tons, John Campbell, fr. GK to VA, in July 1748; Hugh Campbell, fr. GK to VA in Apr. 1753; fr. GK to VA in Apr. 1755; fr. GK to VA in Dec. 1755; fr. GK *with passengers* to VA in Apr. 1756; fr. GK to VA in Jan. 1757; fr. GK to VA in July 1757 [E504.15.2/6/7/8][GJ#759]

ANDROMACHE OF WINDSOR, US brig, Capt. Piercy, fr. GK *with passengers* to NY in June 1802; Elias Fornham, fr Leith to NY 22 Oct.1819, arr. in NY on 7 Feb. 1820 *with 4 passengers* fr. Leith, later in Norfolk, VA. [GkAd#40][USNA.M237/1][pa][E504.22.87]

ANDREW OF PORT GLASGOW, Cap.Brown, fr GK to Boston 22 June 1822. [E504.15.140]

ANECRON OF NEWCASTLE, William Wilson, fr. Tobermory *with 176 passengers* to Pictou and Quebec 5 May 1817. [E504.35.2]

ANGELIE, arr. in SC *with servants* fr. Leith in 1735. [SCGaz,13.12.1735]

ANGERONA OF ST JOHN, NB, 133 tons, George Barclay, fr Aberdeen to St John 17 Mar.1819; fr Aberdeen to St John, NB, 12 July 1820; Alexander Whyte, fr Aberdeen to St John 27 Aug.1822. [E504.1.28/29]

ANN OF EDINBURGH, Robert Bryson, fr. Leith to Boston before 1738. [AC9/1417]

ANNE OF ABERDEEN, 100 tons, John Thomson, fr. Aberdeen to VA in May 1749; fr. Aberdeen to VA in Mar. 1750. [E504.1.3]

ANNE OF GLASGOW, a galley, John Smith, fr. Port Glasgow to MD in May 1743, [E504.28.1]

ANN, a galley, William Wilson, fr. Leith to Carolina by 1750. [AC9/1745]

ANN OF GREENOCK, Thomas Young, fr. GK to Boston in Apr. 1750. [E504.15.4]

ANN OF GREENOCK, 161 tons, Hugh Smith, fr. GK to NFD in Apr. 1787; fr. GK to NFD 2 May 1788; John Barclay, fr. GK to NFD 4 July 1789; fr. GK to NFD 6 Apr. 1791 [E504.15.45/48/51/59]

ANN OF GLASGOW, a snow, 100 tons, John Orr, fr. GK to VA in July 1752; fr. GK via Rotterdam to MD in Mar. 1753; James Cuthbert, fr. GK to MD in June 1754; Neil Jamieson, fr. GK to MD in May 1755; fr. GK to SC in Dec. 1755; Neil Jamieson, arr. in Charleston, SC, in Apr. 1756 fr. Glasgow;

Dugald Shannon, fr. GK to MD in June 1757; fr. GK to SC in
Feb. 1758; fr. GK to SC in Sept. 1759, arr. in Charleston on 19
Nov. 1759; John Wilson, fr. GK to VA in Mar. 1762; fr GK to
VA July 1772. [SCGaz#1140]
[E504.15.5/6/7/8/9/10/21][PRO.CO5.509]

ANN, Andrew Neilson, fr. GK to St Augustine, Fla., on 14 June
1780, [E504.15.33][GM#III.198]

ANN, James Laurie, fr. GK to Bermuda in Oct. 1784; arr. in
Philadelphia during Dec. 1784 fr. Glasgow. [E504.15.39]
[Pa.Merc#18]

ANN, a sloop, Joshua Aitkin, fr. Leith to Boston on 7 May 1764;
arr. in Boston on 20 Aug. 1764 *with 3 passengers* fr. Scotland.
[PAB][E504.22.11]

ANN, William McGill, fr. Port Glasgow to VA in Mar. 1773; fr.
Port Glasgow to VA in July 1774; James Leggat, fr Port
Glasgow to Halifax July 1777; Alexander Huie, fr. Port
Glasgow *with passengers* to the Potomac River, MD and VA,
in Mar. 1786; James Steel, fr. the Clyde to VA on 4 Aug.
1786; fr. Port Glasgow *with passengers* to the James River,
VA, in Feb. 1787; Hugh Douglas, fr. the Clyde to Halifax in
Mar. 1785; fr. the Clyde to VA on 4 Apr. 1789.
[E504.28.21/23/28][E504.15.40] [GM#IX.422.40; 449.254;
468.415; XII.589.118]

ANN OF GREENOCK, John Wilson, fr. GK to NFD July 1777;
Robert Wilson, fr. GK to NFD in July 1782; Alexander
Sutherland, fr. GK to NFD in Apr. 1783; fr. GK to Halifax, NS,
in Apr. 1784; fr. GK to NFD in Mar. 1785; William
Robertson, fr. GK to Halifax on 17 Mar. 1786; Capt. Barclay,
fr. the Clyde to NFD on 1 Aug. 1789; James Law, fr. GK to
Halifax in Apr. 1796 [GM#IX.428.94; XII.606.254]
[E504.15.28/36/37/39/40/42/71/72]

ANN, a brigantine, Hamilton Foster, fr. Port Glasgow *with
passengers* to Norfolk, VA, on 12 Oct. 1786.
[GM#IX.457.320]

ANN, Capt. Lusk, arr. in Norfolk on 24 Oct. 1787 fr. Glasgow.
[Phila.Gaz.#296]

ANN, 300 tons, John Johnston, fr. GK *with passengers* to Quebec
on 12 Apr. 1789. [E504.15.51][GM#XII.578.32/70; 590/126]

ANN, Capt. Crawford, fr. the Clyde to Charleston, SC, in Dec. 1791, was wrecked off the coast of Stranraer, Galloway, in 1791. [CM:#10980; 16.1.1792] [GCr#48/51]

ANN, 250 tons, Andrew Davidson, fr. GK *with passengers* to NY in Aug. 1792.[GCr#136]

ANN, 250 tons, Capt. James Mackie, fr. Queensferry *with passengers* to Wilmington, NC, in Apr. 1804; arr. there before Oct. 1804. [CM#12880][GC:16.10.1804]

ANN OF NEW YORK, John O Yuill, fr. GK *with 6 passengers* to NY 29 Dec. 1810, [E504.15.90]

ANN OF NORTH SHIELDS, James Todd, 295 tons, fr. Stornaway *with 76 passengers* to Pictou, NS, 10 May 1811. [E504.33.3]

ANN OF ST JOHN, NB, 331 tons, George Razer, fr. GK *with 6 passengers* to St Andrews, NB, 21 Sept. 1811; John W. Smith, fr. GK to St John 10 July 1817. [E504.15.93/117]

ANN OF BO'NESS, John Henry, fr GK to Quebec 20 July 1821. [E504.15.137]

ANNE OF GREENOCK, 112 tons, Alexander McVicar, fr. GK to NFD 4 Apr.1818; fr. GK to NFD 19 Sep.1818; fr GK to NFD 6 Feb.1819. [E504.15.119/121/124]

ANN OF QUEBEC, John Ashford, fr GK to Quebec 25 Mar.1822; arr. in New York 11 Feb.1823 *with passengers* fr. Glasgow Michael Barney, arr. in New York 10 Jan.1825 *with passengers* fr. GK. [USNA.M237][E504.15.139]

ANN AND ELIZABETH OF GLASGOW, Alexander Muir, fr GK to VA 5 Apr.1721. [EEC#365]

ANN ELIZABETH OF ABERDEEN, 140 tons, John Gray, fr. Aberdeen to Quebec, 22 Mar. 1816; Benjamin Morgan, fr. Aberdeen via Dundee to NY, 1 Mar. 1817. [E504.1.26; E504.11.20]

ANN GRANT OF GREENOCK, Johnston Hume, fr GK to St John, NB, 22 Aug.1821; fr GK to St John 23 Feb.1822; fr GK to Miramachi Mar.1828; fr GK to Miramachi July 1828. [E504.15.137/139/163/165]

ANNA ROBERTSON OF STORNAWAY, John Mackenzie, fr. Stornaway to Cape Breton 12 Apr. 1825. [E504.33.4]

ANNA MARIA, Robert Kerr, fr. GK to NFD in Mar. 1783. [E504.15.37]

ANNA NANCY OF MONTROSE, 120 tons, arr. in Charleston, SC, 12 July 1736 via London, [PRO.CO5.509]

ANNABELLA OF SALTCOATS, Robert Hamilton, fr. GK to VA in June 1745; fr. Port Glasgow to VA in Apr. 1746; Thomas Knox, fr. GK to VA in Feb. 1747; fr. GK to VA in Oct. 1747; fr. GK to VA, 1748. [AC11/231]; fr. GK to NC in Feb. 1749; fr. Port Glasgow to VA in June 1750; fr. GK to VA in June 1751 [E504.15.2/3/4/5; E504.28.2/4]

ANNABELLA OF CAMPBELTOWN, Dougal Stewart, fr. Campbeltown to St John's, on 27 July 1770. [E504.8.4]

ANNIE, Robert Pollock, fr GK to VA July 1772; fr. Port Glasgow to Port Rappahannock, VA, in Oct. 1773; Patrick Bogle, fr Port Glasgow to Halifax Feb.1777; Archibald Hastie, fr. the Clyde to NFD on 19 May 1780; fr. GK to NFD in Apr. 1782. [E504.15.21/35: 28.25/27][GM#III/166]

ANNISQUAM OF NEW YORK, 245 tons, J. Watkinson, fr. GK *with 26 passengers* to NY 5 Feb.1816. [E504.15.111]

ANSLIE OF LEITH, 80 tons, John Hay, arr. in Charleston, SC, on 27 Nov. 1735 fr. Leith via Madeira, [PRO.CO5.509]

ANTELOPE, Cabel Chapin, from the Clyde to the Chesapeake 21 Oct.1693. [GA.Shawfield MS1/42-43]

ANTELOPE, a snow, Robert Hasty, fr. GK to VA in May 1760; arr. in Annapolis, MD, during July 1761 fr. Glasgow [E504.15.9][MdGaz#845]

APOLLO OF BOSTON/WISCASSET, 111 tons, John F. Hilton, fr. GK *with 60 passengers* to Boston in May 1795; fr. GK to Boston in May 1796. [E504.15.68/72]

APTHORP, Francis Bouchier, fr. GK to Quebec in Feb. 1764; fr. GK to Quebec in July 1764; fr. GK via Belfast to Quebec in Feb.1765 [E504.15.12]

ARAB OF NEW BEDFORD, 351 tons, Warren Daland, fr. GK *with 30 passengers* to New York, 8 June 1812. [E504.15.96]

ARCHIBALD OF SALTCOATS, Robert Crawford, fr. Port Glasgow to Boston in June 1747. [E504.28.3]

ARCHIBALD OF GREENOCK, Robert Watson, fr. GK to Barbados and SC in Sept. 1749. [E504.15.4]

ARDENT OF GREENOCK, 241 tons, James Gunson, fr. GK to NY in Oct. 1805; Thomas Kendall, fr. GK to Quebec 9 Aug.1814; Charles McGlashan, fr. GK *with 5 passengers* to Quebec 15 Mar.1815. [E504.15.74/105/107]

ARGO OF BOSTON, John Bryant, fr Orkney to Boston 12
    Sept.1770. [E504.26.5]

ARGUS, a brig, fr. Dumfries to P.E.I. in 1820. [DWJ: 30.5.1820]

ARGYLE OF GLASGOW, a snow, John McCunn, at Elizabeth
    City in June 1742 [deposition]; Robert Bennet, fr. GK to VA
    in Mar. 1763; Alexander McKirdy, fr. GK to VA in Apr. 1768;
    Capt. Wilson, fr. Leith to Boston in Apr.1771[E504.15.11/15]
    [PaGaz:18.6.1742][GC#67][EA#15/182] [GJ:14.7.1768]

ARGYLL OF CAMPBELTOWN, a snow, Robert Fairy, fr.
    Campbeltown to Philadelphia and return via Belfast in 1754.
    [AC20.2.14]

ARGYLE OF ST JOHNS, 139 tons, Robert Wyllie, fr. GK to NB
    on 20 June 1791. [E504.15.59]

ARGYLL, John Denniston, fr. GK to Quebec and Montreal in Apr.
    1793. [GCr#249]

ARIADNE, fr GK to Quebec Apr.1828; fr GK *with passengers* to
    Quebec Aug.1828. [E504.15.164/165]

ARIEL OF GLASGOW, a brig, Duncan Ritchie, arr. in Savannah
    March 1822 *with 1 passenger* from Glasgow; arr. in NY 20
    July 1822 *with passengers* fr. Dundee; Walter Boag, arr. in NY
    22 Feb.1823 *with passengers* fr. GK; Peter Smith, arr. in NY
    21 May 1829 *with passengers* fr. Port Glasgow.
    [USNA.M575/16; M237]

ARISTIDES OF NEWBURYPORT, 266 tons, George Carter, fr.
    GK *with 39 passengers*to NY 21 May 1817. [E504.15.116]

ASIA OF NEW YORK, 256 tons, John Walter, fr. GK to N.O. 13
    Aug.1817. [E504.15.117]

ATLANTIC, William Fleck, fr. GK to Charleston, SC, in Oct.
    1781. [E504.15.33/35]

ATLANTIC, Alexander Lawson, arr. in NY 19 March 1827 *with
    passengers* fr. Dundee; arr. in NY on 27 Aug.1827 *with
    passengers* fr. Dundee; arr. in NY on 17 May 1828 *with
    passengers* fr. Dundee; arr. in NY 7 Nov.1828 *with
    passengers* fr. Dundee. [USNA.ms237]

ATLAS OF ABERDEEN, a 154 ton brig, James Sanders, fr.
    Aberdeen 5 May 1818, arr. in Quebec on 26 June 1817.
    [MG][E504.1.27]

AUGUSTA OF GREENOCK, Cap. Bruce, fr GK to Quebec 9
    Sep.1822. [E504.15.140]

AUGUSTINA OF SAVANNAH, 255 tons, N. H. McLavige, fr.
GK *with 20 passengers* to NY 12 June 1815. [E504.15.108]

AUGUSTINA, fr. Dumfries to NB in 1817. [DWJ:18.3.1817]

AURORA OF GLASGOW, a 150 ton brigantine, Archibald
Fisher, fr. GK to SC in Oct. 1766; arr. in Charleston on 5 Dec.
1766; William Craig, fr. GK to SC in 5 Nov. 1767, arr. in
Charleston on 6 Feb. 1768; Andrew Lyon, fr GK to MD July
1772; John Johnston, fr GK to Montreal/Quebec Feb.1779;
James Blain, fr. GK *with passengers* NY on 8 June 1781; arr.
in Philadelphia *with passengers* fr. GK on 15 Sept. 1801,
[PAP] [GM#IV.72/198] [SCGaz:5.12.1766/6.2.1768]
[E504.15.13/15/21/30/33] [NLS.ms.Acc10220]

AURORA OF GLASGOW, fr. Fort William *with passengers* to
NS in Sept. 1802; Capt. Thomas Boyd, fr. GK *with passengers*
to Quebec and Montreal on 5 May 1803. [GkAd#74]
[CM#12887]

AURORA OF ABERDEEN, 126 ton brig, Peter Milne, fr.
Aberdeen *with 9 passengers* to NY, 3 July 1816. arr. in NY
with passengers fr. Scotland in 1820; arr. in NY 21 Dec. 1820
with passengers fr. Aberdeen; George Courage, arr. in NY 18
Sept.1821 *with passengers* fr. Aberdeen; Alex Lawson, fr
Aberdeen to Charleston 5 Mar.1822. [E504.1.26/29] [pa]
[USNA.m237]

AURORA OF HALIFAX, 162 tons, Alexander Caven, fr. GK to
Halifax 26 July 1817. [E504.15.117]

AURORA OF GREENOCK, 229 tons, Archibald Craig, fr. GK
with 30 passengers to Quebec 11 July 1811; James McDonald,
fr. GK *with 12 passengers* to Quebec, 2 Apr. 1812; Alan
McKinlay, fr. GK *with 15 passengers* to Charleston 18
Sep.1815; fr GK to Savannah 20 Dec.1817.
[E504.15.93/96/109/114]

AVON OF LEITH, 160 tons, Alexander Urquhart, fr. Leith to
Charleston, SC, on 16 Dec. 1766; arr. in Charleston on 26 Feb.
1767 fr. Leith; fr. Leith to Charleston on 21 Sept. 1767; arr. in
Charleston on 5 Dec. 1767 fr. Leith; to Charleston *with*
passengers in Aug. 1768; arr. in Charleston on 12 Nov.1768
fr. Leith; arr. in Charleston in July 1769; fr. Leith to Charleston
on 14 Dec. 1769; arr. in Charleston in Feb. 1770 fr. Leith; to
Charleston in Aug. 1770, arivedthereinNov. 1770.
[EA#12/328;14/21] [CM#7168/7384]

[SCGaz:24.2.1767/5.12.1767/6.7.1769/27.2.1770/22.11.1770]
[E504.22.13/14/15/16] [SCGaz#1646/1728]
AVON OF GREENOCK, 132 tons, Johnstone Howie, fr. GK *with 5 passengers* to NFD, 15 Apr. 1814. [E504.15.104]
AYRSHIRE OF MONTREAL, 337 tons, James McDonald, fr. GK to Quebec 7 March 1814. [E504.15.103]
BACHELOR OF LEITH, 160 tons, Alexander Urquhart, fr. Leith to Charleston, SC, 9 Nov. 1765; arr. in Charleston on 8 Mar. 1766 fr. Leith;; Alex. Ramage, fr. Bo'ness/Leith to Charleston in Feb. 1772; John Smith, fr. Leith to Cape Fear, NC, in Jan.1774, arr. at Port Brunswick, NC, on 20 Apr. 1774, [E504.22.12/17/18;6/9][EA#17/36] [EA:3.1.1774][NCSA.S8.112][PRO.CO5.511]
BACHELOR OF DYSART, 160 tons, George Barclay, fr. Leith to Edenton, NC, in Jan. 1775, [E504.22.19]
BALCLUTHA, fr GK to NFD Oct.1828. [E504.15.166]
BALFOUR, Andrew Balfour, arr. in Charleston, SC, during Mar. 1742 fr. Leith. [SCGaz#407]
BALTIC OF SALEM, schooner, Edward Allen, fr Orkney to Salem 22 May 1764. [E504.26.4]
BALTIMORE OF GREENOCK, Alexander Campbell, fr. GK to MD in June 1744, fr. GK to MD in May 1745; Thomas Wilson, fr. GK to VA in Dec. 1760 [E504.15.1/2/10; E504.28.2]
BALTIMORE OF LONDON, Andrew Crookshanks, fr. GK to VA in Nov. 1758; Alexander Marquis, fr. GK to VA in Feb. 1758; fr. GK to VA in Feb. 1760 [E504.15.8/9]
BARBADOS OF GREENOCK, 153 tons, Andrew McNeil, fr. GK to VA, 9 July 1787, [E504.15.45]
BARON ARDROSSAN OF SALTCOATS, 137 tons, Archibald Craig, fr. GK to NFD 7 Oct.1817. [E504.15.117]
BARRINGTON, Daniel McKirdy, fr. GK to NY in Aug. 1761; Capt. Butcher, fr. GK *with passengers* to Charleston, SC, on 15 Aug. 1780, [E504.15.10] [GM#III.199, 262]
BARRINGTON, Capt. Stewart, fr. Leith to NY in June 1796, was lost off Cape Sable in Oct. 1796. [CM#11671/11754]
BASSETERRE OF GREENOCK, 123 tons, William McMoreland, fr. GK to Miramachi 15 Aug.1817. [E504.15.117]

BATAVIER, William Jamieson, fr. GK to NY in Feb. 1783.
[E504.15.36]

BATCHELOR, 75 tons, John Ewing, fr. GK to Rhode Island in
Mar. 1754; fr. GK to Boston in July 1755; James Barnhill, fr.
GK to VA in Jan. 1758 [E504.15.6/7/8]

BATCHELOR OF DYSART, George Barclay, fr. Leith *with
passengers* to Edenton, NC, on 10 Jan. 1775. [CM#8289,
19.12.1774]

BATTY, Alexander Marquis, fr. Port Glasgow to America in Mar.
1776. [E504.28.24]

BEDFORD, a snow, Robert Brown, fr. Port Glasgow *with
passengers* to the James River, VA, June 1756; William Clark,
fr. GK to VA in Apr. 1757; fr. GK to VA in Feb. 1758; fr. the
Clyde to VA in 1758, captured by the French but ransomed for
500 guineas; William Clark, fr. GK to the James River, VA, in
Jan. 1759. [E504.15.8/9][GJ#775/811][SM#20.389]
[GAr#TD132/62]

BEE OF GREENOCK, 143 tons, Abram Russell, fr GK to Boston
Feb.1772; fr GK to Boston Aug.1772; fr GK to Boston
Mar.1773; John Baird fr GK to NY Jan.1779; William Eustes,
fr. GK to Charleston, SC, 14 July 1790. [E504.15.21/22/30/56]

BEGGARS BENISON, a brigantine, Patrick Muir, arr. in
Charleston, SC, in Jan. 1770 fr. Irvine; fr. Irvine to Georgia in
Dec. 1772. [SCGaz:20.1.1770][E504.18.8]

BELL OF GLASGOW, 90 tons, David Peter, fr. GK to VA in Feb.
1760; fr. GK to SC in Jan. 1762; arr. in Charleston on 8 May
1762 fr. Glasgow; arr. in Charleston on 13 Dec. 1762 fr.
Glasgow; Capt. Weir, fr. the Clyde to NC in 1768; James
Moody, fr. Port Glasgow to VA in Feb. 1773; fr. Port Glasgow
to York River, VA, in Aug. 1773; fr. Port Glasgow to the York
River, VA, in Feb.1774. [GJ:2.6.1768]
[E504.15.9.10;28.21/22/23][PRO.CO5.509]
[SCGaz#1451/1483]

BELL, John Crawford, fr. GK to St Johns, NFD, in Aug. 1782;
John Cathcart, fr. GK to NFD in Aug. 1784. [E504.15.36/39]

BELLA, Captain Gordon, from Dumfries to VA 1748, captured by
the Spanish and taken to Havannah. [SM.10.651]

BELLE SAVAGE OF BOSTON, 316 tons, Henry Russell, fr. GK
to Boston 30 Nov.1815; fr. GK to NY 10 Sept.1816; fr GK to
NY 25 Aug.1821. [E504.15.109/113/137]

BELMONT, Edward Paul, fr GK to NY June 1828, arr.there 30
Aug.1828 *with passengers*.[E504.15.164] [USNA.m237]

BEN LOMOND OF ST JOHN, NEW BRUNSWICK, 345 tons,
Peter Black, fr. GK to New Brunswick 17 Sept.1816; fr. GK
with 5 passengers to St John 28 Mar.1817; fr. GK to St John,
25 Aug.1817; Laurence Thomson, fr. GK to St John 18
Mar.1818; Henry Rattray, fr GK to Quebec 11 May 1820; arr.
in NY 3 Apr. 1823 *with passengers* fr. GK. [USNA.M237]
[E504.15.113/115/117/119/129]

BERRY CASTLE OF LONDON, 206 tons, David Pratt, fr
Aberdeen to Miramachi 28 Apr.1818.[E504.1.27]

BESS, fr. Tobermory *with 80 passengers* to PEI in 1803. [Telford's
Survey of the Coasts and Central Highlands of Scotland, 2nd
appx., 1803]

BETHIA OF IRVINE, John Craig, fr. GK to Boston in Aug. 1748.
[E504.15.2]

BETHIA, Francis Ellis/Blair?, fr. GK to Charleston, SC, on 4 Oct.
1786 [E504.15.43][GM#IX.457.326]

BETSY, Capt. Hastie, fr. VA to Glasgow in 1758, captured by the
French and taken to Morlaix; Robert Hastie, fr. GK to VA in
Dec. 1763 [SM#20.331] [E504.15.12]

BETSEY, a snow, Hugh Maxwell, fr. GK *with passengers* to the
Rappahannock River, VA, in Apr. 1759. [GJ#920]

BETSY, a brigantine, Duncan Campbell, arr. in Charleston, SC, on
22 Nov. 1763 fr. Glasgow. [SCGaz#1532]

BETSY, William Anderson, fr. GK to VA in Mar. 1758; Andrew
Anderson, fr. GK to VA in Feb. 1759; James Orr, fr. GK to
VA in June 1759; fr. GK to VA in July 1760; James Scott, fr.
GK to VA in July 1761; fr. GK to VA in Feb. 1762; Robert
Hastie, fr. GK to VA in May 1763; fr. GK to VA in Aug. 1764;
James Cuthbert, fr. GK to VA in Nov. 1764; Robert Hunter, fr.
GK to VA in Jan. 1765; John Gillies, fr. GK *with passengers*
to the James River, VA, 31 July 1767; James Leitch, fr. GK to
St Augustine and NY in Apr. 1777; John Marquis, fr. GK to
VA in Nov. 1794; fr. GK to VA in Aug. 1796.
[NLS.ms.Acc.10220] [E504.15.9/10/11/12/27/67/73][GC#19]

BETSY OF MARBLEHEAD, Samuel Forster, fr Orkney to
Marblehead 9 Aug.1764. [E504.26.4]

BETSY, James Scott, fr. GK to VA in Apr.1760; fr. GK to VA in

June 1762; Robert Hunter, fr. GK to VA in Mar.1764; James Scott, fr. the Clyde for VA 26 Apr.1768; Thomas Muir, fr. GK to Halifax in Jan.1777; William Fleck, fr. GK to NY in Dec.1779; fr. GK to NY on 20 Jan.1781; fr. the Clyde to NY in 1781 when captured and taken to Salem. [GC#67] [E504.15.9/11/12/27/28/33][SM#43.614][GM#IV/30]

BETSY, Capt. Warden, fr. VA to the Clyde in 1760, captured by the French and taken to France. [SM#22.334]

BETSY OF GREENOCK, a brig, John Smith, fr. GK to Boston in Feb. 1768; arr. in Boston on 12 May 1768 *with 2 passengers* fr. GK; James Leitch, fr. GK to Halifax, NS, in May 1756. [PAB] [E504.15.15/26]

BETSY OF LONDON, James Pearson, fr. Kirkcaldy to Boston in Feb. 1772. [E504.20.8]

BETSEY OF GREENOCK, John Dunnet, fr. Port Glasgow to VA in Aug. 1772; John Ramsay, fr. Port Glasgow to VA in July 1774; William Colville, fr GK to Salem Sep.1775; William Drummond, fr GK to St John's, NFD, Aug.1778; James Leitch, fr GK to NY Mar.1779 [E504.28.21/23; E504.15.25/29/30]

BETSEY, Capt. Patrick, arr. in NC fr. the Clyde in 1786. [GM: 7.9.1786]

BETSY OF ROTHESAY, 84 ton brig, Daniel Duncan, arr. in Port Brunswick, NC, on 28 Aug. 1789 fr. GK, [NCSA.S8.112]

BETSEY OF GREENOCK, a 188 ton brigantine, James Leitch, fr GK to Quebec Mar.1778; fr GK to NFD May 1779; fr. GK *with passengers* to Halifax in May 1780; James Young, fr. GK to Halifax, NS, in Sept. 1783; Robert Hyndman, fr. GK to Halifax in Sept. 1783; fr. GK to Halifax in July 1784; fr. GK to NFD on 16 Mar. 1786; fr. GK *with passengers* to Halifax on 20 Sept. 1786; fr. GK to Halifax in Mar. 1787; Thomas Ferrie, fr. GK to VA on 13 Oct. 1787; Capt. McCunn, fr. the Clyde to VA on 31 Mar. 1789; fr. GK to VA in Aug. 1789; arr. in Norfolk, VA, on 25 Oct. 1789 fr. Glasgow; John McLean, fr. GK to Montreal in Apr. 1795. [PIG#1225] [E504.15.31/39/42/43/44/46/52/68][GM#III/117;#IX.429.94/310; XII.588.110]

BETSEY OF GREENOCK, a 120 ton brig, Robert Cross, fr. GK to NFD in Sept. 1789; George Philips, fr. GK to NFD 26 Mar. 1791; fr. GK to NFD 10 Oct. 1791; Capt. Cullen, fr. GK to NFD in Apr. 1792; Robert Lyon, fr. GK to NFD in June 1795;

fr. GK to NFD in May 1796. [E504.15.52/58/60/68/72]
[GCr#114]

BETSY OF GREENOCK, 91 tons, John McKie, fr. GK to NFD in
Sept. 1796. [E504.15.73]

BETSY, a 220 ton US ship, John Savage, fr. GK to Wiscasset 27
Sept. 1790. [NAS,E504.15.56]

BETSEY, 200 tons, George Caithness, fr. Leith to Montreal on 1
May 1797. [CM#11801]

BETSEY OF HULL, 219 tons, Thomas Lowdon, fr. GK to
Montreal in Apr. 1806. [E504.15.77]

BETSEY OF DUNDEE, Peter Nucator, fr. Dundee to NY *with
passengers* on 19 Sept. 1807.[DW#263/269]

BETSY OF AYR, John Bell, fr. Ayr to Falmouth, NE, in Apr.
1769. [E504.4.5]

BETSY, Ronald McAllister, arr. in Bath, NC, on 3 July 1785, fr.
Glasgow; fr. GK to NC 9 May 1786. [NCSA/S8/112]
[GM:4.5.1786][E504.15.43]

BETSY, a brig, Peter Brown, fr. GK to the Potomac River, MD and
VA on 29 July 1786. *"NB the Betsey has good
accommodation for passengers and shipping to Baltimore or
the Eastern Shore have daily opportunities of craft going fr.
the Potomac to these places"* [E504.15.43][GM#IX.438.175;
448.246]

BETSEY OF BOSTON, William Shackleford, fr. GK *with 24
passengers* to Wilmington 26 July 1811. [E504.15.93]

BETSEY OF GREENOCK, Capt. Wither, fr Oban to Quebec 24
June 1820. [E504.25.3]

BETSY AND MOLLY, Thomas Calvert, fr. the Clyde to Norfolk,
VA, on 27 Oct. 1775. [AC7/72]

BETTY, a doggar, John Somerville, fr. the Clyde to NE in 1731.
[AC9/1425]

BETTY, a brigantine, master Robert Boyd, arr. in Charleston in
July 1733 fr. Glasgow. [SCGaz.14.7.1733]

BETTY, John Conochie, arr. in Charleston, SC, in May 1747 fr.
Leith. [SCGaz#686]

BETTY OF GLASGOW, 140 ton, John Gray, fr. Port Glasgow to
VA in Mar. 1743; fr. GK to VA in Mar. 1744; Robert Brown,
fr. GK to VA in Oct. 1744; Capt. Aitken, fr. the Isle of May to
VA in 1748, taken by the Spanish but escaped and arr. in NY
27 July 1748; Henry Scott, fr. GK to MD in June 1749;

Robert Warden, fr. GK to MD in July 1750; Robert Warden,
fr. GK to VA in July 1751; John Morison, fr. GK to MD in
July 1755; fr. GK to VA and MD in Sept. 1756; Robert Hastie,
fr. GK to MD in Nov. 1757; William Warden, fr. GK to MD in
Oct. 1759; Thomas McCunn, fr. GK to NC in Sept. 1762;
Duncan Campbell, fr. GK to SC in Aug. 1763.
[SM#10.651][E504.15.2/4/5/7/8/9/11; E504.28.1]

BETTY OF BOSTON, schooner, John Cathcart, fr Orkney o
Boston 14 November 1761. [E504.26.4]

BETTY OF LEITH, 80 ton snow, Angus McLarty, arr. in
Charleston, SC, on 5 Nov. 1767 fr. Glasgow, [PRO.CO5.511]

BETTY OF GREENOCK, a 182 ton snow, Angus McLarty fr.
Leith to VA 2 Apr. 1766; arr. in Charleston, SC, on 4 Nov.
1766 fr. Glasgow; fr. GK to SC in Sept. 1767; arr. in
Charleston on 17 Jan. 1768 *with passengers* fr. Glasgow; fr.
GK to Charleston, SC, in Sept. 1768; arr. in Charleston on 9
Dec. 1768 fr. Glasgow; arr. in Charleston during Sept. 1769 to
Cape Fear, NC, *with 120 passengers* fr. Leith; Robert McLarty,
fr. GK to VA in Jan. 1771; fr. GK to VA, 4 Aug.1788.
[SCA][E504.15.14/16/19/48;E504.22.12]
[SCGaz:3.11.1766/14.1.1768/9.12.1768/14.9.1769]

BETTY, James Malcolm, fr. GK for VA via Jamaica in Oct. 1763.
[E504.15.12]

BETTY OF GREENOCK, 75 ton brigantine, arr. in Charleston,
SC, on 24 Nov. 1763 fr. Glasgow; Duncan Campbell, arr. in
Charleston on 25 June 1764 via St Kitts; Robert McLarty, fr.
GK to VA in July 1771; William Kinnear, fr GK to Cape Fear,
NC, in Sept.1773; fr. Port Glasgow to Charleston in Oct. 1774.
[PRO.CO5.510/511]
[GJ:26.8.1773][E504.15.20/23;E504.28.22/24]

BETTY, James Gardner, fr Port Glasgow to NFD Sep.1776; John
McDougald, fr GK to NFD May 1778; fr GK to Quebec
Feb.1779. [E504.28.26;15.29/30]

BETTY AND JEAN OF LARNE, Hugh Shutter, fr. GK to NY in
May 1748. [E504.15.2]

BETTY AND MOLLY, a brigantine, Peter McIntosh, fr. GK to
Philadelphia in May 1784; arr. in Philadelphia during Aug.
1784 *with 70 servants and passengers* fr. GK.
[E504.15.39][Pa.Merc.#2]

BETTY CATHCART, William Chisholm, fr. GK to VA in Aug. 1789; arr. in Norfolk, VA, in Nov. 1789. [E504.15.52][PIG#1216]

BEVERLEY, Robert Montgomery, fr. GK to MD and VA in Jan. 1760; fr. GK to VA in Oct. 1761 [E504.15.9/10]

BINNING OF GLASGOW, 160 tons, Robert Steel, fr. GK to VA in Mar. 1751; fr. GK to VA in Nov. 1754; fr. GK to VA in May 1755; James Colquhoun, fr. GK to VA in May 1758; fr. GK to VA in Feb. 1761; fr. GK to VA in Oct. 1761; fr. GK to VA in June 1762 [E504.1.5/7/8/10/11]

BIRD OF GLASGOW, 255 tons, John Galt, fr. GK to NFD in July 1784; fr. GK to NFD in July 1785; fr. GK to NFD in July 1786; fr. GK to NFD 14 Aug. 1787, [E504.15.39/41/43/45]

BIRMINGHAM PACKET OF CHARLESTON, 266 tons, Robert Bowden, fr. GK *with 6 passengers* to Charleston, 8 Feb. 1806. [E504.15.77]

BLACK PRINCE OF PORTSMOUTH, 86 ton brigantine, Henry Fraser, arr. in Charleston, SC, on 18 Nov. 1763 fr. Dunbar. [SCGaz#1531][PRO.CO5.510]

BLACKBURN OF GLASGOW, 85 tons, Arthur Tran, fr. GK to VA in June 1751; Robert Graham, fr. GK to VA in Jan. 1752; fr. GK to VA in Apr. 1753; fr. GK via France to VA in Mar. 1754; James Ewing, fr. GK to VA and MD in May 1755; fr. GK *with passengers* to the Rappahannock River, VA, in Aug. 1756; fr. GK to VA in July 1757; fr. GK to VA in Apr. 1758; Edward Morrison, fr. GK to Boston in July 1767 [E504.15.5/6/7/8/13][GJ#779]

BLAKELY OF BOSTON, John Burril, fr Dundee to NO 8 Mar.1821, [E504.11.22]

BLANDFORD, James Cuthbert, fr. GK to VA in Jan. 1763; Andrew Troup, fr. Port Glasgow to VA in July 1772; Andrew Troop, fr GK to VA Mar.1773; fr. the Clyde to VA 12 Mar. 1786; fr. Port Glasgow *with passengers* to the James River, VA, on 4 Aug. 1786; arr. in Norfolk, VA, on 20 Oct. 1787 fr. Glasgow; fr. Port Glasgow *with passengers* to the James River, VA, on 14 Mar. 1789; fr. Port Glasgow *with passengers* to the James River, VA, in Aug. 1789; John Morris, fr. Port Glasgow *with passengers* to the James River, VA, in Mar. 1792; fr. Port Glasgow *with passengers* to the James River, VA, in Feb. 1793. [E504.15.11/22/28.21] [GCr#70/198] [GM#IX.428.86;

444.223; 449.254; XII.581.55; 586.94; 603.232]
[PhilaGaz#291/319]

BLESSING, a brigantine, John Gordon, arr. in Pennsylvania *with servants* fr. Aberdeen in May 1741. [PaGaz,28.5.1741]; John Gordon, arr. in Philadelphia *with Scotch servants* fr. Aberdeen in May 1742. [PaGaz:28.5.1742]

BOGLE OF GLASGOW, Andrew Sym, fr GK to VA May 1743; fr. Port Glasgow to VA in Apr. 1744; James Fleming, fr. Port Glasgow to VA in Mar. 1746; fr. Port Glasgow to VA in Aug. 1747; fr. Port Glasgow to VA in Jan. 1750, [E504.28.1/2/3/4; E504.15.1,2]

BOGLE, James Montgomery, fr. GK to MD in May 1755, arr. there in July 1755; William Dunlop, fr. GK to VA in Sept. 1759, [E504.15.7/9][SCGaz#534

BOGLE, George Hunter, fr. Port Glasgow *with passengers* to the Rappahannock and Potomac Rivers, VA, in July 1759; Robert Muir, fr. Port Glasgow to the Rappahannock River, VA, in Aug. 1773; fr GK to VA Mar.1774. [GJ#931] [E504.28.22; E504.15.23]

BOLIVAR, James McDonald, arr. in NY 19 May 1826 *with passengers* fr. Dundee. [USNA.M237]

BONNY LASS OF LIVINGSTONE, Francis Bouchier, fr. GK to Quebec in Mar. 1763; fr. GK to Quebec in Aug. 1763; Hugh Wilson, fr. GK to Quebec in Apr. 1764 [E504.15.11/12]

BOSTON PACKET OF GLASGOW, William Lang, fr. GK to Boston in Mar. 1751, [E504.15.5]

BOSTON, John Hunter, fr. GK to Boston in May 1784. [E504.15.39]

BOWLING OF GLASGOW, 190 tons, Alexander Campbell, fr. GK to VA in Apr. 1753; Robert Douglas, fr. GK to VA in Apr. 1755; fr. GK to NY in May 1756; arr. in NC fr. the Clyde in 1756; James Porteous, arr. in MD in July 1761 fr. Glasgow. [E504.15.6/7][MdGaz#847][GJ#809]

BOWLING, a barque, fr. Glasgow *with passengers* to Montreal on 5 Apr. 182. [GSP#712]

BOWMAN, 300 tons, Allan Stevenson, fr. Port Glasgow *with passengers* to the James River, VA, in Aug. 1768; Humphrey Taylor, fr. Port Glasgow to VA in Oct. 1772; James Paterson, fr. Port Glasgow *with passengers* to Baltimore, MD, in Feb. 1786; James Longmuir, fr. Port Glasgow *with passengers* to

the James River, VA, in Oct. 1786; arr. in Norfolk, VA, during
Dec. 1786 fr. Glasgow. [E504.28.21][GM#IX.418.7;
454.290][GC#80] [Phila.Gaz.#204]

BOYD OF GLASGOW, a 200 ton galley, James Main, fr. Port
Glasgow to VA in Mar. 1743; fr. Port Glasgow to VA in Mar.
1744; Ninian Bryce, fr. GK to VA in Dec. 1746; Patrick
Campbell, fr. GK to VA in Jan. 1749; fr. Port Glasgow to VA
in Mar. 1750; fr. GK to VA in Mar. 1751; fr. GK to VA in
Mar. 1754; John Douglas, fr. GK to VA in May 1755;
Andrew Lindsay, fr. Port Glasgow to Philadelphia in Sept.
1759; William Dunlop, fr. Leith to Philadelphia in Aug. 1763;
William Dunlop, fr. Leith to VA on 14 Apr. 1764; [GJ#936]
[E504.15.3/4/5/6/7; E504.22.10/11; E504.28.1/4]
[GAr.B10.15.5523]

BOYD, 200 tons, Robert Dunlop, fr. Port Glasgow to VA in Sept.
1772; fr. Port Glasgow to VA in Apr. 1773; fr. Port Glasgow to
the Rappahannock River, VA, in Oct. 1773; fr. Port Glasgow to
VA in July 1774; James Boyd, fr. Port Glasgow *with*
passengers to the Rappahannock River, VA, on 19 Mar. 1786;
fr. Port Glasgow *with passengers* on 20 Aug. 1786.
[E504.28.21/22/23/25][GM#IX.422.39; 428.94; 448.247;
451/270]

BOYD, fr. GK to Wilmington, NC, in Feb. 1802. [GkAd#4]

BOYD, Capt. Barclay, fr. GK to Boston 9 Mar. 1802. [GkAd#19]

BRANDY WINE MILLER, a US brig, George Fram, fr. GK *with*
passengers to NY 6 Feb. 1802; Robert Dunlevy, fr. Port
Glasgow *with passengers* to Philadelphia in Aug. 1802.
[GkAd#3/59]

BRAVE CORSICAN OF GREENOCK, 115 tons, John Wallace,
fr. GK to NC in Mar. 1770; fr. GK to Boston in Sept. 1771;
John Dean, fr. GK *with passengers* to Wilmington and Cape
Fear, NC, 10 Mar. 1774, arr. at Port Brunswick, NC, on 31
May 1774 [E504.15.18/20/23]
[GJ:22.3.1770; 24.3.1774] [NCSA.S8.112]

BRILLIANT OF NEW YORK, Richard Jeffery, fr Orkney to NY
19 Aug.1756. [E504.6.3]

BRILLIANT OF GLASGOW, Robert Bennet, fr. Port Glasgow to
VA in July 1772; fr. Port Glasgow to the James River, VA, in
Apr. 1774; Alexander McPherson, fr. Port Glasgow/Greenock

'with troops' to North America in Mar. 1776.
[E504.28.21/23/24]

BRILLIANT, Alexander Ferguson, fr. GK to NY in Dec. 1794.
[E504.15.67]

BRILLIANT, Hosea Winsor, arr. in NY 19 March 1828 *with passengers* fr. Port Glasgow. [USNA.M237]

BRISBANE OF PORT GLASGOW, 140 tons, James Hamilton, fr. Port Glasgow to VA and MD in 1727. [AC7/36/328]

BRISCOE, William McKenzie, fr. Port Glasgow to MD in Apr. 1773; Neil McMillan, fr. Port Glasgow to MD in July 1774. [E504.28.22/23]

BRISTOL OF NEW YORK, William Briggs, fr. GK to NY 3 Feb.1818. [E504.15.119]

BRITANNIA, schooner, Jonathan Freeman, fr Orkney to Boston 8 Aug.1761. [E504.26.3]

BRITANNIA OF GREENOCK, James Shaw, fr. GK to VA in Mar.1749; John Thomson, fr. GK to MD in May 1755; James Kerr, fr. GK to VA in Apr. 1767; fr GK to SC 5 Nov.1767, arr. in Charleston, SC, on 5 Feb.1768 fr. Glasgow; fr. GK to SC in Dec. 1768; arr. in Charleston on 3 Mar. 1769; John Denniston, fr. GK to SC in Sept. 1769; arr. in Charleston on 13 Nov.1769 [NLS.MS.Acc.10220][E504.15.4/7/14/16/17] [SCGaz#1746/1782:5.2.1768]

BRITANNIA OF GLASGOW, John Simpson, fr. GK to VA in Apr. 1752; fr. GK to VA and MD in Mar. 1753; Alexander Marquis, fr. GK *with passengers* to the James River in Dec. 1756 [E504.15.5/6/8][GJ#798]

BRITANNIA OF PHILADELPHIA, William Montgomery, fr. GK *with passengers* to NY and Philadelphia in Jan. 1768 [E504.15.15] [GC#46]

BRITANNIA OF WHITEHAVEN, John Watson, fr GK to MD Nov.1774. [E504.15.24]

BRITANNIA, Capt. Scott, fr. the Clyde *with passengers* to America in 1772. [GJ:13.8.1772]

BRITANNIA, a 250 ton brig, David Galbreath, fr. GK *with passengers* to VA on 26 Mar. 1786; David Hunter, fr. GK to NFD 16 Aug. 1790; Daniel Martin, fr. GK to NY in July 1791; fr. GK *with passengers -'excellent accommodation for cabin and steerage passengers who may depend on Capt. Martin's good usage'* to NY in July 1792; fr. GK *with passengers* to NY

in Feb. 1793. [GCr#122/205]
[E504.15.42/56/60][GM#IX.424.55; 430.102]

BRITANNIA, Capt. Hunter, fr. Port Glasgow *with passengers* to the James River, VA, on 25 July 1789; arr. in the Cermuda Hundred during Oct. 1789 fr. Glasgow; John Duncan, arr. in Port Brunswick, NC, on 10 Jan. 1790 fr. Port Glasgow; Adam Pearson, fr. Port Glasgow *with passengers* to the Potomac River in Feb.1792.[GM#XII.598.192][Phila.Gaz.#319] [GCr#46] [NCSA.S8.112]

BRITANNIA, Capt. Millar, fr. Port Glasgow to VA 3 Feb. 1802. [GkAd#36]

BRITANNIA OF MONTREAL, 172 tons, John Sterrat, fr. GK to Quebec and Montreal 26 Aug. 1813; fr. GK to Quebec 16 Apr. 1814. [E504.15.101/104]

BRITANNIA OF CARLISLE, 200 tons, Jonas Neilson, fr. GK to Quebec 2 Aug.1815. [E504.15.109]

BRITANNIA OF GREENOCK, 174 tons, Charles Spence, fr. GK *with 5 passengers* to Quebec 1 Aug.1816. [E504.15.113]

BRITANNIA OF SALTCOATS, 131 tons, William Barclay, fr. GK to Quebec 14 Apr.1819. [E504.15.124]

BRITANNIA OF DUMFRIES, a brig, Cap. McDowall,fr. Dumfries *with 31 passengers* to Miramachi, NB, in Apr.1820, arr. in P.E.I. on 22 May 1820. [DWJ:1.2.1820]

BRITISH KING, John Young, arr. in NY 4 Apr. 1827 *with passengers* fr. Dundee. [USNA.M237]

BRITISH QUEEN OF GREENOCK, 191 tons, John McCall, fr. GK to Wilmington, NC, in Jan. 1787, arr. in Port Brunswick, NC, on 19 Apr. 1787; John Denniston, fr. GK to Charleston on 14 June 1788; arr. in Charleston *with passengers* fr. Glasgow in Sept. 1788; fr. GK *with passengers* to Charleston in Feb. 1789; fr. GK *with 30 passengers* to Quebec 14 July 1790; fr. GK to Halifax, NS, in Sept. 1791. [PIG#896] [NCSA.S8.112] [E504.15.44/48/50/56/60] [GM.XII.580.47][GCr#3]

BRITISH QUEEN OF SOUTH SHIELDS, Charles Thompson, fr Leith to Halifax 17 June 1818. [E504.22.81]

BROADSTREET OF NEW YORK, Fleming Colgan, fr Orkney to NY 15 Sep.1760. [E504.26.3]

BROCK, J. McCulloch, arr. in NY 19 Aug.1823 *with passengers* fr. GK. [USNA.M237]

BROKE OF GREENOCK, 252 tons, Dougal Swan, fr. GK to NFD 7 Oct.1815; fr. GK to NFD 1 Aug.1817; Alexander Hardie, arr. in NY 16 July 1829 *with passengers* fr. GK. [USNA.M237][E504.15.109/117]

BROTHERS OF GREENOCK, 50 ton brig, Robert Arthur, arr. in Charleston, SC, on 12 Apr. 1727 fr. GK. [PRO.CO5.509]

BROTHERS, Capt. Aitken, fr. Scotland to VA in 1744, captured by the French and taken to NFD. [SM#6.440]

BROTHERS OF AYR, a snow, arr. at Port South Potomac, VA, via Dieppe, on 7 Aug. 1752; William Andrew, *with passengers* to the Potomac River in March 1756. [VG#94][GJ#761]

BROTHERS, Capt. Anderson, fr. GK to VA in Apr. 1759; Capt. Bogle, fr. Glasgow to Carolina in 1766, arr. in Charleston in Jan. 1767; Capt. Baillie, arr. in Carolina fr. the Clyde in 1770; Alexander Maclarty, fr GK to NY and St Augustine Mar.1779. [GJ: 922; 13.11.1766; 8.3.1770][SCGaz.12.1.1767] [E504.15.30]

BROTHERS OF GREENOCK, 120 ton brigantine, Patrick Bogle, arr. in Charleston, SC, on 31 Jan. 1763 fr. Glasgow; fr. GK to VA in Aug. 1763; James Bog, fr. GK to VA in Mar. 1765; arr. in Charleston in Jan. 1766, fr. Glasgow; Patrick Bogle, arr. in Charleston on 8 Jan. 1767 fr. Glasgow; Captain Baillie, arr. in Charleston in Jan. 1770 fr. Glasgow; Moses Crawford, fr. GK to Pensacola in June 1777; John Heastie, fr GK to Pensacola Oct.1778; James Crawford, fr GK to Halifax May 1779; Donald Hastie, fr. GK to St Johns, NFD in Mar. 1782; John Kerr, fr. GK to NFD in Mar. 1783; Capt. Longmuir, fr. the Clyde to VA on 7 Oct. 1786; John Wallace, fr. Port Glasgow *with passengers* to the Rappahannock River, VA, on 19 July 1789. [SCGaz:17.1.1766; 13.1.1770] [SCGaz#1640] [E504.15.11/12/30/31; 8.27/35/37] [GM#IX.457.326; XII.600.207; 604.238][PRO.CO5.509]

BROTHERS, a US ship, Capt. Withers, fr. Glasgow *with passengers* to Philadelphia in Aug. 1802, arr. there on 2 Oct. 1802. [GkAd#58][PAP]

BROTHERS OF GREENOCK, 196 tons, Archibald McNair, fr. GK to NFD 3 May 1814; fr. GK to NFD 20 June 1815; Alexander Shand, fr. GK to NFD 9 May 1816; Robert Kerr, fr. GK to Savannah 16 Apr.1819. [E504.15.104/108/112/124]

BROTHERS ADVENTURE, a snow, R. Patterson, fr. Glasgow, wrecked off Charleston, SC on 5 May 1756. [SCGaz#1141]

BROUGHTY CASTLE, Andrew Law, arr. in NY 18 Dec.1826 *with passengers* fr. Dundee. [USNA.M237]

BROWN, Colin Buchanan, fr. GK to Boston in Apr.1759. [E504.15.9][GJ#922]

BRUNSWICK OF GLASGOW/GREENOCK, 624 tons, Robert Steel, fr. GK to VA in June 1765; fr. GK *with passengers* to the James River, VA, Feb. 1767; fr. GK to VA *with passengers* in Feb. 1768; Robert Watson, fr. GK to VA in Mar. 1769; Alexander McLarty, fr. GK to VA in June 1770; fr. GK to VA in Jan. 1771; fr. GK to VA in Dec. 1771; fr GK to VA June 1772; fr GK to VA Jan.1773; fr GK to James River, VA, Aug.1773; fr GK to VA May 1774; James Service, fr GK to Halifax Mar.1776; fr. GK to NFD and Halifax in Apr. 1777; William Milne, fr. GK *with 20 passengers* to Halifax, NS, 2 Apr.1791.[CM#7142] [GC#57] [E504.15.12/15/16/18/19/20/21/22/23/24/26/27/58/59]

BRUTUS, John Keiller, arr. in NY 5 Sept.1827 *with passengers* fr. Dundee; arr. in NY 6 May 1828 *with passengers* fr. Dundee. [USNA.M237]

BUCHANAN OF GLASGOW, 250 tons, John Orr, fr. GK toVA via France in May 1750; David Hunter fr. GK to VA in Feb. 1752; fr. GK to MD and VA in Feb. 1753; Robert Steel, fr. GK to VA in May 1757; fr. GK to VA in Nov. 1758; fr. GK to VA in Nov. 1759; fr. GK to VA in May 1760; fr. GK to VA in July 1761; fr. GK to VA in Mar. 1762; fr. GK to VA in Jan. 1763; Thomas Cochrane, fr. GK to NY in May 1765; fr. GK to Philadelphia in June 1766; fr. GK to NY in May 1767; fr. GK to NY in Oct. 1767; fr. GK to NY in May 1768; fr. GK to NY in Nov. 1768; fr. GK to NY in July 1769. [CM#7154] [E504.15.4/5/6/8/9/10/11/12/13/14/15/16]

BUCHANAN OF GREENOCK, James Moody, fr GK to Philadelphia Mar.1772; fr GK to NY Apr.1773. [E504.15.21/22]

CAESAR OF GLASGOW, a 99 ton snow, Richard Hunter, arr.in Charleston, SC, on 6 Jan. 1762 fr. Glasgow; William Hume, fr. GK to NC in May 1763; fr. GK to NC in Nov. 1765; arr. in NC in Feb.1766 fr. Leith. [NCGaz#70] [SCGaz1433] [CM#6544][E504.15.13][PRO.CO5.509]

CAESAR OF GLASGOW, Alexander Rankin, fr. GK to Pictou 12 Oct.1818. [E504.15.122]

CALEDONIA OF GLASGOW, 100 tons, Walter Corry, fr GK to Boston in Apr.1753; fr. GK to Boston in Oct. 1753; fr. GK to Boston in Oct. 1753; William Warden, fr. GK to Boston in July 1754; fr. GK *with passengers* to Boston in Mar. 1755; fr. GK *with passengers* to Boston in Mar. 1756; William Warden, fr. GK *with passengers* to Boston in Feb. 1757; David Stirrat, fr. GK to Boston in Oct. 1757; fr. GK to Boston in Aug. 1759; fr. GK to MD in Apr. 1760; fr. GK to MD in Mar. 1761; fr. GK to MD and VA in Feb. 1762; fr. GK to MD in Sept. 1762 [E504.15.6/7/8/9/10/11] [GJ#701/756/800]

CALEDONIA, fr. Glasgow *with 100 passengers* to Shelbourne in 1785; Lewis Colquhoun, fr. GK to NY in May 1785; fr. GK to Baltimore on 24 Aug. 1786, [E504.15.41/43][GM#IX.451/278][Times#270]

CALEDONIA OF GREENOCK, 623 tons, Thomas Boag, fr. GK to New Brunswick 8 May 1813; fr. GK to Halifax 2 Feb.1814; arr. in Philadelphia on 11 Nov. 1816 *with passengers* fr. GK [E504.15.100/103][PAP]

CALEDONIA OF AYR, 177 tons, David Wilson, fr. Ayr to Quebec, 20 Mar. 1806. [E504.4.11]

CALEDONIA OF ST JOHN, NB, 348 tons, Thomas Boag, fr. GK to NY 1 Nov.1815.[E504.15.109]

CALEDONIA OF IRVINE, 154 tons, James Reid, fr. GK *with 30 passengers* to Montreal 29 Apr. 1816; James Neil, fr. GK *with 4 passengers* to Montreal 15 Apr.1817. [E504.15.112/115]

CALEDONIA OF GLASGOW, 111 tons, Peter Campbell, fr. GK to NFD 7 March 1815; William Daw, fr. GK to NFD 13 Nov.1815; fr. GK *with 15 passengers* to Philadelphia 20 Aug.1816; John McNish, fr. GK to Chaleur Bay 6 June 1818. [E504.15.107/109/113/120]

CALEDONIA OF GREENOCK, 131 ton snow, John Potter, fr. GK to NFD 30 Aug.1816; fr. GK to NFD 19 Mar.1818; fr GK to NFD Dec.1828. [E504.15.113/119/166]

CALEDONIA, 282 tons, John McFarlane, fr. GK to Quebec 7 June 1814. [E504.15.104]

CALEDONIA OF PETERHEAD, 155 tons, John Thom, fr. Aberdeen to P.E.I. 20 Mar. 1816. [E504.1.26]

CALEDONIA OF DUNDEE, 132 tons, Robert Fleming, fr Dundee
with passengers to NY 20 Apr.1819. [E504.11.21][CE70.1.15]
CALEDONIA OF PERTH, 136 tons, Cap. Mearns fr Dundee *with
passengers* to Philadelphia 28 Apr.1819, arr. in Philadelphia on
6 Aug. 1819 *with passengers* fr. Dundee;
[PAP][E504.11.21][CE70.1.15]
CALEDONIA, Cap.Kerr, fr Dundee to Restigouche Apr.1823.
[E504.11.23]
CALEDONIA fr GK to Montreal Apr.1828. [E504.15.166]
CALLIDEN, David Stirrat, fr. GK *with passengers* to Boston in
May 1759. [GJ#923]
CALLIOPE, William C. Waters, arr. in NY 15 Aug.1827 *with
passengers* fr. Glasgow. [USNA.M237]
CAMBRIA OF ABERDEEN, a 118 ton brig, Alexander
Lawrence, fr. Aberdeen *with 12 passengers* to Miramachi, NB,
25 May 1816; Capt. Wilson, fr. Aberdeen *with 15 passengers*
to Quebec, arr. there on 9 Aug. 1817; fr Aberdeen to Quebec 3
July 1818. [E504.1.26/27][MG]
CAMILLA OF GREENOCK, 294 tons, Duncan McArthur, fr.
GK to NFD 29 Aug.1814; fr. GK to N.B. 31 May 1815; fr. GK
to Savannah 8 Sept.1817; fr. GK to Quebec 2 May 1818; fr GK
to St John, NB, Aug.1828. [E504.15.105/108/117/120/165]
CAMILLUS OF NEW YORK, 338 tons, Joseph Boyer, fr GK to
Charleston 9 Mar.1819; fr. GK to NY 17 Aug.1819; fr GK to
NY 12 Feb.1820; fr GK to NY 11 Aug.1820, arr. in NY 9
0ct.1820 *with passengers* fr. GK; fr GK to NY 25 Jan.1821,
Norman Peck, fr GK to NY 27 June 1821, arr. in NY 6
Apr.1821 *with passengers* fr. GK; Norman Peck, arr. in NY 6
Apr.1821 *with passengers* fr. GK; arr. 10 Sept. 1821;fr GK to
NY 22 Jan.1822, arr. NY 6 Apr.1822 *with passengers* fr. GK;
arr. NY 28 Apr.1823 *with passengers* fr. GK; arr. 17
Sept.1823 *with passengers* fr. GK; Norman Peck, arr. NY 28
Apr.1824 *with passengers* fr. GK; arr. NY 18 Nov.1824 *with
passengers* fr. GK; arr. NY 7 March 1825 *with passengers* fr.
GK; arr. NY 27 July 1825 *with passengers* fr. GK; arr. NY 10
Dec.1825 *with passengers* fr. GK; ; arr. NY 27 June 1826 *with
passengers* fr. GK; arr. NY 9 May 1827 *with passengers* fr.
GK; arr. NY 12 Sep.1827 *with passengers* fr. GK; arr. NY 3
May 1828 *with passengers* fr. GK; John West, fr GK to NY
July 1828, arr. NY 8 Sep.1828 *with passengers* fr. GK; fr GK

to NY Dec.1828; John Niven, arr. NY 29 Jan.1829 *with passengers* fr. GK; N. Peck, ; arr. NY 27 Oct.1829 *with passengers* fr. GK [pa] [USNA#m237] [E504.15.123/125/128/131/134/136/139/163/166]

CAMPVERE PACKET, a brigantine, Andrew Govan, arr. in Charleston in July 1747 fr. Leith. [SCGaz.27.7.1747]

CANADA OF NEW YORK, Thomas Erskine, fr Orkney to NY 10 Aug.1762. [E504.26.4]

CANADA OF GREENOCK, 205 tons, David Harvie, fr. GK *with passengers* to Montreal on 4 Apr. 1789; fr. GK *with 30 passengers* to Quebec 2 Apr. 1791; fr. GK *with passengers* to Quebec in Apr. 1792; fr. the Clyde to NY in Sept. 1802. [GCr#64/70] [E504.15.50/58][GM#XII.578.32; 589.118] [GkAd#81]

CANADA OF ABERDEEN, 287 tons, Alexander Robertson, fr. Aberdeen to St John, NB, 24 Feb. 1817; fr Aberdeen to St John, NB, 26 Feb.1819. [E504.1.26/28]

CAPRICE OF GREENOCK, 139 tons, John McKie, fr. GK to Montreal in Apr. 1796. [E504.15.72]

CAROLINA, a brigantine, James Maitland, arr. in Charleston in March 1741 fr. Scotland. [SCGaz.12.3.1741]

CAROLINA OF PORT GLASGOW, 130 ton brig, John Gardner, fr. the Clyde to NC on 15 Sept. 1786; arr. in Port Brunswick, NC, on 15 Nov. 1787 fr. Glasgow; arr. in Port Brunswick, on 5 Nov. 1788 fr. Port Glasgow; arr. in Port Brunswick, on 17 Aug. 1789 fr. Port Glasgow; Capt. Ritchie, fr. the Clyde to NC in Dec. 1792; fr. the Clyde to NC 17 Oct. 1793. [GCr#207][NCSA.S8.112] [GM:7.9.1786; 19.9.1793]

CAROLINA OF ABERDEEN, 170 tons, Alexander Duncan, fr. Aberdeen to Pictou, NS, 25 Mar. 1817. [E504.1.26]

CAROLINA MERCHANT, James Gibson, fr. Glasgow *14 servants* to Charleston, SC, in 1684. [AC7/8]

CAROLINA PACKET OF NORTH CAROLINA, a brigantine, Malcolm McNeill, to Wilmington, NC, in Oct. 1774. [GJ:3.11.1774][E504.15.24]

CAROLINA PLANTER OF GLASGOW, a snow, John Wilson, fr. GK to SC in Nov. 1769; arr. in Charleston, SC, in Jan. 1770 fr. Glasgow; Capt. Jamieson, to NC in 1771. [E504.15.17] [SCGaz:14.1.1770] [GJ:21.11.1771]

CAROLINA OF ABERDEEN, 170 tons, J. Duncan, fr. Aberdeen *with 25 passengers* to Quebec and Montreal, 30 Mar. 1816; A.L.Duncan, jr., fr Aberdeen to Pictou Mar.1817. [E504.1.26]

CAROLINA OF NEW YORK, William Steel, fr. GK to N.O. July 1818. [E504.15.121]

CAROLINE OF GREENOCK, 142 tons, Thomas Crawford, fr. GK to St Andrews, NB, on 14 May 1791. [E504.15.59]

CARRON OF GREENOCK, Robert Lindsay, fr GK to NY and St Augustine Feb.1779. [E504.15.30]

CARY OF GLASGOW, 100 ton snow, Robert Brown, fr. GK to VA in Mar. 1753; fr. GK to VA in Jan. 1754; fr. GK to VA in July 1754; fr. GK to VA in Mar. 1755; fr. GK *with passengers* to VA in Mar. 1756; fr. Port Glasgow *with passengers* to the James River in Sep. 1756; Joseph Tucker, fr. Glasgow to VA in 1758, captured by the French but ransomed. [SM#20.275]; Joseph Tucker, fr. GK to VA in Nov. 1759, [E504.15.6/7/9][SM#20.275][GJ#746/783]

CASSANDRA, fr. Port Glasgow to Philadelphia on 15 Aug. 1752, [E504.28.7]; William Smith, fr. GK to VA in May 1757, captured by the French and taken to Cape Breton. [SM#19.613][E504.15.8]

CASTLE SEMPLE, Capt. McKinley, fr. the Clyde to Wilmington in Sept. 1792. [GCr#161]

CATHCART, Robert Rae, fr GK to VA Feb.1724. [RH18/3/344]

CATHCART OF GLASGOW, 123 tons, John Buchanan, fr. GK to VA in Apr. 1753; fr. GK to MD in Apr. 1754; James Barnhill, fr. GK to VA in Oct. 1756; fr. GK to VA in Feb. 1757; James Lyon, fr. GK to VA in Jan. 1762; fr. GK to VA and MD in May 1764; William Gilkison, fr. GK to MD in Feb. 1765; fr. GK to VA in Jan. 1766 [E504.15.6/10/12]

CATHCART OF GREENOCK, 90 tons, James Barnhill, fr. GK to VA in Aug. 1753; fr. GK *with passengers* to the James River in Jan. 1757 [E504.15.6][GJ#800]

CATHERINE OF GLASGOW, John Philp, fr. Glasgow to Charlestown, NE, on 25 Apr. 1673. [E72.16.4]

CATHERINE, 80 ton snow, Neil Jamieson, fr. GK to Boston in Apr. 1753; Hugh Wyllie, fr. GK to SC in Jan. 1755, arr. in Charleston in March 1755; fr. GK *with passengers* to the Potomac River, MD, in June 1756; Hector Carswell, fr. GK to VA in Mar. 1757; William Warden, fr. GK to MD in Aug.

1760; fr. GK to Quebec in Mar. 1761; fr. GK to VA in Mar.
1762; John Harrison, fr. GK to Casco Bay in July 1765; Hugh
Morris, fr. GK to NC in Mar. 1766; to NC in Sept. 1767; Capt.
Neil, to NC in Feb. 1769; arr. in Roanoke, NC, 28 Mar. 1769
fr. Glasgow; arr. in Roanoke, NC on 25 Jan. 1770 fr. Glasgow;
James Kippen, fr. GK to VA in Sept. 1771; fr GK to VA
Apr.1773; James Patrick, fr. GK to Halifax in Feb. 1777; John
Tarbert, fr. Port Glasgow *with passengers* via Cork to NY in
Apr. 1780; fr. Port Glasgow *with passengers* to NY in Apr.
1781 , [GJ:774; 26.1.1769] [GM#III/117;IV.119/174]
[CM:20.8.1767] [E504.15.6/7/8/9/10/13/20/22/27]
[NCSA/PC67/21]

CATHERINE OF NEW YORK, brigantine, Frederick Becker, fr
    Orkney to NY 15 Sep.1756; John Waldron, fr Orkney to NY 18
    June 1759; Nathaniel Laurence, fr Orkney to NY 9 Sept.1763;
    fr Orkney to NY 3 Dec.1765. [E504.6.4]

CATHERINE, Capt. McMillan, fr. VA to Glasgow, taken by the
    French near the Capes on 6 July 1760. [SM#23.335]

CATHERINE OF GLASGOW, 100 ton snow, John Love, arr. in
    Charleston, SC, on 7 Apr. 1763 fr. Glasgow; arr. in Charleston
    on 22 Dec. 1763 fr. GK; Hugh Morris, arr. in Boston on 29
    Aug. 1768 *with 4 passengers* fr. Scotland. [SCGaz#1499]
    [PAB][PRO.C05.510]

CATHERINE BANKS OF CHARLESTON, Thomas H. Jervey,
    fr. GK to Charleston, SC, 24 Oct. 1810, [E504.15.90]

CATO OF GREENOCK, 180 tons, John Wood, fr. GK to NY in
    Nov. 1771; John Dennistoun, fr. GK to NC in Aug. 1774, arr.
    in Port Brunswick, NC, on 1 Dec. 1774 *with 312 passengers* fr.
    Skye. [E504.15.20/24] [GJ: 18.8.1774] [NCSA.S8.112]

CATO OF MONTEGO BAY, 181 tons, J. Robinson, fr. GK to
    Newfoundland and Jamaica 17 Aug.1819. [E504.15.125]

CATO, David Ritchie jr. arr. NY 8 Aug.1825 *with passengers* fr.
    Dundee; arr. NY 12 May 1826 *with passengers* fr. Dundee.
    [USNA.M237]

CENTURION OF WHITEHAVEN, fr. Glasgow to VA in 1729.
    [AC9/1070]

CERBERUS OF NEW BRUNSWICK, 214 tons, A, Thomson, fr.
    GK to New Brunswick on 27 March 1813. [E504.15.99]

CERES, Archibald Robertson, fr. GK to VA in Jan. 1762
    [E504.15.10]

CERES, George Jamieson, fr. GK to NFD in Mar. 1784,
[E504.15.39]

CERES OF ABERDEEN, 220 tons, David Raitt, fr. Aberdeen to
St John, NB, 26 Feb. 1817. [E504.1.26]

CESSNOCK OF IRVINE, 135 tons, Archibald Stewart, fr. GK to
NY 8 Apr.1817.[E504.15.116]

CHAMPION, Cap. Reid, fr Montrose to St John, NB, 14 June
1826. [NAS.E504.24.21]

CHANCE OF DUNDEE, George Smith, fr Orkney to
Charleston,SC, 17 May 1758. [E504.26.3]

CHANCE OF ORKNEY, 160 tons, Charles Smith, arr. in
Charleston, SC, on 10 Jan. 1758 fr. Orkney; arr. in Charleston
on 16 Aug. 1758 fr. Kirkwall; arr. in Charleston on 4 Jan. 1760
with passengersi fr. Orkneys; arr. in Charleston in June 1761
fr. Orkney; arr. in Charleston on 22 Jan. 1762 fr. Orkney; arr.
in Charleston on 16 Nov. 1762 fr. Orkney; arr. in Charleston on
5 Mar. 1766 fr. Kirkwall. [PRO.CO5.509/511]
[SCGaz#1325/1406/1435/1479]

CHANCE OF GREENOCK, Capt. Wardrope, fr. the Clyde to VA
23 Dec. 1767; Abram Hunter fr GK to Boston Aug.1772; fr
GK to Oxford, MD, Aug.1773; John Simpson, fr. GK to New
York Aug. 1777; a brigantine, John Simpson, fr. the Clyde to
Mobile in 1778; Alexander Wyllie, fr GK to R.I. and Quebec
mar.1779; Capt. Williamson, fr. the Clyde to Halifax on 28
Apr.1780. [GC#50]
[E504.15.21/28/30][AC9/3032][GM#III/142]

CHANCE, a brig, Capt. Wilson, arr. in Philadelphia in May 1790
fr. Glasgow; arr. in Philadelphia in Apr. 1793 fr. Glasgow.
[PIG#1396/1443]

CHARLES OF DANVERS, Capt.Brown, fr GK to Boston 8 June
1822. [E504.15.140]

CHARLESTOWN OF GREENOCK, 135 tons, Alexander
McKellar, fr. GK to Charleston, SC, on 15 Oct. 1787; fr. GK to
Charleston in Oct. 1788; fr. GK to Charleston 27 Apr. 1789; fr.
GK *with passengers* to Charleston on 2 July 1789; fr. GK to
Charleston in Jan. 1792, wrecked on the Irish coast.
[CM#10980; 16.1.1792][GC:12.1.1792] [GM#XII.588.111;
601.214] [E504.15.46/49/51]

CHARLESTON OF HALIFAX, 156 tons, Hugh Watt, fr. GK to
Pictou 27 Aug. 1813. [E504.15.101]

CHARLOTTE OF AYR, William Fleck, fr. Ayr to West Fla. in Apr. 1769. [E504.4.5]

CHARLOTTE OF FALMOUTH, George Smith, fr. GK to VA in Feb. 1770 [E504.15.18]

CHARLOTTE OF PHILADELPHIA, 204 tons, Peter Bell, fr. GK *with 80 passengers* to Philadelphia in Feb. 1796; fr. GK *with 60 passengers* to Philadelphia in Aug.1796. [E504.15.71/73]

CHARLOTTE OF CHARLESTON, Joseph W. Clark, fr. GK *with 16 passengers* to Amelia Island, GA, 25 Sept. 1811. [E504.15.93]

CHARMING ANN, John Aitken, fr. GK to Quebec in Apr. 1763 [E504.15.11]

CHARMING BETTY, a snow, James Murray, arr. in Charleston, SC, in Dec. 1753 fr. Leith. [SCGaz#1019]

CHARMING JANET OF LEITH, 180 tons, John Brown, fr. Leith to VA in Feb. 1769. [E504.22.14]

CHARMING LILLIE OF GLASGOW, David Cunningham, fr. Port Glasgow to VA in Feb.1749. [E504.28.4]

CHARMING MOLLY, from Fort William to America in 1736. [NRAS#1279]

CHARMING NANCY OF NEW YORK, Andrew McLean, fr Orkney to NY 19 Sep.1757; John Taylor, fr Orkney to NY 9 July 1763. [E504.26.3/4]

CHARMING SALLY, James Montgomery, fr. Port Glasgow *with passengers* to the Potomac River, MD, in Apr. 1757. [GJ#814]

CHARMING SALLY OF NEW YORK, Isaac Mund, fr Orkney to NY 4 Aug.1757. [E504.26.3]

CHARMING SALLY, William Whitely, fr GK *with troops* to North America May 1778. [E504.15.29]

CHEERFUL OF KIRKCALDY, 211 tons, George Beveridge, fr Leith *with 51 passengers* to New York 6 May 1816; fr. GK *with 4 passengers* to Montreal 19 Apr.1817. [E504.15.116; E504.22.73]

CHEROKEE, Capt. Boyd, fr. GK to Savannah, GA, on 26 May 1780, captured and taken to Corunna, Spain. [GM#III/174][SM#42.446]

CHERUB OF GLASGOW, 269 tons, Allan Stevenson, fr. GK

with 12 passengers to Montreal 29 Mar.1817; fr. GK to
Charleston 24 Sept.1817; fr. GK to Montreal 8 Mar.1818;
William Rayside, fr. GK to Quebec 22 July 1819; fr GK to
Montreal 21 Feb.1820; fr GK to Quebec 3 Aug.1820; fr GK
to Montreal 2 Mar.1821; fr GK to Quebec 13 Aug.1821; fr
GK to Montreal 2 Mar.1822; fr GK *with passengers* to
Montreal Apr.1828; fr GK *with passengers* to Montreal
Aug.1828. [E504.15.115/117/119/125/131/137/139/163/164]

CHRISTIAN OF FORT WILLIAM, Hugh Hill, fr GK to VA 5
Apr.1721. [EEC#365]

CHRISTIAN, John Petticrew, fr GK to VA Jan.1744; fr GK to SC
Feb.1746, arr.in Charleston in May 1746; fr GK to VA
Feb.1748. [E504.15.1/2][SCGaz.5.5.1746]

CHRISTIAN OF LEITH, a 110 ton snow, George Watt, arr. in
MD during Feb.1757 fr. Leith; Henry Steel, fr. Leith to VA
in Apr. 1763; fr. Leith to Philadelphia 23 July 1765.
[MdGaz#615][E504.22.10/12]

CHRISTIAN OF AIRTH, James Brown, Bo'ness to VA 23 Apr.
1771 [E504.6.9]

CHRISTIAN OF IRVINE, a brigantine, James Neilson, fr. Ayr to
Charleston, SC, in Nov. 1769; arr. in Charleston, on 27 Dec.
1769 fr. Irvine; Patrick Muir, fr. Ayr via Dublin to GA in
Nov.1770; fr. Airth to VA in 1772.
[AC7/55][SCGaz#1789][E504.4.5]

CHRISTIAN OF WHITEHAVEN, John White, fr GK to Halifax,
NS, Sep.1775. [E504.15.25]

CHRISTIAN OF SALTCOATS, Robert Sheddan, fr GK to
Halifax Apr.1776. [E504.15.26]

CHRISTIAN OF KIRKCALDY, 158 tons, master Charles
Patterson, fr. GK *with 2 passengers* bound for NFD 6 Apr.
1813. [E504.15.100]

CHRISTIAN AND PEGGY, a 120 ton brigantine, Walter
McPherson, fr. GK *with passengers* to Charleston, SC, 6
Sept. 1786. [E504.15.43][GM#IX.444.223; 454.291]

CHRISTIE OF GREENOCK, a 77 ton brigantine, Andrew Lee,
fr. Port Glasgow to MD/NY in Apr. 1774; fr. Port Glasgow
to Baltimore, MD, in Jan. 1775; Hugh Rellie, fr GK to GA
Apr.1775; Andrew Lee, fr GK to GA July 1775; John
McCaul, fr. GK to Halifax and New York Sept.1777; fr GK to
Halifax Jan.1779; John Sharp, fr. GK to NFD in June 1784;

John Bruce, fr. GK to Wilmington, NC, *with passengers* on 3
Nov. 1786, arr. in Port Brunswick, NC, on 30 Jan. 1787.
[NCSA.S8.112] [E504.28.23/24/39/44;15/24/28/30]
[GM:5.10.1786; 2.11.1786]

CLANSMAN, fr GK to Savannah in Oct.1828. [E504.15.166]

CLARISSA ANN OF NEW ORLEANS, Nathaniel Green, fr GK
to NO 25 June 1821; fr GK to NY 11 Apr.1822.
[E504.15.136/140]

CLARKSTON OF LONDON, 251 tons, James Service, fr GK to
Quebec 18 Aug.1820. [E504.15.131]

CLEMENTINA OF GREENOCK, Dick Weir, fr. Port Glasgow
with passengers to NC 1 Mar. 1774, arr. at Port Brunswick,
NC, on 25 May 1774; John McKellar, fr. GK to NY and GA
in Nov. 1779, [E504.15.32; E504.28.23]
[CM#8156][GJ:17.3.1774][NCSA.S8.112]

CLINTON OF GREENOCK, George Innes, fr GK to St
Augustine and NY Mar.1779. [E504.15.30]

CLYDE, a brigantine, Archibald Riddell, fr GK to SC July 1743,
arr. in Charleston in Oct. 1743; Thomas Watson, fr. GK *with*
passengers to the James River, VA, 28 July 1746; fr GK to
VA July 1747. [GC#41][SCGaz.3.10.1743][E504.15.1/2]

CLYDE, John Aitken, fr. GK to Boston in Apr.1761. [E504.15.10]

CLYDE, John Smith, fr. Port Glasgow to VA in Apr. 1773;Thomas
Bolton, fr. Port Glasgow to VA in July 1774.
[E504.28.22/23]

CLYDE OF GREENOCK, 169 tons, William McKissock, fr. GK
to NFD in Oct. 1805. [E504.15.75]

CLYDE OF GLASGOW, 204 tons, John Paterson, fr. GK to
Charleston 8 Jan.1816. [E504.15.111]

CLYDE OF KIRKCALDY, 133 tons, Walter Greig, fr. GK to
NFD 2 Apr. 1816. [E504.15.111]

CLYDE OF ST JOHN, N.B., 330 tons, Alexander McLauchlan,
fr. GK *with 50 passengers* to St John, 26 March 1817; fr. GK
with 17 passengers to St John 13 Sept.1817; fr GK to St John
4 Feb.1819; J. Morison, fr. GK to St John 4 Sep.1819; fr GK
to St John 21 Mar.1822. [E504.15.115/117/123/125/139]

COCHRANE OF GLASGOW, Archibald Steel, fr. Port Glasgow
to VA in Mar. 1750; John Ewing, fr. GK to VA in May 176;
Robert Duthie, fr. GK to VA in July 1771 [E504.15.9/20;
E504.28.4]

COCHRANE, Thomas Bolton, fr. Port Glasgow to VA in Mar.
1773, [E504.28/21]

COCHRANE OF GREENOCK, 269 tons, Robert Stevenson, fr.
GK to Quebec on 9 June 1786; fr. GK *with passengers* to
NFD and Quebec in Mar.1787; Archibald Boag, fr. GK to
NFD on 20 Mar. 1788; fr. GK to NFD on 3 Mar. 1789;
Robert Burns, fr. GK to NFD 15 June 1791; fr. the Clyde to
NFD in June 1792. [E504.15.43/44/47/50/59]
[GM#IX.437.157/190/391; XII.584.78] [GCr#127]

COLLINGWOOD OF GREENOCK, 221 tons, James Gilchrist,
fr. GK *with 25 passengers* to Quebec 16 Mar. 1811; fr. GK
to Quebec 1 Apr. 1813; fr. GK to Quebec 4 Aug. 1813.
[E504.15.90/99/101]

COLOGNE, James McLean, fr. Port Glasgow *with passengers* to
Quebec in 1781. [GM#III.368]

COLOSSUS, Solomon Maxwell, arr. NY 5 June 1827 *with
passengers* fr. Glasgow. [USNA.M237]

COLUMBIA, John Watt, fr. GK *with passengers* to Charleston,
SC, in Dec. 1802. [GkAd#98]

COLUMBUS, 200 tons, John Bell, fr. GK to Wilmington, NC, 5
Jan. 1775, arr. in Port Brunswick on 25 Apr. 1775.
[GJ:15.12.1774][NCSA.S8.112]

COLUMBUS OF GREENOCK, 272 tons, John Donaldson, fr.
GK to VA 1 Apr.1788; fr. GK to VA in Feb. 1789; fr. GK
with passengers for Norfolk, VA, inAug.1792.
[GCr#145][E504.15.47/50][GM#XII.581.54]

COLUMBUS, Cap.Bisset, fr Dundee to Miramachi Apr.1823.
[E504.11.23]

COLUMBUS, A. Fleck, fr. Tobermory, Mull, *with 228 passengers*
to Cape Breton Island on 11 Aug. 1827. [E504.35.2]

COMELY OF DUNDEE, 144 tons, George Morrison, fr Dundee
with passengers to Charleston 31 Aug.1818; Cap. Gray fr
Dundee to Charleston Aug.1820; fr Dundee to NY 15
Nov.1821; fr Dundee to NO Sep.1822. [E504.11.20/21/22]
[CE70.1.15]

COMET OF ST JOHN, N.B., 420 tons, Robert Gillies, fr. GK to
N.B. 9 Aug.1815; Cap. Ritchie, fr GK to St John 17 Feb.1819.
[E504.15.109/123]

COMET OF ABERDEEN, 212 tons, William Leisk, fr. Aberdeen
to Miramachi, NB, 25 Mar. 1817. [E504.1.26]

COMMERCE OF GLASGOW, David Conkie, fr. GK to VA in
Feb. 1771; fr. GK to VA in Aug. 1771; [E504.15.19/20]

COMMERCE, Robert Hastie, fr. Port Glasgow to VA in Nov.
1772; fr. Port Glasgow to VA in May 1773. [E504.28.21/22]

COMMERCE OF GREENOCK, Gabriel Wood, fr GK to NY
Feb.1774; Capt. Ferguson, to NY *"with 250 emigrants -
weavers, spinners, blacksmiths, joiners, shoemakers, tailors,
hatters and farmers"* in 1774; to NY 14 Apr. 1775.
[E504.15.23][GJ:17.2.1774][EA#23/237]

COMMERCE OF GREENOCK, a 133 ton brigantine, James
Kerr, fr. GK to Boston 5 Nov. 1787; William McIntyre, fr. GK
to Wilmington, NC, 3 Nov. 1790; fr. GK to the Rappahannock
River, VA, in Apr. 1792; James Kerr, fr. GK *with 10
passengers* to Charleston, SC, in July 1791; fr. GK *with
passengers* to Charleston in Sept. 1792.
[E504.15.46/57/59][GCr#89/156]

COMMERCE OF AYR, 121 tons, John McMicken, fr. GK to
Quebec 27 Apr. 1814. [E504.15.104]

COMMERCE OF GREENOCK, 423 tons, John Wilson, fr. GK to
N.B. 23 Jan.1815; fr. GK *with 44 passengers* to Charleston 5
Sep.1815; H.Covendale, fr. GK to St John, NB, 4 Sept.1819;
fr GK to NFD Oct.1828. [E504.15.107/109/125/166]

COMMERCE OF ST JOHN, N.B, 420 tons, Thomas Boag, fr. GK
to Norfolk, VA, 14 Oct. 1817. [E504.15.114]

COMMERCE, Duncan Ritchie, arr. NY 17 July 1823 *with
passengers* fr. GK, [USNA.M237]

CONCORD OF ARBROATH, John Fraser, fr. Montrose to
Boston in May 1744; arr. in MD during Aug. 1745 fr.
Montrose. [E504.24.1][MdGaz#16]

CONCORD OF AYR, Hugh Moodie, fr. GK to VA in July 1756;
fr. the Clyde to VA in 1756, captured by the French and taken
to Marseilles. [E504.15.7] [SM#18.571]

CONCORD OF LEITH, 140 tons, Alexander Ramage, fr. Leith to
Boston on 12 Sept. 1767; fr. Leith to Charleston in Oct. 1771;
James Watt, fr. Leith to NC in Feb. 1772; fr. Leith to
Charleston in Nov. 1774 [E504.22.13/17][EA#16/230]

CONCORD, James Laurie, fr GK to Salem Sep.1775; Archibald
McCormick, fr GK to NFD Aug.1779; [E504.15.25/31]

CONCORD OF DYSART, 148 tons, Daniel McKinlay, fr. GK
with 19 passengers to Quebec 17 June 1811. [E504.15.92]

CONCORD OF DUNDEE, Robert Lithgow, fr Dundee *with passengers* to NY 1816. [CE70.1.14]

CONCORD OF PHILADELPHIA, Benjamin Cozens, fr. GK to Philadelphia 7 Aug.1818, arr. in Philadelphia on 16 Nov. 1818 *with passengers* fr. GK; fr GK to NY 29 Mar.1821, arr. NY 4 June 1821 *with passengers* fr. GK. [NAS,E504.15.122/135] [PAP][USNA.M237]

CONESTOGA OF PHILADELPHIA, 265 tons, master H. Marshall, fr GK to Philadelphia 16 Aug.1820. [E504.15.131]

CONFIDENCE, John Wesley, arr. NY 5 Sep.1828 *with passengers* fr. Dundee. [USNA.M237]

CONVENOR, Robert Dickie, fr. Leith to Carolina and MD in July 1740. [CM#3154]

CONVENTION, US ship, Thomas Snow, fr. Port Glasgow *with passengers* to NY on 24 Mar. 1789. [GM#XII.582.63; 587.102]

COQUETTE OF GLASGOW, 244 tons, J. McLean, fr. GK to N.O. 7 Feb.1816. [E504.15.111]

COQUET, Thomas Cowans, arr. NY 6 June 1827 *with passengers* fr. Dundee. [USNA.M237]

CORDELIA OF PHILADELPHIA, 252 tons, Walter Medlin, fr. GK *with 38 passengers* to Philadelphia, 9 June 1812, arr. there on 10 Aug. 1812 *with passengers*; fr. GK *with 100 passengers* to NY 19 June 1816. [PAP][E504.15.96/112]

CORNELIA, William Adam, fr. GK to St Augustine, Fla., in Oct. 1779; fr. the Clyde to NY in 1780 when captured. [E504.15.32][SM#42.332]

CORNWALLIS OF GREENOCK, brig, Robert McKinlay, fr GK to Halifax Oct.1777; fr GK to St Augustine Sep.1779; fr. GK to St John, NFD, on 3 Sept. 1781; Capt. Nixon, arr. in Beaufort, NC, on 26 Oct. 1789 fr. Glasgow. [E504.15.27/31/33][GM#IV.286] [NCSA/S8.112]

CORSAIR, fr GK to Chaleur Bay Aug.1828. [E504.15.165]

COSSACK OF GREENOCK, 177 tons, fr. GK to NFD 10 March 1814. [E504.15.103]

COUNTESS OF CRAWFORD, a brig, Capt. Brown, fr. Port Glasgow to the Rappahannock River, VA, in Mar. 1792. [GCr#73]

COUNTESS OF DARLINGTON, David Wilson, fr. GK *with passengers* to Montreal in Apr. 1802. [GkAd#22/25]

COUNTESS OF DUMFRIES OF AYR, David Spirling, fr. Ayr to Falmouth, NE, in Apr. 1769; fr. Ayr to Falmouth in Mar. 1770; fr. Ayr to Falmouth, in Mar. 1771; Capt. Esson, fr. Port Glasgow to SC in Oct. 1774; arr. in Charleston during Dec. 1774 *with passengers* fr. Scotland. [E504.4.5/24/E504.28.24] [SCGaz#2023]

COUNTESS OF EGLINTON, a brig, Matthew Brown, fr. Port Glasgow *with passengers* to the Potomac River, MD, and VA on 28 Feb. 1789. [GM#XII.584.78; 575.7]

COUNTESS OF HADDINGTON OF GREENOCK, 183 tons, Thomas Workman, fr. GK to Petersburg, VA, in July 1786; fr. GK to Charleston, SC, on 21 Nov. 1787; fr. GK *with passengers* to NY and the James River, VA, in Feb. 1789; Robert Boyd, fr. GK to Boston on 9 May 1791 [E504.15.46/50/59][GM#IX.441.191; XII.577.24; 581.54]

COURIER OF GREENOCK, 128 tons, David Hogg, fr. GK to NFD 1 Feb. 1814. [E504.15.103]

COURIER, Pulaski Benjamin, arr. NY 26 June 1827 *with passengers* fr. Glasgow. [USNA.M237]

COUTTS, William King, fr. GK to VA in July 1757; fr. GK to VA in May 1758. [E504.15.8]

CRANSTON, Robert Johnston, arr. in Charleston in July 1754 fr. Leith. [SCGaz.1.8.1754]

CRAWFORD OF GLASGOW, a 75 ton brigantine, Hugh Wyllie, fr. GK to SC in Aug. 1751, arr. in Charleston in Oct. 1751; William Smith, fr. GK to Gibralter, the Canaries and SC, in June 1752, arr. in Charleston, SC, in Dec. 1752 fr. Glasgow; James Barton, fr. GK to VA in Mar. 1753; Walter Corrie, fr. GK to Boston in Aug. 1754; fr. GK *with passengers* to Boston in July 1755; John Tran, fr. GK *with passengers* to Boston in Sept. 1756 [E504.15.5/6/7][SCGaz#967; 30.10.1751][GJ#722/783]

CRAWFORD, James McLean, fr. Port Glasgow to MD in Nov. 1772; fr. Port Glasgow to MD in Aug. 1774; John Montgomery, fr GK to Salem Sep.1775. [E504.28.21/23/25]

CRAWFORD OF GREENOCK, 110 tons, Archibald McNair, fr. GK *with 2 passengers* to Quebec on 12 June 1812; fr. GK to NFD 13 Feb.1813; Alexander Shannan, fr. GK to NFD 22 Feb.1815. [E504.15.96/99/107]

CROWN POINT OF NEW YORK, Thomas Lawrence, fr Orkney to NY 24 Sep.1756. [E504.6.3]

CRUICKSTON CASTLE, fr GK to Halifax Mar.1828. [E504.15.163]

CULLODEN, Peter Wallace, arr. NY 17 May 1828 *with passengers* fr. Alloa. [USNA.M237]

CUMMING, 110 tons, Stephen Carpenter, fr. GK to Edenton, NC, on 3 Oct. 1787, arr. in Port Roanoke, NC, on 21 Dec. 1787 fr. GK, [E504.14.45] [NCSA.S8.112]

CUNNINGHAM OF GREENOCK, 267 tons, Robert Montgomery, fr. GK to VA in Mar. 1762; Patrick Robertson, fr. Port Glasgow *with passengers* to the James River, VA, in Sept. 1769; Walter Buchanan, fr. Port Glasgow to VA in Mar. 1773; fr. Port Glasgow to VA in Mar. 1774; John McKindlay, fr. GK to Halifax in Mar. 1782; Hugh Smith, fr. GK to Halifax in Apr. 1783; James King, fr. GK to NY in June 1784; Theophilius Pyle, fr. GK to VA in July 1786; James Paterson, fr. GK *with passengers* to VA on 29 Oct. 1786; fr. GK to Halifax in July 1787; William Milne, fr. GK to Halifax on 19 Mar. 1788. [GM#IX.461.350] [GJ#31.8.1769] [E504.15.10/35/37/39/43/44/45/47; E504.28.21/23]

CURLER, J. R. Jones, fr GK to NY May 1828, arr. NY 19 July 1828 *with passengers* fr. GK. [USNA.M237][E504.15.164]

CURLEW, John Young, fr. GK *with 205 passengers from Perthshire* to Upper Canada in July 1818. [PRO.384/3; CO226/36]

CYGNET OF DUNDEE, 144 tons, John Henderson, fr Dundee to NY May 1817; fr Dundee to Quebec/Montreal 22 Feb.1820. [E504.11.20/21]

CZAR, A. Russell, arr. NY 29 Aug. 1829 *with passengers* fr. GK. [USNA.M237]

DALMARNOCK OF ALLOA, 315 tons, James Cumming, fr GK to Miramachi 14 Mar.1820; fr GK to NY 12 Jan.1821;   John Kinnemont, arr. NY 24 Oct.1826 *with passengers* fr. GK; James Cummins, arr. NY 17 May 1822 *with passengers* fr. Leith; John Kinnemont, ; arr. NY 23 May 1823 *with passengers* fr. Alloa; arr. NY 11 Dec.1828 *with passengers* fr. Alloa.[E504.15.128/134] [USNA.M237]

DANIA, fr GK to Boston Apr.1828. [E504.15.164]

DAPHNE, Capt. Wilkie, fr. GK to NFD on 13 Mar. 1802.
[GkAd#18]

DAPHNE OF ABERDEEN, 129 tons, George Philip, fr. Aberdeen
to Miramachi, NB, 3 Mar. 1817. [E504.1.26]

DART OF GREENOCK, Alexander Kerr, fr. GK to NFD 7
Aug.1818. [E504.15.122]

DAVID OF KINCARDINE, 189 tons, Archibald Forrester, fr Leith
to Miramachi 19 Apr.1816; Adam Drysdale, fr. GK to Halifax
7 March 1817. [E504.22.73; E504.15.115]

DAVID AND ANNE OF LEITH, 150 tons, David Howison, fr.
Leith to VA in Apr. 1771; Alexander Ritchie, fr. Leith to NY in
Aug. 1773; fr. Leith via Fort George, *with 250 emigrants from
Sutherland* arr. in Philadelphia in 1774.
[GC:9.6.1774][GJ:9.6.1774][E504.22.16/18]

DAVID DENOON, a brigantine, Alexander Donaldson, fr.
Inverness on 7 Sept. 1773 *with over 200 passengers* to NY,
delayed at Orkney, to proceed to NY on 22 Mar. 1774.
[SCGaz:21.3.1774]

DEFENCE, George Rodger, arr. NY 13 Dec.1827 *with passengers*
fr. Leith. [USNA.M237]

DEFIANCE OF RHODE ISLAND, Oliver Champlen, fr Orkney
to NY/RI 7 June 1758; James Duncan, fr Orkney to RI 12 June
1764. [E504.6.3/4]

DELAWARE, US ship, Bezzabel Beebe, fr. GK *with passengers* to
NY in Dec. 1802. [GkAd#94]

DENNISTOUN OF BOSTON, 90 ton snow, Colin Campbell, arr.
in Charleston, SC, on 29 Jan. 1759 fr. Glasgow; Hugh Porter,
arr. in Charleston on 27 Nov. 1762 fr. Glasgow; arr. in
Charleston on 27 Feb. 1764 fr. Glasgow.
[SCGaz#1480/1545][PRO.CO5.509/511]

DIADEM OF ST JOHN, N.B., 319 tons, Henry Colburn, fr. GK to
Halifax 1 Oct. 1813; George Wells, fr. GK to Halifax 8 May
1815; fr. GK to Halifax 24 Jan.1816; fr. GK *with 2 passengers*
to Halifax 5 Aug.1816. [E504.15.101/108/111/113]

DIAMOND OF GREENOCK, James Weir, fr. GK to the Potomac
River in 1738 [AC79/1443]

DIAMOND, James Boyd, fr. GK to VA in Aug. 1761; fr. GK to
VA in Aug. 1762; fr. GK to VA in Feb. 1764
[E504.15.10/11/12]

DIANA, brigantine, Robert Curtis, fr Orkney to NY 17 July 1762; fr Orkney to NY 20 June 1764. [E504.26.4]

DIANA OF GREENOCK, 80 ton brig, Alexander Bain, fr. GK to Boston in Aug. 1760; William Montgomery, fr. GK to NFD in May 1767;Capt. Montgomery, fr. the Clyde to Quebec 29 Apr. 1768; John Denniston, fr GK to NY July 1773; fr GK to Philadelphia Mar.1774; Dugald Ruthven, fr GK to NC in Sept. 1774, arr. at Port Brunswick, NC, on 10 Dec. 1774 fr. GK Capt. Elphinston, fr. the Clyde to NC in June 1775. [NCSA.S8.112] [CM#8362] [GJ: 15.9.1774] [GC#67][E504.15.9/14/23/24]

DIANA OF GREENOCK, 115 tons, J. Kerr, fr. GK to VA in May 1787; fr. GK to the Rappahannock, VA, 4 Oct. 1788; A.Houston, fr. GK to Wilmington 3 Feb. 1791 [E504.15.45/48/58]

DIANA, a 350 ton US ship, Capt. James Tibbets, fr. GK *with passengers* to NY on 5 June 1805. [CM#13053]

DIANA, a schooner, S. W. MacPherson, arr. in NY *with passengers* fr. Scotland in 1820. [pa]

DIANA OF GREENOCK, 294 tons, John Ferguson, fr. GK to NFD 28 July 1814; fr. GK to NFD 4 July 1815; fr. GK to New York 12 Feb.1817; fr. GK to NFD 29 July 1818; fr GK to NFD 27 Apr.1819; fr GK to NFD July 1828 [E504.15.105/108/115/122/124/164]

DIANA OF DUMFRIES, a 226 ton brig, John Martin, fr. Carsethorn, Dumfries-shire, *with 53 passengers* to P.E.I. and the Bay of Chaleur, NB, in 1821. [DCr:30.1.1821]

DIANA, Cap. Fyffe, fr Dundee to Miramachi Mar.1824 [E504.11.23]

DILIGENCE OF GLASGOW, John Hamilton, fr. the Clyde to the Potomac River, VA, before 1725. [AC9/925]

DILIGENCE OF ABERDEEN, a 80 ton brigantine, Alexander Gordon, arr. in Philadelphia in Oct. 1736 *with servants* fr. Aberdeen; George Duncan, fr. Aberdeen to VA in Mar. 1749; arr. in MD during May 1749 fr. Aberdeen, [George Duncan, fr. Aberdeen to MD by 1750. [PaGaz,14.10.1736] [AC9/1748] [E504.1.3] [MdGaz#214]

DILIGENCE OF GLASGOW, 100 tons, James Dunlop, fr. GK to MD in Apr. 1749; fr. Port Glasgow to VA in Mar. 1750; Charles Robertson, fr. GK to Boston in Sept. 1763, arr. in

Boston *with 3 passengers* on 15 Nov. 1763; arr. in Charleston, SC, on 29 Apr. 1764 via St Kitts, [E504.15.4/11; E504.28.4][PAB][PRO.CO5.511]

DILIGENT, 89 ton brig, John Kean, fr. GK to Wilmington, NC, in May 1787, arr. in Port Brunswick, NC, on 16 July 1787, [E504.15.45][NCSA.S8.112]

DISPATCH, James Mudie, arr. in Charleston, SC, in Aug. 1740 fr. Montrose. [SCGaz#337]

DISPATCH OF NEWCASTLE, Alexander Thistlewaite, fr. Aberdeen to VA in May 1749. [E504.1.3]

DISPATCH, Capt. Farrie, fr. the Clyde to Pensacola on 24 Apr. 1781, [GM#IV/135]

DOLLY, William Morrison, fr. GK to NC in Mar. 1758; fr. GK to NC in May 1759, [E504.15.8/9]

DOLPHIN, Capt. Robert Franklin, arr. in SC *with women servants* fr. Leith in Aug. 1745. [SCGaz#595]

DOLPHIN, a snow, David Alexander, arr. in MD during June 1747 fr. Glasgow. [MdGaz#110]

DOLPHIN OF CHARLESTON, 60 ton brigantine, James Rea, arr. in Charleston, SC, on 22 Feb. 1763 fr. Dundee; arr. in Charleston on 21 Nov. 1763 fr. Dundee; Robert Stirling, arr. in Charleston, SC, on 26 Nov. 1764 fr. Dundee. [SCGaz#1493/1532/1560][PRO.CO5.509/510]

DOLPHIN OF GLASGOW, Quintin Leitch, fr. GK *with passengers* to Philadelphia in Sept. 1768; James Noble, fr. GK to Philadelphia in Sept. 1769; John Shiels, fr GK to NFD. [GC#77/80] [E504.15.16/17/26]

DOLPHIN OF AYR, Andrew Burns, fr. Ayr via Waterford to NFD, in Mar. 1772, William Thomson, fr. Ayr to NFD in Apr. 1776. [E504.4.6]

DOLPHIN, 94 tons, James McCunn, fr. GK to VA in Aug. 1785; fr. GK to VA 21 Aug. 1787; Duncan McRobb, fr. GK to Halifax, NS, 28 Aug. 1788. [E504.15.41/45/48]

DOMESTIC, a brig, P. Barney, arr. in NY *with passengers* fr. Scotland in 1820. [pa]

DONALD OF GLASGOW, 160 tons, John Andrew, fr. GK to VA in Aug. 1749; fr. GK to VA in July 1750; fr. GK to VA in Apr. 1751; fr. GK to VA in Mar. 1752; fr. GK to VA in Feb. 1753; fr. GK to VA in Aug. 1753; fr. GK to VA in Mar. 1754; fr. GK to VA in Dec. 1754; fr. GK *with passengers* to the James

River, VA, on 20 Mar. 1755; fr. GK to VA in Aug. 1755; fr.
GK *with passengers* to VA in Apr. 1756; fr. GK *with
passengers* to VA in Oct. 1756; fr. GK to VA in July 1757; fr.
GK to VA in May 1758; Thomas Archdeacon [John
Paterson?], fr. GK *with passengers* to the James River, VA, in
July 1759; John Patterson, fr. GK to VA in Jan. 1761; Robert
Lees, fr. GK to VA in Jan. 1762; fr. GK to VA in Aug. 1762;
William Morrison, fr. GK to VA in June 1764; fr. GK to VA in
June 1765; James Bog, fr. GK to VA in Jan. 1766; fr. GK to
VA in July 1766; James Leitch, fr. GK to VA in Jan. 1767; fr.
GK to VA in July 1767; fr. GK to VA in Jan. 1768; David
Andrew, fr. GK to VA in July 1768; Andrew Lee, fr. GK to
VA in Mar. 1769; Thomas Ramsay, fr GK to VA June 1772;
James Pasteur, fr. Port Glasgow to VA in Nov. 1772; Thomas
Ramsay fr GK to VA Jan.1773; Thomas Ramsay, fr GK to
James River, Jamaica, Mar.1774; John Heartwell, fr. Port
Glasgow to VA in Aug. 1774; Capt. Ramsay, fr. the Clyde to
VA in Apr. 1775, [E504.28.21/23]
[E504.15.4/5/6/7/8/9/10/11/12/13/14/15/16/21/22/23]
[EA#23/1180][GJ#730/760/778/928]

DOROTHY OF GLASGOW, James Thomson, fr. GK to NC in
Dec. 1771; Capt. Dunlop, arr. at Cape Fear, NC, fr. the Clyde
before May 1772. [E504.15.20] [GJ:14.5.1772]

DOROTHY, John Butler, fr. Leith *with passengers* to Cape Fear,
NC, 10 Mar. 1775, arr. in Port Brunswick, NC, on 8 July 1775.
[CM#8311, 8.2.1775] [EA#23/160][NCSA.S8.112]

DORSET OF GRANGEMOUTH, Andrew Scott, fr Leith *with 83
passengers* to Halifax 1 May 1816. [E504.22.73]

DOVE, a snow, John Andrew, arr. in Nansemond in Jan. 1740 fr.
Glasgow. [VG#181]

DOUGLAS, James Montgomerie, arr. in Boston on 28 Oct. 1763
with 24 passengers fr. Scotland; Robert Manderston, fr. GK to
Boston in May 1764; fr. GK to Boston in Apr. 1765; fr. GK to
NC in Nov. 1765; fr. GK to NC in July 1767.
[PAB][E504.15.12/13]

DOUGLAS OF ABERDEEN, 135 tons, John Moir, fr Aberdeen
with 7 passengers to Halifax 12 Apr.1818. [E504.1.27]

DRAGON OF GREENOCK, Thomas Bolton, fr GK to NY
Feb.1779. [E504.15.30]

DRAPER, a US ship, Ormand Noble, fr. GK *with passengers* to
   NY on 20 Apr. 1802; Peter Taylor, fr. GK *with passengers* to
   NY in Aug. 1802. [CM#12576][GkAd#25/68]

DREGHORN OF GLASGOW, William Andrew, fr. GK to VA in
   May 1748; fr. Port Glasgow to VA in Feb. 1749; fr. GK to VA
   in July 1750; fr. GK to VA in Mar. 1751; fr. GK to VA in June
   1752; fr. GK to VA in Aug. 1756. [E504.15.2/4/5/7;
   E504.28.4]

DRUMMOND OF GLASGOW, fr. Glasgow to VA before 1722,
   [AC8.285]

DUBLIN OF NEW YORK, snow, William Moore, fr Orkney to
   NY 1 Nov.1760. [E504.26.3]

DUBLIN OF GREENOCK, John Cunningham, fr. GK to NC in
   Sept. 1770; Matthew Orr fr GK to Halifax Mar.1779.
   [E504.15.18/30][GJ:27.8.1770]

DUCHESS, Arthur Young, fr. GK to VA in Mar. 1758; Archibald
   Hamilton, fr. GK to Boston in May 1758 [E504.15.8]

DUCHESS OF ARGYLL, 80 ton brig, Andrew Miller, arr. in Port
   Brunswick, NC, *with 80 passengers* fr. Campbeltown, on 19
   Oct. 1785. [NCSA.S8.112]

DUCHESS OF RICHMOND OF GREENOCK, 319 tons, Cap.
   Cook, fr GK to Quebec 1 June 1820; fr GK to Quebec June
   1828; fr GK to NS Dec.1828.[E504.15.129/164/166]

DUCHESS OF GLOUCESTER, John King, arr. NY 1 Dec.1823
   with passengers fr. Glasgow. [USNA.M237]

DUCHESS OF PORTLAND, James Hall, arr. NY 30 Oct.1826
   with passengers fr. Glasgow. [USNA.M237]

DUKE, Robert Jamieson, arr. in Charleston in Dec. 1751 fr.
   Glasgow.[SCGaz#916]

DUKE OF ARGYLL, Capt. King, arr. at Sandy Hook on 3 Nov.
   1756 *with troops* fr. the Clyde. [GJ#809]

DUKE OF ATHOLL OF BO'NESS, a brigantine, R. Grindlay, to
   SC in Sept. 1768; arr. in Charleston, SC, on 6 Dec. 1768 fr.
   Bo'ness; to Charleston in July 1769; arr. in Charleston, in Oct.
   1770;Robert Grindlay, fr Bo'ness to Charleston 20 Apr.1771,
   arr. in Charleston during Aug. 1771, fr. Bo'ness.
   [SCGaz:6.12.1768/15.10.1770/1.8.1771][CM#7194/7325][E50
   4.6.9]

DUKE OF ATHOL, Capt. Russell, fr. Grangemouth to Quebec 3
   Mar. 1802. [GkAd#22]

DUKE OF BUCINGHAMSHIRE OF MONTREAL, 593 tons,
William Philips, fr. GK *with 20 passengers* to Quebec 13 May
1815. [E504.15.108]

DUKE OF CUMBERLAND OF GLASGOW, 200 tons, Hugh
Brown, fr. GK to VA in Sept. 1747; fr. GK to VA in Mar.
1749; fr. Port Glasgow to VA in Mar. 1750; fr. GK to VA in
June 1753; John Dunlop, fr. GK to VA in Apr. 1754; fr. GK to
VA, in Jan. 1755; fr. Port Glasgow *with passengers* to the
James River, VA, in Aug. 1755; fr. GK to NY in May 1756
[E504.15.2/4/6/7; E504.28.4][GJ#728]

DUKE OF GLASGOW, Robert Jamieson, fr. GK to VA in Mar.
1750; fr. GK to SC in Oct. 1751; fr. GK to VA in June 1752
[E504.15.4/5]

DUNDEE OF DUNDEE, Robert Anderson, fr. GK to NY 17 Oct.
1810, [E504.15.90]

DUNKIRK OF GREENOCK, a brigantine, John Henderson, fr.
GK to Charleston, SC, in Nov. 1771; arr. in Charleston during
Mar. 1772 fr. GK. [SCGaz:10.3.1772][E504.15.20]

DUNLOP OF GLASGOW, a snow, David Alexander, fr. GK to
MD in Mar. 1747; fr. Port Glasgow to MD in Oct. 1747; fr.
Port Glasgow to VA in July 1749; fr. Port Glasgow to VA in
July 1750; Ralph Boyle, arr. in Charleston, SC, in June 1756
fr. Glasgow; arr. in Charleston in Nov. 1759 fr. Glasgow; John
Hartwell fr GK to VA Aug.1774; fr GK to Quebec May 1776
[SCGaz#1145; 17.11.1759] [E504.15.2/24/26; E504.28.3/4]

DUNLOP OF GLASGOW/GRANGEMOUTH, 331 tons, John
McKenzie, fr. GK *with 5 passengers* to Quebec 16 Aug.1811;
William Abram, fr. GK *with 24 passengers* to Montreal 13
Apr.1812; fr. GK to Quebec 23 July 1813; fr. GK to Quebec 7
June 1814; fr. GK *with 4 passengers* to Quebec and Montreal
28 Feb.1815; John Brown, fr. GK *with 22 passengers* to
Halifax 3 Apr.1817; fr. GK to St John, NB, 25 Aug.1817.
[E504.15.93/96/101/104/107/115/117]

DUNLOP OF GREENOCK, John Brown, fr. GK to Halifax 5
Feb.1818; John Banner, fr. GK to Quebec 1 Aug.1818; John
Brown, fr GK to St John, NB, 7 Aug.1821; fr GK to Halifax
and St John, NB, 5 Mar.1822 [E504.15.119/122/137/139]

DUNMOOR, James Ewing, fr. GK to VA in May 1760; fr. GK to
VA in Apr. 1762; fr. GK to VA in Jan. 1763; fr. GK to VA in
Sept. 1764 [E504.15.9/10/11/12]

EAGLE OF GLASGOW, 223 tons, William Dunlop, fr. GK to
VA in Mar. 1770; fr. GK to VA in Aug. 1770; fr. GK to VA in
June 1771; fr. GK to VA in Oct. 1771; John Blain, fr. GK to
NY in June 1784; fr. Glasgow *with 300 passengers, mostly
mechanics* to NY, arr. there in Aug. 1784; John Blain, fr. GK
to Baltimore in Feb. 1785; fr. GK to Baltimore in Aug. 1785;
fr. GK to NY in Mar. 1786; arr. in NY *with passengers* during
May 1786 fr. Glasgow; Capt. Scotland, to NC on 23 Oct. 1786;
Lewis Colquhoun, fr. GK to NY on 14 Mar. 1789.
[CM:20.10.1784] [PennMerc#93]
[E504.15.18/19/20/39/40/42/45/50] [GM] [GM#IX.460.342;
#XII.586.94]

EAGLE OF HALIFAX, 298 tons, Alexander Liddle, fr. GK *with
5 passengers* to Halifax, NS, in Apr. 1796. [E504.15.72]

EAGLE, William Morrison, fr. GK to Norfolk, VA, in Mar. 1802.
[GkAd#18]

EAGLE, Capt. Connoly, fr. GK *with passengers* to Quebec in Apr.
1802. [GkAd#18]

EAGLE, Abraham B. Cary, arr. NY 10 Aug.1825 *with passengers*
fr. Glasgow. [USNA.M237]

EARL OF ABERDEEN, George W.Legerwood, fr. Aberdeen to
Miramachi 1 Apr.1820. [E504.1.28]

EARL OF DALHOUSIE OF ABERDEEN, 183 tons, John Livie,
fr Aberdeen *with 24 passengers* to Halifax 1 July 1818; fr
Aberdeen to Quebec 19 Mar.1819; fr Aberdeen to Miramachi
22 Aug.1821; fr GK *with passengers* to Montreal July 1828.
[E504.1.27/28/29; 15/165]

EARL OF GLENCAIRN, Alexander McCall, fr GK to St
Augustine and NY May 1779. [E504.15.31]

EARL OF LOUDOUN, Capt. Erskine, fr. VA to Glasgow in 1757,
captured by the French and taken to Cape Breton. [SM#19.613]

EARL OF MANSFIELD, 800 tons, James Robertson, fr. GK *with
passengers* to St John's, NB, in Mar. 1792. [GCr#68]

ECHO OF GREENOCK, 129 tons, Robert Thynne, fr. GK *with 5
passengers* to Quebec, 20 Mar.1812; Robert Lyon, fr. GK to
NFD 29 Jan.1813; fr. GK to NFD 8 Feb.1814; Charles
McGlashan, fr. GK *with 6 passengers*to Montreal 5 Apr. 1816.
[E504.15.95/99/103/111]

ECLIPSE OF AYR, 190 tons, James Moore, fr. GK to Quebec 2
Apr. 1816; fr. GK to Quebec 5 Mar.1818. [E504.15.111/119]

ECONOMY, Capt. Frazer, fr. Tobermory, Mull, *with 258 passengers* to Pictou, NS, 2 Aug. 1819. [E504.35.2]

ECONOMY, Cap. Balfour, fr Dundee to St John, NBr. 26 Mar.1821. [E504.11.22]

EDDYSTONE OF LONDON, 245 tons, Thomas Ramsay, fr. Stornaway *with 27 passengers* to Hudson Bay on 24 July 1811. [E504.33.3]

EDINBURGH OF GLASGOW, 140 ton brigantine, John Lyon, fr. GK to SC in Jan. 1751; arr. in Charleston in Apr. 1751 fr. Glasgow; fr. GK to SC in Oct. 1751; arr. in Charleston in Dec. 1751 fr. Glasgow; Alexander Ritchie, fr. GK to SC in Nov. 1754; arr. in Charleston in Feb. 1755 fr. Glasgow; arr. on 3 Dec. 1759 fr. Kirkcaldy; R. Alexander, arr. in Charleston in Sept. 1769; arr. in Charleston in Oct. 1770 *with passengers* fr. Leith; Alexander McCroskie, fr. GK *with passengers* to Quebec 23 Apr.1781.[GM#IV.95/135] [PRO.CO5.509][SCGaz#883/916/1079/1320; 21.9.1769/18.10.1770]   [E504.15.5/7/33]

EDINBURGH OF LEITH, 100 tons, Robert Alexander, fr. Leith to Charleston, SC, in July 1769; fr. Leith to Charleston 2 Aug. 1770, arr. in Oct. 1770. [CM#7315][E504.22.15/16][SCGaz.18.10.1770]

EDINBURGH OF CAMPBELTOWN, 70 tons, John McMichael, fr. Campbeltown *with 70 passengers* to St John's, 27 July 1771. [E504.8.4]

EDWARD AND ANN OF LONDON, 238 tons, Thomas Gull, fr. Stornaway *with 61 passengers* to Hudson Bay 24 July 1811. [E504.33.3]

EGLINTON OF PORT GLASGOW, a 70 ton snow, Duncan McCausland, fr. GK to SC in Jan. 1750, arr. in Charleston in Mar. 1754 fr. Glasgow; arr. in Charleston in Aug. 1755 fr. GK via Bordeaux; arr. in Charleston in Feb. 1756 fr. Glasgow; Archibald Fisher, fr. GK *with passengers* to MD in May 1756; Duncan McAusland, fr. GK to Boston in Mar. 1757; Alexander Witherspoon, fr. GK to VA in Jan. 1758; George Buchanan, fr. GK to MD/VA in Apr. 1759; Capt. Roberton, fr. Carolina to Glasgow when taken by the French but ransomed for £200 in 1761. [E504.15.4/7/8/9] [SM#23.335] [SCGaz#1030/1130; 1.9.1755][GJ#762/922]

EGLINTON OF SALTCOATS, William Dunlop, fr. Port
Glasgow to VA in Feb. 1743; Henry Scott, fr. Port Glasgow to
VA in May 1744; John Scott, fr. Port Glasgow to Boston in
Aug. 1746; Patrick Wodrow, fr. Saltcoats *with passengers* via
Liverpool to VA in Feb. 1786; William Hamilton, fr. Port
Glasgow to Boston in Aug. 1802. [E504.23.1; E504.28.2]
[GM#IX.420.33][GkAd#64]

ELDON, John Cooper, arr. NY 21 Aug.1827 *with passengers* fr.
Dundee. [USNA.M237]

ELEANOR OF WORKINGTON, Edward Wallace, fr. GK to
Antigonish 5 May 1818. [E504.15.120]

ELEANOR OF QUEBEC, Robert Bell, fr GK to Quebec 31 July
1821. [E504.15.137]

ELEPHANT OF GREENOCK, 471 tons, Thomas Crawford, fr.
GK *with passengers* to VA on 24 Dec. 1786; William Tarbert,
fr. GK to NY on 9 Jan. 1789.
[E504.15.44/50][GM#IX.460.343; 468.414; XII.575.14]

ELIZA OF SALTCOATS, a 150 ton brigantine, Robert
Cunningham, fr. GK to SC in Sept. 1770; Robert Jack, fr. Port
Glasgow to Port Humphrey, VA, in Aug. 1773; fr. Port
Glasgow via Waterford to NFD in Mar. 1774; Robert Jack, fr.
GK to Quebec in Mar. 1777; fr. GK *with passengers* to
Charleston on Oct. 1786; James Morrison, fr. GK to
Charleston, SC, in Apr. 1787 [E504.15.18/27/45]
[E504.28.23/25] [GM#IX.454.295]

ELIZA OF GLASGOW, David Blair, fr. Port Glasgow to VA in
Mar. 1743; fr. Port Glasgow to VA in Feb. 1745; fr. Port
Glasgow to VA 31 Dec. 1746; fr. Port Glasgow to VA in Aug.
1747, [E504.28.1/2/3]

ELIZA OF SALTCOATS, Robert Jack, fr GK to NFD Mar.1774;
fr GK to Halifax Dec.1777; fr GK to Halifax Jan.1778.
[E504.15.23/28/29]

ELIZA, Capt. McAlister, fr. Port Glasgow to Pictou, NS, in Apr.
1802. [GkAd#32]

ELIZA OF PETERHEAD, 132 tons, John Innes, fr. Aberdeen to
Quebec, 10 Apr. 1816. [E504.1.26]

ELIZA OF ST JOHN, NB, 304 tons, George Kelly, fr. GK to St
John, NB, 19 Sept.1816. [E504.15.113]

ELIZA OF CHARLESTON, Jonathan A. Tupper, fr. GK to
Savannah 13 Jan.1818. [E504.15.119]

ELIZA OF DUNDEE, William Wrongham, fr Dundee *with passengers* to NY 30 May 1818; Theo. Burgess, arr. NY 23 Dec.1822 *with passengers* fr. Dundee; George Hynd, fr Dundee to NY Dec.1824; arr. NY 9 May 1827 *with passengers* fr. Dundee; arr. NY 31 July 1828 *with passengers* fr. Dundee.[E504.11.20/23] [USNA.M237][CE70.1.15]

ELIZA OF BOSTON, Cap.Burgess, fr Dundee to NY Oct.1822. [E504.11.22]

ELIZA OF THURSO, fr. Thurso_*with 8 passengers* to Canada in May 1823. [E504.7.6]

ELIZA ANN OF GREENOCK, 306 tons, Thomas Little, fr. GK to Savannah 17 Sept.1817; Cap.Little, fr GK to Savannah 24 mar.1819; Andrew Grierson, fr. GK to Quebec 17 May 1819. [E504.15.117/123/124]

ELIZA JANE OF NEW YORK, 194 tons, Samuel Rose, fr. GK to NY 12 Sep.1815; W. Ferrier, fr GK to NO 8 Mar.1821. [E504.15.109/135]

ELIZABETH OF GREENOCK, a brigantine, James Hasty, fr. GK via Belfast and the Isle of May to Carolina in Oct. 1741; fr. GK *with passengers* to MD in Aug. 1742. [GJ#12/53]

ELIZABETH OF BOSTON, John McKay, fr. Port Glasgow to Boston in Nov. 1742, [E504.28.1]

ELIZABETH OF GLASGOW, Andrew Geills, fr. GK to VA in Mar. 1744; James Heastie, fr. GK to VA in Dec. 1744; Andrew Geills, fr. GK to VA in Feb. 1745; James Heastie, fr. GK to VA in Aug. 1745; fr GK to VA in July 1747; John Morison, fr. GK to MD in Apr. 1749; William Kerr, fr. GK to VA in July 1769; fr. GK to NC in July 1770. [E504.15.2/4/17/18]

ELIZABETH OF GREENOCK, David Taylor, fr GK to St Augustine Aug.1779. [E504.15.31]

ELIZABETH, a brig, Capt. Donald Clark, arr. in Charleston, SC, during Nov. 1740 fr. Glasgow; Hercules Angus, arr. in Charleston on 18 Nov. 1764 fr. Bo'ness; arr. in Charleston in Nov. 1765 fr. Bo'ness; arr. in Charleston in Nov. 1766 fr. Bo'ness; James Angus, arr. in Charleston in Nov. 1767 fr. Bo'ness; J. Martin, arr. in Charleston in Feb. 1768 fr. Dundee; Thomas Cunningham, arr. in Charleston in Feb. 1771 fr. GK. [SCGaz:#352; 17.11.1765/6.11.1766/ 24.11.1767/5.2.1768 /7.2.1771][PRO.CO5.511]

ELIZABETH, Capt. Orr, fr. Glasgow to VA in 1746, captured by the French or Spanish. [SM#8.450]

ELIZABETH, William Morris, fr. GK to VA in Aug. 1752. [E504.15.5]

ELIZABETH OF BO'NESS, a brigantine, Hercules Angus, arr. in Charleston, SC, on 7 Nov. 1767 fr. Bo'ness, [PRO.CO5.511][SCGaz.30.11.1767]

ELIZABETH OF GREENOCK, Alexander Kerr, fr. GK to VA in July 1762; fr. GK to VA in Apr. 1763; fr. GK to VA in Jan. 1764; fr. GK to VA in Jan. 1765;arr. in Charleston on 14 Dec. 1766 fr. Glasgow; arr. in the James River, VA, on 15 Dec. 1768 fr. Glasgow; James Leitch, fr. GK to VA in June 1769; Thomas Archdeacon, fr. GK to VA in Nov. 1771; James Rankin, fr GK to VA July 1772; John Warden, fr. GK to Wilmington, NC, *with passengers* 1 Feb. 1773; James Rankin, fr GK to James River, VA, July 1773; John Warden, fr GK to Falmouth, VA?, Apr.1774; Robert Hunter, fr. GK to New York and Halifax Aug. 1777; James Rankin fr GK to NY and St Augustine Jan.1778. [GJ:14.1.1773] [SCGaz#1636] [E504.15.11/12/16/20/21/22/23/28/29] [PaGaz#2091]

ELIZABETH OF DUNDEE, Andrew Peddie, fr. Dundee *with passengers* to Edenton, NC, 14 Apr. 1775. [CM#8333. 1.4.1775]

ELIZABETH OF GREENOCK, 107 tons, Thomas Adair, fr. GK to Baltimore, 24 July 1787; Alexander Houstoun, fr. GK to Pictou, NS, on 6 Aug. 1788; John McKie, fr. GK to NFD in Apr. 1795; fr. GK to NFD in Mar. 1796. [E504.15.45/48/68/71]

ELIZABETH OF BATH, a brig, Hugh Houstoun, arr. in Port Brunswick, NC, on 27 Sept. 1788 fr. Glasgow, [NCSA.S8.112]

ELIZABETH, brig Richard Neilson, fr. the Clyde for NC on 24 Mar. 1789, arr. in Port Brunswick, NC, on 15 May 1789 fr. Port Glasgow; arr. in Port Brunswick on 26 Oct. 1789 fr. Glasgow; James McCunn, fr. the Clyde *with passengers* to the James River, VA, in Sept. 1789. [GM#XII.587.102;606.255] [NCSA.S8.112]

ELIZABETH OF GREENOCK, 214 tons, Archibald McNeill, fr. GK to VA in Sept. 1789; fr. Port Glasgow *with passengers* to the James River, VA, in Oct. 1791; fr. Port Glasgow *with passengers* to the James River in Aug. 1792. [E504.15.52][GCr#8/126]

ELIZABETH, John Galt, fr. GK to NFD in Aug. 1789; James
    Farrie, fr. GK to NFD in July 1791. [E504.15.52/60]

ELIZABETH OF PORT GLASGOW, 107 tons, John Hartwell,
    fr. GK to Wilmington, NC, on 23 July 1790. [E504.15.56]

ELIZABETH OF ST JOHNS, 197 tons, Robert Lusk, fr. GK to
    NFD 3 May 1791. [E504.15.59]

ELIZABETH, William Milne, fr Oban *with 96 passengers from*
    *Mull and Colonsay*to PEI August 1808. [PAPEI.RG9]

ELIZABETH OF NEWCASTLE, 242 tons, Cap. Beckington, fr.
    GK to Pictou 14 Jan.1819. [E504.15.123]

ELIZABETH, a brig, G. Thomson, fr. Glencaple *with passengers*
    to America in 1821;fr. Glencaple, Dumfries-shire, to NB in
    1822. [DCr: 30.1.1821]
    [DWJ: 29.1.1822]

ELIZABETH AND JANET, James Orr, fr. GK to Boston in June
    1757. [E504.15.8]

ELIZABETH AND KATHERINE, in Virginia by July 1678.
    [RH9.8.229]

ELIZABETH AND MARY, Henry Walker, arr. NY 20 Mar.1828
    with passengers fr. Port Glasgow. [USNA.M237]

ELIZABETH AND PEGGY, a snow, Walter Scott, arr. in
    Charleston, SC, in Oct. 1753 fr. Leith. [SCGaz#1008]

ELK OF HALIFAX, John Edington, fr. GK *with 3 passengers* to
    NB 22 Mar. 1811, [E504.15.90]

ELLIOT OF GREENOCK, a snow, William Clark, fr. GK to VA
    in Aug. 1761; fr. GK to VA in May 1762; Alexander Ferry, fr.
    GK to VA in Feb. 1763; fr. GK to VA in Jan. 1764; fr. GK to
    VA in Feb. 1765; fr. GK *with passengers* to the James River,
    VA, on 14 July 1767; John Speir, fr. GK to VA in May 1769;
    fr. GK to VA in Feb. 1770; Archibald Bog, fr. GK to
    Falmouth, VA in Aug. 1770; John Nicol, fr GK to Boston
    Sep.1772. [E504.15.10/11/12/14/16/17/18/21]
    [GC#19][NLS.ms.Acc.10220]

ELRICK OF ABERDEEN, Frances McLean, fr Dundee *with*
    passengers to NY 5 June 1818. [E504.11.20][CE70.1.15]

EMBLEM, William Henderson, arr. NY 18 June 1825 *with 2*
    passengers fr. Glasgow. [USNA.M237/7]

EMILIA, a snow, John Hay, arr. in Charleston in Nov.1735 fr.
    Leith. [SCGaz.22.11.1735]

EMPEROR ALEXANDER OF GREENOCK, 327 tons, Hugh

Morris, fr. GK to NY 27 Aug.1816;   Alexander McLea, fr.
  GK to NFD 18 Sep.1818. [E504.15.113/121]
ENDEAVOUR OF ABERDEEN, John Thomson, fr. Aberdeen to
  VA in June 1747. [E504.1.2]
ENDEAVOUR OF GREENOCK, John Andrew, fr. GK to
  Philadelphia in Feb. 1747; fr. GK to VA in Oct. 1747; John
  Simpson, fr. GK to VA in July 1748. [E504.15.2/3]
  [GAr.B10.12.2, fo.55]
ENDEAVOUR, James Nicholls, fr. Scotland via Boston to
  Philadelphia in Mar. 1747. [PaGaz:24.3.1747]
ENDEAVOUR, a snow, William Watson, arr. in Charleston, SC, in
  Oct. 1753 fr.Leith; arr. in Charleston in Feb. 1756 fr. Leith;
  arr. in Charleston in Dec. 1757 fr. Leith; arr. in Charleston in
  Feb. 1756 fr. Leith. [SCGaz#1010/1067/1131]
ENDEAVOUR, John Speir, fr GK to St Augustine Mar.1779;
  James Robertson, fr GK on 29 May 1781 to Halifax, NS,
  when captured and taken to Beverley, America. [E504.15.33]
  [SM#44.110][GM#IV.174]
ENTERPRISE, John Campbell, fr. GK to Charleston, SC, *"Good*
  accommodation for passengers" on 26 May 1781, fr. the
  Clyde to Charleston in 1782 when captured and taken to N.C.
  [E504.15.33][GM#IV.72/174][SM#44.164]
ENTERPRISE, T. Cumming, fr. GK to New York in Nov. 1802.
  [GkAd#82]
ENTERPRISE OF BOSTON, Cap. Crowell, fr Dundee to Mobile
  Oct.1823. [E504.11.23]
EQUITY OF GREENOCK, 119 tons, James Stewart, fr. GK to
  Quebec 12 Sept.1814. [E504.15.105]
ESSEX, William Scott, fr. GK to VA in Apr. 1762; fr.GK to VA in
  Mar. 1763;fr. GK to VA in Feb. 1764; fr. GK to VA in Feb.
  1765. [E504.15.10/11/12]
ESTHER OF AYR, 130 tons, Robert Leyburn, fr. GK to Halifax 4
  March 1814. [E504.15.103]
EUNICE, Silvanus Briggs, arr. NY 13 Dec.1827 *with passengers*
  fr. Glasgow. [USNA.M237]
EUPHEMIA OF GLASGOW, a 70 ton snow, James Lyon, at
  Charleston, SC, in Apr. 1732; fr. Leith to Charleston in 1731,
  arr. in Charleston during Apr. 1732, left to Cape Fear.
  [PRO.CO5/509 [SCGaz#15] [AC9/6455]

EUPHEMIA OF GREENOCK, Duncan Wilkie, fr. GK to
  Savannahh, GA, 15 Oct. 1810, [E504.15.90]

EUPHRATES, Capt. Stoddard, arr. in NY *with passengers* fr.
  Scotland in 1820 [pa]

EUROPE OF AYR, 158 tons, Gilbert Dick, fr. GK to Quebec 18
  March 1814; James Hannah, fr. GK to Miramachi 1 Sept.1814.
  [E504.15.103/105]

EVANDER OF ABERDEEN, 141 tons, Andrew Deary, fr
  Aberdeen to St John, NB, 27 Feb.1822; fr Aberdeen to St John
  12 July 1822. [E504.1.29]

EVERTHORP, arr. in Philadelphia on 12 July 1816 *with
  passengers* fr. the Clyde, [PAP]

EXERTION, a schooner, James Windsor, arr. in Boston *with
  passengers* fr. Scotland in 1820. [pa]

EXPEDITION OF GLASGOW, 80 tons, William Dunlop, arr. in
  Charleston, SC, during 1717 fr. Glasgow, [PRO.CO5/508]

EXPEDITION, Peter Milne, arr. NY 19 May 1828 *with
  passengers* fr. Aberdeen. [USNA.M237]

EXPERIMENT OF ST JOHNS, 55 tons, James McLean, fr. GK
  to St Johns, 10 Sept. 1788; Walter Black, fr. GK to NFD on 21
  Apr. 1789 [E504.15.48/51][GM#XII.591.134]

EXPERIMENT OF CHEPSTOW, 206 tons, John Chapman, fr.
  GK to NB 16 Apr. 1816. [E504.15.112]

EYDER, Benjamin Merrill, arr. NY 7 Aug.1826 *with passengers*
  fr. Port Glasgow. [USNA.M237]

FACTOR, a 300 ton US ship, Josiah Caldwell, fr. GK *with
  passengers* to NY in Oct. 1802. [GkAd#73]

FAIR CANADIAN, Capt. Crawford, fr. the Clyde to Quebec on 24
  Mar. 1780; fr. Rothesay *with passengers* to Quebec on 10 June
  1780. [GM#III/117, 190] [NRAS.0067/2]

FAIR LADY, Isaac Foster, arr. in Halifax, NS, in June 1749 *with
  10 passengers* fr. Glasgow. [CNSHS]

FAIR LILLY, Robert Morrison, fr. GK to MD in Jan. 1760; fr. GK
  to VA and MD in July 1760; fr. GK to VA in Mar. 1761; fr.
  GK to MD in Apr. 1762; fr. GK to MD in Sept. 1762; fr. GK to
  MD in Oct. 1763; Alexander Marquis, fr. GK to MD in Apr.
  1766 [E504.15.9/10/11/13]

FAIR PENITENT, Alexander Taylor, fr. GK *with passengers* to
  Norfolk, VA, on 11 June 1789. [GM#XII.594.158/183]

FAIR SUSANNAH OF LEITH, a snow, James Strachan, fr. GK
 via Madeira to SC in Aug. 1751; arr. in Charleston, SC, in Nov.
 1751 fr. Glasgow; arr. in Charleston in Oct. 1752 fr. Leith.
 [SCGaz#914/957] [E504.15.5]

FAIR TRADER, from Port Glasgow to NY Nov.1818.
 [E504.28.103]

FAIRFIELD OF ABERDEEN, William Farrie, fr Aberdeen via.
 GK to Quebec 26 Mar.1781.[E504.15.33;1.26][GM#IV.102]

FAIRFIELD OF ABERDEEN, 350 tons, James Morrice, fr.
 Aberdeen *with 13 passengers* to Quebec, 25 Mar. 1817; James
 Work, fr Aberdeen to St Andrews, NB, 28 Mar.1820.
 [E504.1.26/28]

FALMOUTH OF GLASGOW, 80 tons, John Anderson, fr. GK to
 VA in Feb. 1753; John McWhae, fr. GK to Casco Bay in Aug.
 1769; fr. GK to Casco Bay in Mar. 1770; John McWhae, arr.
 in Charleston, SC, in Jan. 1772 fr. GK. David Stirrat, fr. GK to
 Halifax in Apr.1777. [E504.15.6/17/18/27] [SCGaz:7.1.1772]

FALMOUTH OF GREENOCK, Archibald Bog, fr. GK to
 Quebec in Mar. 1777. [E504.15.27]

FAME OF DUNDEE, W. Thornton, arr. in Charleston, SC, in June
 1771 fr. Dundee; to Charleston in Jan. 1773; arr. in Charleston
 in Apr. 1773 fr. Dundee; fr. Port Glasgow to the Rappahannock
 River, VA, in Nov. 1773 [GC#358][SCGaz:
 6.6.1771/30.4.1773][EA#18/383][E504.28.22]

FAME OF GREENOCK, 219 tons, J.Leitch, fr. GK via Skye *with
 250 passengers* to Wilmington, NC, 7 July 1788; arr. in
 Wilmington on 18 Oct. 1788; fr. GK to Wilmington and
 Grenada in Sept. 1789, arr. in Port Brunswick, NC, on 14 Nov.
 1789. [E504.15.48/52][NCSA.S8.112]

FAME OF NEW YORK, 134 tons, William Hervey, fr. GK to NY
 on in Apr. 1790; fr. GK to NY on 25 Sept. 1790; Abraham
 Lewis, fr. GK to NY 25 Mar. 1791. [E504.15.55/56/58]

FAME, a brigantine, fr. GK *with passengers* to Charleston, SC, in
 Dec. 1802. [GkAd#89]

FAME, a 100 ton schooner, Holmes Whitemars, fr. Port Glasgow
 to America in 1792. [GCr#119]

FAME OF PHILADELPHIA, 257 tons, Robert Dunlevy, fr. GK
 with 35 passengers to Philadelphia 11 June 1811,
 [E504.15.92]

FAME OF GREENOCK, 248 tons, William Gemmill, fr. GK to
   NFD 30 Sep.1815. [E504.15.109]
FAME OF KIRKCALDY, 204 tons, J. Cummings, fr. GK to
   Montreal 21 March 1816. [E504.55.111]
FAME OF QUEBEC, 204 tons, William Abrams, fr. GK *with 12
   passengers*to Quebec 25 March 1816; fr. GK *with 15
   passengers* to Quebec 1 Aug.1816; fr. GK to NFD 11
   Oct.1817; fr. GK to Quebec 17 Mar.1818; fr. GK to Quebec
   July 1818. [E504.15.111/113/118/119/121]
FANCY OF ABERDEEN, 141 tons, James Stratton, fr. GK to
   Quebec and Montreal 25 May 1816. [E504.15.112]
FANCY OF GREENOCK, Henry Rattray, fr. GK to NFD 3
   Sept.1818. [E504.15.122]
FANNY OF GLASGOW, 160 tons, Archibald Galbraith, fr. GK to
   VA in Dec. 1759; fr. GK to VA in June 1760; fr. GK to VA in
   Mar. 1761; fr. GK to VA in May 1763; fr. GK to VA in Feb.
   1764; fr. GK to VA in Feb. 1765; fr. GK to SC in Oct. 1766;
   arr. in Charleston on 11 Dec. 1766; arr. in Charleston on 21
   Dec. 1767 fr. GK; fr. GK to VA in Feb. 1768; Angus McLarty,
   fr GK to VA July 1773; fr. GK *with passengers* to the
   Rappahannock and Potomac Rivers, VA, in Jan. 1774;
   William Robertson, fr. GK to Halifax in Oct. 1776; John
   Campbell, fr. GK to Charleston or Georgia in Oct. 1780; fr. GK
   to VA in Mar. 1787; fr. GK *with passengers* to the
   Rappahannock River, VA, in Jan. 1792.
   [SCGaz#1636][GM#III.256][PRO.CO5.511]
   [E504.15.9/10/11/12/13/15/22/23/27/44][GCr#49/358]
FANNY OF GREENOCK, a 122 ton brigantine, George
   Henderson, fr. GK to the Cape Fear River, NC, *with
   passengers* in Jan. 1787, arr. in Port Brunswick, NC, on 11
   Apr. 1787, fr. GK to VA 7 July 1788; William Tarbert, fr. GK
   to VA 7 Jan. 1791; Robert Houston, fr. GK *with 1 passenger*
   to NFD in June 1796 [E504.15.44/48/58/72/73]
   [GM:30.11.1786] [NCSA.S8.112]
FANNY OF NEW YORK, a 230 ton US ship, Daniel Braine, fr.
   GK *with passengers* to NY in Sept. 1792; fr. GK *with 70
   passengers* to NY in July 1795, arr. there in Oct. 1795; fr. GK
   to NY in Feb. 1796; fr. GK *with 50 passengers* to NY in July
   1796; fr. GK *with passengers* to NY , arr. there on 5 Apr.
   1801; fr. GK *with passengers* to NY in Mar. 1802; Peter

Taylor, fr. GK *with 10 passengers* to NY in Nov.1805; M N
Burke, fr. GK *with 40 passengers* to NY 19 Mar. 1811;
A.G.Jennings, fr. GK *with 50 passengers* to NY 29 June 1812;
William H. Forman, fr. GK *with 54 passengers* to NY 7
Oct.1815; fr. GK to NY 20 Apr. 1816; fr. GK *with 10
passengers*to NY 7 Apr.1817; fr. GK *with57 passengers* to NY
9 July 1817; fr. GK to NY July 1818; fr GK to NY 2 Feb.1819.
[ANY#1.327/351][CM#11672] [GkAd#9] [GCr#165]
[E504.15.71/73/75/90/96/109/111/115/117/121/123]

FARMER, a brig, Capt. Jamieson, arr. in Norfolk, VA, on 20 Oct.
1787 fr. Glasgow. fr. Port Glasgow to Norfolk and the James
River, VA, on 29 Jan. 1789.
[Phila.Gaz#291][GM#XII.575.6/38]

FARMER OF SALTCOATS, Andrew Low, fr. GK to NFD 16
Sep.1818. [E504.15.122]

FAVOURITE, Capt. Nicol, fr. the Clyde to NC in Apr. 1775.
Patrick Beatson, fr. GK to VA in Sept. 1785. [E504.15.41]
[CM#8340]

FAVOURITE, Robert Boag, fr. GK to Quebec in Mar. 1802; fr.
GK *with passengers* to NY in Sept. 1802; Archibald Shannon,
fr. GK to Charleston, SC, 26 Oct. 1810; James Dornan, fr. GK
to NY 21 Nov.1815. [GkAd#11/66] [E504.15.90/109]

FAVOURITE OF PETERHEAD, 202 tons, William Sellar, fr.
Aberdeen to Miramachi, 4 Mar. 1816. [E504.1.26]

FAVOURITE OF ABERDEEN, 124 tons, Alexander Henderson,
fr. Aberdeen to Shediac, NB, 19 Mar. 1817. [E504.1.26]

FAVOURITE OF AYR, James Gray, fr. GK to Quebec 27
Apr.1818. [E504.15.120]

FAVOURITE OF PORT GLASGOW, 391 tons, Johnstone
Horne, fr. GK to St John, NB, 15 Sep.1818; fr. Port Glasgow to
St John, NB, in Apr. 1820. [E504.28.108; E504.15.122]

FAVOURITE, Henry Bearns, arr. NY 12 May 1823 *with
passengers* fr. GK. [USNA.M237]

FAVOURITE, fr GK to Montreal Apr.1828; fr GK *with passengers*
to Montreal August 1828. [E504.15.164/165]

FERDINAND, a snow, John Ryburn, arr. in Charleston, SC, in Feb.
1760 fr. Glasgow. [SCGaz#1330]

FIELDING OF GREENOCK, 146 tons, John Murchie, fr. GK to
NFD 27 Mar.1815. [E504.15.107]

FILIPE OF AMELIA ISLAND, Francisco Aruffe, fr. GK to
   Amelia Island 20 Dec. 1814.[E504.15.106]

FINDLAY, Capt. Philips, fr. the Clyde to NS in Aug. 1792.
   [GCr#157]

FISHER AND FRIENDSHIP, a 100 ton brigantine, William
   Forrester, fr. Leith to GA in Jan. 1772; fr. Leith to Charleston,
   SC, in Dec. 1773; arr. in Charleston *with passengers* during
   Mar. 1774 fr. Leith. [SCGaz:14.3.1774][EA#16/383; 20/333]
   [E504.22.17/18]

FLORA OF GREENOCK, J.Simson, fr. GK to the Cape Fear
   River, NC, in Mar. 1773. [GJ:28.1.1773; 25.3.1773]
   *"For Cape Fare River, N.C., the Flora {now lying at
   Greenock} John Simson master will be ready to take on board
   goods by 1ˢᵗ Feb. and clear to sail by 20ᵗʰ of the said month.
   For freight or passage apply to James Gemmill and Co.
   merchants in Greenock"* [Glasgow Journal, 28 Jan. 1773]
   [E504.15.22]

FLORA, A.Henry, fr. the Clyde to NFD on 21 June 1786; fr. the
   Clyde *with passengers* to Quebec in Mar. 1787; fr. GK to
   Quebec in Mar. 1788; fr. the Clyde to NFD on 12 Apr. 1789;
   Capt. Ewing, fr. the Clyde to NFD 18 Sept. 1791. [GCr#9]
   [E504.15.47][GM#IX.442.206/399; XII.590.126]

FLORA OF GREENOCK, 258 tons, G.Alexander, fr. GK to
   Newfoundland 28 Jan.1815.[E504.15.107]

FLORA OF ABERDEEN, 147 tons, A.Henderson, fr. Aberdeen to
   Quebec and Montreal on 1 Apr. 1816; R.Work, fr Aberdeen to
   Savannah 1 March 1820; fr Aberdeen to Savannah 21
   Sept.1820. [E504.1.26/28]

FLORENZO, Russell E. Glover, arr. NY 29 June 1826 *with
   passengers* fr. GK. [USNA.M237]

FLY OF BOSTON, brigantine, John Easterbrook, fr Orkney to
   Boston 17 Oct.1760; John Hunt, fr Orkney to Boston 15
   Aug.1764. [E504.26.3]

FLY OF GREENOCK, 169 tons, Alexander Dow, fr. GK to NFD
   7 Feb.1815. [E504.15.107]

FLY OF PETERHEAD, 120 tons, James Thom, fr. Aberdeen to
   Quebec, 10 Apr. 1816. [E504.1.26]

FORTH, fr GK to St Johns Sep.1828. [E504.15.165]

FORTITUDE OF GREENOCK, 85 tons, David Hunter, fr. GK to
   VA on 15 July 1786; Alexander Kerr, fr. GK to Wilmington,

NC, in Apr. 1790; Capt. Blane, fr. the Clyde to Boston in Aug.
1792. [E504.15.43/55][GM#IX.446.280] [GCr#147]

FORTUNE OF GLASGOW, fr. Glasgow to VA in 1729.
[AC9/1085]

FORTUNE OF ABERDEEN, 60 tons, Harry Elphinstone, fr.
Aberdeen to VA in Mar. 1748. [E504.1.2]

FORTUNE, John McLeod, fr. Skye via the Clyde *with 300*
passengers to Wilmington, NC, in Aug. 1791.
[TGSI.55.343][E504.15.60]

FORTUNE OF GREENOCK, a brigantine, John Smith, fr. Jura
with 417 passengers [180 fr. Jura, 55 fr. Coll, 78 fr. Islay, 91
fr. Navdale, and 13 fr. Luing] to Wilmington, NC, in 1792.
[PRO.HO102/5]

FORTUNE OF DUNDEE, Alexander Craig, fr Dundee to
Charleston Apr.1816. [CE70.1.14]

FOUR BROTHERS OF WHITBY, William Jackson, fr. GK to
VA in Nov. 1758. [E504.15.9]

FRANCES OF NEW YORK, 292 tons, Daniel H. Braine, fr. GK *with 34*
passengers to NY in Feb. 1806; fr. GK *with passengers* to NY, arr.
there in 1810; Peter Taylor, fr. GK *with 36 passengers* to NY 31 Jan.
1811. [E504.15.77/90][ANY#2.158]

FRANCES OF NEW ORLEANS, 338 tons, Joseph Boyer, fr. GK with *24*
passengers to NY 15 July 1812, to settle in Columbiana County,
Ohio. [SHR#63/53][E504.15.97]

FRANCES OF NEW YORK, 317 tons, Jacob Foreman, fr GK to NY 7
June 1820, arr. NY 17 Aug.1820 *with passengers.*
[USNA.M237][E504.15.129]

FRANCES, Cap. Paterson, fr Dundee to Charleston Nov.1822.
[E504.11.22]

FRANCES ANNE OF IRVINE, John Stobo, fr. Fort William *with*
136 passengers to Pictou, NS, on 12 Aug. 1817. [E504.12.6]

FRANCIS AND ELIZABETH, Capt. Service, fr. Dumfries to VA
in 1744, captured by the French and taken to NFD.
[SM#6.440][CM:17.8.1744]

FRANKLIN, Joshua Drew, arr. NY 6 Apr.1826 *with passengers* fr. GK.
[USNA.M237]

FREDERICK, a 300 ton brigantine, Robert Boyd, fr.Port Glasgow
with passengers to the James River, VA, on 31 July 1789;
arr. in Cermuda Hundred in Oct. 1789 fr. Glasgow.
[GM#XII.598.198/246] [PIG#2000] [Phila.Gaz.#319]

FREEMASON OF GLASGOW, James Crawford, fr.GK to VA in
Feb. 1743; Robert Jamieson, fr. GK to VA in Apr. 1746; fr.
GK via the Isle of May to VA in Dec. 1746; John Patterson,
fr. GK via the Isle of Man to VA in Jan. 1748.
[E504.15.1/2/3]

FREETOWN OF HALIFAX, 166 tons, George Wright, fr. GK to Halifax
4 March 1814; John Archibald, fr. GK to Halifax 5 Sep.1818.
[E504.15.103/122]

FRIENDLY THOMAS, a snow, Philip Ball, arr. in Charleston fr.
Scotland *with passengers* in Oct. 1752 to Cape Fear, NC.
[SCGaz#958]

FRIENDS, a 250 ton brigantine, James Sinclair, fr. Port Glasgow
with 2 passengers to Quebec in Mar. 1780, captured by the
French on 8 Apr. 1780 and taken to Bergen, Norway
[GM#III/105] [SM#42.332] [GM#III/126]

FRIENDS, a brig, fr. Kirkcudbright to NS in 1801 [DWJ: 5.5.1801]

FRIENDS OF SALTCOATS, John How, fr. Fort William *with*
passengers to Quebec in July 1802. [GkAd#59]

FRIENDS OF WORKINGTON, a snow, John Harrison, fr. GK to
NFD 8 Mar.1818. [E504.15.119]

FRIENDS OF NEW YORK, 403 tons, fr GK to NY 2 Aug.1821,
Thomas Choate, arr. NY 24 Sept.1821 *with passengers* fr.
GK; fr GK to NY 15 Mar.1822, arr. NY 29 Apr.1822 *with*
passengers fr. GK; arr. NY 28 Sep.1822 *with passengers* fr.
GK; arr. NY 10 May 1823 *with passengers* fr. GK; arr. NY
15 Mar.1824 *with passengers* fr. GK; arr. NY 16 Aug.1824
with passengers fr. GK; arr. NY 31 Jan.1825 *with*
passengers fr. GK; Jacob A. Warnock, arr. in NY on 13 June
1825 *with 48 passengers* fr. GK; Thomas Choate, arr. NY
21 Oct.1825 *with passengers* fr. GK; arr. NY 12 May 1826
with passengers fr. GK; arr. NY 7 July 1827 *with passengers*
fr. GK.[USNA.M237] [E504.15.137/139]

FRIENDS ADVENTURE OF NEW YORK, a 40 ton sloop,
Edward Barber,arrived in Barbados on 27 September 1698
with 50 men and boys from Scotland bound for Virginia.
[PRO.CO33/13]

FRIENDS GOODWILL OF LEITH, 120 tons, JohnThomson, fr.
Leith via Orkney to NY in Aug. 1763; fr. Leith to VA 25
June 1765. [E504.22.10/12]

FRIENDSHIP OF LEITH, Archibald Galbraith, fr. Leith to MD before 1711. [AC7/17/270-275]

FRIENDSHIP OF GLASGOW, 180 tons, fr. Glasgow to VA
Mar.1737. [GAr.B10.15.5178, 5229]

FRIENDSHIP OF AYR, a brigantine, John Aitken, to VA before
1742; fr Port Glasgow to VA in July 1743; James Moody, fr.
Ayr to VA via Dieppe in Apr. 1769; fr. Ayr to VA in Feb.
1770; James Montgomerie, fr. Ayr to VA in June 1772; John
Smith, fr GK to Quebec Mar.1775; fr. Ayr to Halifax, NS, in
Mar. 1776; fr. Ayr to VA by Aug. 1777; John Smith, fr. GK
to Montreal in Mar. 1777; [E504.15.25/27; E504.4.5/6;
E504.28.1] [AC9/1483; AC7/56]

FRIENDSHIP, John Aiken, fr. GK to VA in July 1743; John
Shannon, fr.GK toVA in Apr. 1744; Capt. Lockhart, fr.
Scotland to VA in 1744, captured by the French and taken to
NFD. [SM#6.440] [E504.15.1]

FRIENDSHIP OF GLASGOW, 80 tons, John Shannan, fr. Port
Glasgow to VA in Apr. 1743; James Colhoun, fr. GK to VA
in May 1748; fr. GK to VA in Feb. 1749; John Paterson, fr.
GK to VA in Mar. 1750; fr. GK to VA in Mar. 1751; John
Morrison, fr. GK to Boston in Aug. 1757; fr. GK to VA in
Mar. 1758; James Baird, fr. GK to VA in Sept. 1761
[E504.15.2/4/5/8/10; E504.28.1]

FRIENDSHIP OF BO'NESS, 240 tons, William Miller, arr.
Charleston on 9 Jan. 1760 *with passengers* fr. Leith;
Hercules Angus, arr. in Charleston on 21 Apr. 1763 fr.
Bo'ness; James Cowan, fr. Bo'ness *with passengers* in Aug.
1768; arr. in Charleston on 12 Nov. 1764 fr. Bo'ness; to
Charleston in July 1768; James Cowan, arr. in Charleston on
12 Oct. 1768 fr. Bo'ness; to Charleston in Sept. 1769; James
Cowan, arr. in Charleston on 28 Jan. 1769 fr. Bo'ness; James
Cowan, arr. in Charleston in Nov.1769 fr. Bo'ness; fr.Bo'ness/
Leith to VA and MD in Sept. 1771.[PRO.CO5.510][E504.6.9]
[SCGaz#1326/1501/28.11.1769/1557/1785] [GC#78]
[CM#7122/7350][EA#10/22; 12/135; 16/119] [SC#1725]

FRIENDSHIP OF ANSTRUTHER, 100 tons, Andrew Reid, fr.
Leith to VA in July 1769. [E504.22.15]

FRIENDSHIP OF PHILADELPHIA, 120 tons, William
McCulloch, fr. GK to Philadelphia in Mar. 1771.
[E504.15.19]

FRIENDSHIP, fr. Scotland *with passengers* to NY, arr. there in

June 1771. [ANY#2.164]

FRIENDSHIP OF GLASGOW, Robert Park, fr. Port Glasgow to VA in Feb. 1773; fr GK to VA Apr.1774; fr. Port Glasgow to VA in Apr. 1774; fr. Port Glasgow to VA in Aug. 1774; John Smith, fr. Port Glasgow to Quebec in Mar. 1775. [E504.28.21/23/24;E504.15.23]

FRIENDSHIP OF PHILADELPHIA, John McAdam, fr.GK to Philadelphia in Apr. 1784; fr. GK to Philadelphia in Apr. 1785. [E504.15.39/40]

FRIENDSHIP OF GREENOCK, a brig, Robert Erskine, fr GK to Boston Mar.1774; fr. Port Glasgow to Charleston, SC, in Sept. 1774; arr. in Charleston, in Dec. 1774 fr. Glasgow. [E504.28.23; E504.15.23] [SCGaz:28.12.1774]

FRIENDSHIP OF LEITH, Capt. Jann, to Philadelphia 31 Mar.1775, [EA#23/207]

FRIENDSHIP, Peter Muir, fr. GK to NFD in July 1782. [E504.15.36]

FRIENDSHIP, Adam Corsan, fr. GK to Charleston, SC, in 1787. [AC7/64]

FRIENDSHIP OF GREENOCK, Henry Rattray, fr. GK to NFD 28 Mar.1818;Alexander McLarty, fr. GK to NFD in July 1818; fr. GK to NFD 18 June 1819. [E504.15.119/121/124]

FUNCHAL OF GREENOCK, 215 tons, James Gilchrist, fr. GK to NFD 4 July 1815;John Crews, fr. GK to NFD 7 May 1816; fr. GK to NFD 21 Feb.1817; fr. GK to NFD 23 Feb.1818. [E504.15.108/112/115/119]

GALATE, a brig, Paul Pandely, arr. in New Orleans on 1 Sept. 1827 *with 4 passengers* fr. Glasgow. [USNA.M259/6]

GANGES OF ABERDEEN, 210 tons, Alex. Martin, fr. Aberdeen to St John, NB, 20 Mar. 1817; fr Aberdeen to St John, NB, 15 Mar.1819. [E504.1.26/28]

GARLAND OF SUNDERLAND, Rt. Robertson, fr Leith to Halifax/Quebec/Montreal 24 June 1819. [E504.22.85]

GENERAL GOLDIE, a schooner, fr. Dumfries to Canada in 1817. [DWJ: 3.6.1817]

GENERAL HOWE OF LONDON/GREENOCK, Thos Salkeld, fr.GK to Halifax in July 1776; fr. GK to NY and St Augustine in Apr. 1777 [E504.15.26/27]

GENERAL KNOX OF BOSTON, 254 tons, E. L. Scott, fr. GK to Boston 19 July 1815. [E504.15.109]

GENERAL LESLIE, a snow, Rt. Eson, fr. GK to Charleston, SC, in Mar. 1781. [GM#IV/39]

GENERAL PIKE OF KENNEBUNK, 207 tons, Ismail Credifors, fr. GK to N.O. 18 Sep.1818; fr GK to N.O. 1 Apr.1819. [E504.15.121/123]

GENERAL WASHINGTON OF ROANOKE, 125 ton brig, Joseph Bryan, fr. GK to Wilmington, NC, on 25 July 1789, arr. in Port Brunswick, NC, on 28 Sept. 1789. [E504.15.52] [GM#XII.605.246][NCSA.S8.112]

GENERAL WASHINGTON OF WILMINGTON, 198 tons, James Miller, fr. GK to Wilmington on 4 Aug. 1791. [E504.15.60]

GENERAL WELLESLEY OF GREENOCK, 221 tons, J. Irving, fr. GK to NFD 6 Feb.1813. [E504.15.99]

GENERAL WOLFE, J. MacLean, arr. in Charleston, SC, on 29 Sept. 1767 *with 60 Highlanders* fr. Jura, Argyll, to Cape Fear, NC, sailed for Cape Fear on 7 Oct. 1767. [SCGaz:28.9.1767, #1671][SCGaz.5.10.1767]

GEORGE OF GLASGOW, 249 tons, James Crawford, fr. GK to VA in Mar. 1745; fr. GK to VA in Aug. 1745; fr. GK to VA in Mar. 1746; fr. GK to VA in Aug. 1746; fr. GK to VA in May 1747; fr. GK to VA in Dec. 1747; fr. GK to VA in Aug. 1748; fr. GK to VA in May 1749; John McLean, fr. GK to VA in Dec. 1759; fr. GK to VA in Aug. 1760; fr. GK to VA in June 1761; fr. GK to VA in Apr. 1762; fr. GK to VA in Feb. 1763; fr. GK to VA in Oct. 1763; fr. GK to VA in July 1764; fr. GK to VA in Apr. 1765; Peter Patterson, fr. GK to VA in Jan. 1766; Peter Paterson, fr. GK to VA in July 1766; fr. GK to VA in Apr. 1767; James Coats, fr. GK to VA in Dec. 1767; Peter Paterson, fr. GK to VA in Dec. 1768; James Coats, fr. GK to VA in Aug. 1769; fr. GK to VA in Mar. 1770; fr. GK to VA in Aug. 1770; fr. GK to VA in Apr. 1771; fr GK to VA Aug.1772; John McWhae, fr GK to NC Dec.1772; John Hunter, fr. GK to NY in Oct. 1786; fr. GK *with passengers* to NY in May 1787; arr. in NY on 20 June 1787 fr. GK; John Hunter, fr. GK to NY 15 Oct. 1787; fr. GK to NY in Apr. 1788; fr. GK *with passengers* to NY in Mar. 1789; fr. GK *with 20 passengers* to NY 10 Feb. 1791; fr. GK *with passengers* to NY in Mar. 1792. [GCr#70][GAr#TD132/66] [E504.15. 10/11/12/13/14/15/16/17/18/19/22/44/45/46/48/50/58]

[GM#IX.455.303; XII.578.46/64][GJ#2444] [Phila.Gaz.#255]

GEORGE OF GLASGOW, arr. in Wilmington, NC, *with passengers* fr. Glasgow 22 Oct. 1775. [JLQ#212]

GEORGE OF GREENOCK, James Kerr, fr. GK to GA and SC in Oct. 1770; fr GK to Boston Apr.1772; Archibald Bog, fr GK to NY May 1774 [E504.15.19/21/24]

GEORGE OF GREENOCK, 255 tons, D. McTaggart, fr. GK to NFD in Feb. 1806. [E504.15.77]

GEORGE OF LEITH, 180 tons, Capt. Watson, fr. Leith to Charleston, SC, in Feb. 1769, arr. in Charleston on 14 June 1769 fr. Leith; Alexander Alexander, fr. Leith to Charleston in Sept. 1770; fr.Bo'ness/ Leith to Charleston in Oct. 1771; fr. Leith to Charleston in Sept. 1772, arr. in Charleston in Dec. 1772 fr. Leith; fr. Leith to Charleston in Aug. 1773, arr. in Charleston during Nov. 1773 fr. Leith; arr. in Charleston in Oct. 1774 fr. Leith; Andrew Clunie, fr. Leith to Charleston in Aug. 1774. [E504.22.14/17/18/19; 6/9] [EA#11/61; 14/183; 16/182; 18/78] [CM#7258] [SCGaz:14.6.1769/20.12.1772/30.11.1773/24.10.1774]

GEORGE, Capt. Waters, fr. Glasgow to NY in 1780 when captured and taken to Dunkirk. [SM#42.561]

GEORGE, Donald Campbell, fr. GK *with passengers* to NY in Feb. 1802; fr. GK *with passengers* to NY in Nov. 1802. [GkAd#4/85]

GEORGE OF GREENOCK, 117 tons, Peter Jason, fr. GK to NFD 27 Aug.1814; fr. GK to NFD 16 Aug.1815; Cap.McAlpin, fr GK to Quebec 30 May 1822. [E504.15.105/109/140]

GEORGE OF NEWBURYPORT, 145 tons, Samuel Walton, fr. GK *with 8 passengers* to NO 1 Aug.1815. [E504.15.109]

GEORGE AND JAMES OF IRVINE, Robert Montgomery, fr. GK to Boston in Aug. 1764; arr. in Boston on 3 June 1766 *with 8 passengers* fr. Scotland; fr. GK to Boston in Mar. 1766; arr. in Boston on 15 Nov. 1766 *with 72 indentured servants* fr. Glasgow; Matthew Robinson, fr. GK to VA in June 1769, [E504.15.12/13/16] [PAB]

GEORGE AND MARY OF SALTCOATS, James Cunningham, fr. GK to VA in Apr. 1745. [E504.15.2]

GEORGE AND WILLIAM, Dougall Matheson, fr. Leith to Halifax in Aug. 1775. [E504.22.20]

GEORGE CUMING OF GREENOCK, 485 tons, Thomas Potter, from Greenock to Miramachi 28 Mar.1820; fr GK to Miramachi 26 Mar.1822; fr GK to Quebec May 1828. [E504.15.128/139/164]

GEORGE YORK, fr. GK *with passengers* to NY in 1810, to settle in Columbiana County, Ohio. [SHR#63/53]

GEORGIA OF GREENOCK, Thomas Bolton, fr GK to GA July 1775. [NAS,E504.15.25]

GIBRALTER OF ABERDEEN, 157 tons, James Lindsay, fr. Aberdeen to Miramachi, NB, 28 Mar. 1817. [E504.1.26]

GIRZIE, Archibald Hamilton, fr. Port Glasgow to VA in Oct. 1749; Capt. Dunlop, fr. the Clyde to VA in Feb. 1759; John Sproull, fr. Port Glasgow to Charleston, SC, in Oct. 1772; Andrew Sym, fr. Port Glasgow to VA in Jan. 1773; fr. Port Glasgow to the James River, VA, in July 1774, [E504.28.4/21/23][GJ#917]

GLASGOW OF GLASGOW, 130 ton snow, Andrew Gray, arr. in the Upper James River, VA, on 2 June 1737 fr. Glasgow; John Sommerville, fr. Port Glasgow to MD in Apr. 1743; Alexander Montgomery, fr. Port Glasgow to MD in June 1746; William McCunn, fr. GK to Boston in Apr. 1751; Patrick Campbell, fr. GK to Boston in Mar. 1752; fr. GK to Boston in Oct. 1752; William Clark, fr. GK to VA in Aug. 1754; fr. GK *with passengers* to MD in Mar. 1756; William Miller, fr. GK *with passengers* to the James River Dec. 1756; James Coats, fr. GK to VA in Feb. 1757; fr. GK to VA in Aug. 1757; fr. GK to VA in Apr. 1758; John Dunn, fr. GK to Boston in Apr. 1767; fr. GK to Boston in Sept. 1767; arr. in Boston on 18 Nov. 1767 *with 2 passengers* fr. Glasgow; fr. GK to Boston in Mar. 1768; arr. in Boston on 28 May 1768 *with 3 passengers* fr. Glasgow; fr. GK to Boston in Sept. 1768; arr. in Boston on 28 Nov. 1768 *with 1 passenger* fr. Glasgow; to Boston in Mar. 1769, arr. in Boston on 2 June 1769 *with 3 passengers* fr. Glasgow; John Dunn, fr. GK to Boston in Apr. 1769; fr. GK via Belfast to Boston in July 1770; Richard Tucker, fr. GK to Boston in Apr. 1771; Alexander Marquis, fr. GK to Boston, NY and Philadelphia in Sept. 1771; William Hume, fr GK to Boston May 1772; Alexander Marquis fr GK to NY Dec.1772; fr. GK *with passengers* to NY on 15 Sept. 1773; Robert Craig, fr GK to NY Nov.1774. [VG#40][PAB]

[E504.15.5/6/7/8/14/15/16/18/19/20/21/23/24;
E504.28.1/2][CM#7187/7270][GC#346][GJ#757/797]

GLASGOW, Capt. Montgomery, fr. Glasgow to VA in 1746, captured by the French or Spanish off the Capes of VA in Mar. 1747. [SM#8.549][PaGaz:24.3.1747] [MdGaz#99]

GLASGOW, 80 ton snow, W. Clark, fr. GK to VA in Aug. 1755; fr. GK *with passengers* to the Potomac River in March 1756; J. Coats, fr. GK to VA in Aug. 1757. [E504.15.7/8] [GJ#757]

GLASGOW PACKET, Alexander Porterfield, fr GK to Salem Mar.1775; fr GK to Salem Sep.1775. [E504.15.25]

GLASGOW, John Harrison, fr GK to St Augustine and NY Apr.1778.[E504.15.29]

GLASGOW, James Patrick, fr. GK to VA in June 1783; John Bowie, fr. GK to Halifax in June 1784. [E504.15.38/39]

GLASGOW, US brig, Capt. Thomas, fr. Port Glasgow *with passengers* to MD 15 Aug. 1790; Harding Williams, fr. GK *'elegantly equipped for passengers'* to Philadelphia in July 1792; fr. GK *with passengers* to Philadelphia in Mar. 1793, *'20 guineas for cabin passengers, 6 guineas for steerage passengers'*. [GJ#2613] [GCr#121/205/239]

GLASGOW, Capt. Williams, arr. in Philadelphia in Sept. 1790 fr. Glasgow. [PIG#1411]

GLASGOW OF DUNDEE, 165 tons, R.Kidd, fr Dundee *with passengers* to Quebec 1816; A.Craig, fr Dundee to N.Br. 17 Mar.1818; fr Dundee to St John, NBr.12 Mar.1820; fr Leith to Halifax/Quebec 13 June 1820. [E504.11.20/21; 22.90] [CE70.1.14]

GLASSFORD, 150 tons, William Hume, fr. GK to MD in Aug. 1757; arr. in Charleston, SC, on 6 June 1758 fr. Glasgow; Robert Hall, fr. GK to SC in Jan. 1759, arr. in Charleston in Apr. 1759. [E504.15.8/9][PRO.CO5.509] [SCGaz.14.4.1759]

GLEANER, fr GK to NFD Apr.1828. [E504.15.164]

GLENCAIRN, Hugh Porter, arr. in Charleston on 12 Jan. 1767 fr. Glasgow. [SCGaz#160]

GLENDOICK, C.Campbell, fr. GK to VA in Apr.1759; fr.GK to VA in Mar. 1761; John McRae, fr. GK to VA in Jan. 1762; A. Gray, fr. GK to VA in Mar. 1763 [E504.15.10/11][GJ#922]

GLENTANNAR, Capt. Murray, fr. Tobermory, Mull, *with 141 passengers* to Quebec on 1 July 1820. [E504.35.2]

GLENTHORN OF HARTFORD, Francis Stillman, fr. GK to NY
    7 May 1818. [E504.15.120]

GOLDEN RULE OF WHITEHAVEN, Christopher Cragg, fr.
    Kirkcudbright to NY on 2 June 1774. [E504.21.4]

GOOD INTENT, R.Beverley, fr. Fort William *with 69 passengers*
    to Pictou, NS, 19 Aug.1816. [E504.12.6]

GOOD INTENT OF ABERDEEN, 159 tons, Alexander Rogers,
    fr. Aberdeen *with 30 passengers* to Pictou, NS, 1 Mar. 1817;
    Daniel Mearns, fr Aberdeen to Pictou 2 Mar.1819; fr
    Aberdeen to Pictou 20 Mar.1820; fr Aberdeen to Shediac,
    NB, 7 May 1821. [E504.1.26/28/29]

GOSPORT OF PHILADELPHIA, Isaiah Bunker, fr. GK to
    Philadelphia 20 May 1818. [E504.15.120]

GOVERNOR CARLETON, Capt. Udney, fr. GK to Norfolk, VA,
    in Nov. 1802. [GkAd#93]

GOVERNOR FERNOR, fr GK to N.O. Oct.1828. [E504.15.166]

GOUDIES OF GREENOCK, 354 tons, Thomas McCulloch, fr.
    GK to Boston 27 Sept.1816; fr. GK to Charleston 2
    Oct.1817; James Wyllie, fr GK to Charleston 23 Sep.1819.
    [E504.15.113/118/125]

GOWAN, 144 tons, James Webster, fr Dundee to Quebec 17
    Mar.1818. [E504.11.20]

GRAEMIE OF GLASGOW, George Hunter, fr. Port Glasgow to
    VA in Feb. 1749, [E504.28.4]

GRACE OF ARBROATH, 130 tons, Charles Mill, fr. GK *with 2*
    passengers to Pictou, 30 Mar.1812. [E504.15.95]

GRANADA, William Noble, fr. GK to VA in Jan. 1765.
    [E504.15.12]

GRANDVALE OF GLASGOW, James Wallace, fr GK to Salem
    Oct.1774; fr GK to NFD Aug.1775; fr. GK to St Johns, NFD,
    and Jamaica in July 1776 [E504.15.24/25/26]

GRANDVILLE OF GREENOCK, 184 tons, Alexander Huie, fr.
    GK to Charleston, SC, 11 Feb. 1791. [E504.15.58]

GRANITE OF ABERDEEN, 127 tons, Alexander Scorgie, fr.
    Aberdeen *with 6 passengers* to Miramachi, NB, 28 Mar.
    1816; fr Aberdeen to Miranmachi 19 Apr.1818.
    [E504.1.26/27]

GRATITUDE OF DUNDEE, 155 tons, John Kinnear, fr Dundee to
    NY May 1817; John Goodlet, fr Dundee to NO 20 Feb.1821;
    John Young, arr. NY 25 June 1822 *with passengers* fr.

Dundee; Cap. Gellatly fr Dundee to Montreal June 1824.
[E504.11.20/22/23] [USNA.M237]

GRAY OF GLASGOW, snow, Thomas Woodrop, fr.Ayr to Cape
Fear, NC, in Nov. 1770; arr. in Charleston, SC, in Mar. 1771
en route for Cape Fear, NC. [SCGaz:17.3.1771] [E504.4.5]

GREENFIELD OF IRVINE, 114 tons, James Holmes, fr. GK *with
29 passengers* to Quebec and Montreal 22 Apr. 1816; fr. GK
to Quebec 11 Aug.1818; fr GK to Quebec 16 Feb.1818.
[E504.15.112/122/123]

GREENOCK OF GREENOCK, 100 ton snow, J.McCunn, fr. GK
to Boston and VA in May 1750; fr. GK to VA in Jan. 1751; fr.
GK to VA in Mar. 1752; A.Roberton, fr. GK to SC in Nov.
1752; J.McCunn, fr. GK to MD in Apr. 1755, arr July 1755; fr.
GK to VA in Mar. 1757; R.Knox, fr. GK to VA in Dec. 1757;
H. Carswell, fr. GK to VA in Feb. 1758; T. Archdeacon, fr. GK
to Falmouth, Casco Bay, in May 1770; J. Scott, fr. GK via
Oporto to SC in July 1771; T.Hunter, fr. GK to SC in Dec.
1771; J.Shields, fr GK to Charleston and Savannah in
Sept.1773, arr. in Charleston Jan.1774. [SCGaz.27.1.1774]
[E504.15.4/5/6/7/8/18/20/22][MdGaz#534]

GREENVALE OF AYR, John Bowie, fr. Ayr via Dieppe to VA in
Sept. 1770; fr. Ayr to VA in July 1771. [E504.4.5]

GREGORY, fr. GK to NC in June 1742. [GJ#46]

GREYHOUND OF VIRGINIA, John Jeffrey, fr. GK to VA 28
May 1788; fr. GK to VA 20 Jan. 1789, [E504.15.48/49]
[GM#XII.575.14]

GRISSIE, a snow, John Cameron, fr. Saltcoats *'passengers,
redemptioners or servants may apply'* to Philadelphia in Mar.
1755, [GJ#710]

GRIZELL OF GLASGOW, Archibald Hamilton, fr. GK to VA in
Dec. 1749, [E504.15.4]

HAMILTON OF GREENOCK, 151 tons, William Jack, fr. GK
with 15 passengers to Montreal, 11 Apr. 1812; fr. GK to
Montreal 23 March 1813. [E504.15.96/99]

HAMMER OF BOSTON, J.M.Pollard, fr Leith to Boston 11
Sep.1820. [E504.22.91]

HANNAH OF BOSTON, schooner, Jonathan Freeman, fr Orkney
to Boston 14 Sep.1758; fr Orkney to Boston 1 Sep.1759.
[E504.26.3]

HANNAH OF GREENOCK, Dugald Shannon, fr. GK to VA in
Apr. 1762; fr. GK to SC in Nov.1764, arr. in Charleston in
Feb.1765; arr. in Charleston on 7 July 1765 fr. Glasgow; John
McNachtane, fr. GK to NFD and Barbados in July 1776;
Thomas Wilkie, fr Port Glasgow to Halifax Dec.1778.
[E504.15.10/12/26; 28/30] [SCGaz#1570]

HANNAH, 137 tons, Anthony Nutter, fr. GK to Wiscasset in Aug.
1796. [E504.15.73]

HANNAH OF GREENOCK, 101 tons, C. Duggan, fr. GK to NFD
in Mar. 1806. [E504.15.77]

HANNAH OF ABERDEEN, 202 tons, Alexander Black, fr Leith
to St John, NB, 9 Sep.1819; fr Aberdeen to Quebec 29
Mar.1820. [E504.22.86; E504.1.28]

HANNAH, Alexander Martin, fr Dundee to NY June 1823, arr. NY
16 Sep.1823 *with passengers* fr. Dundee.
[E504.11.23][USNA.M237]

HANNIBAL OF NEW YORK, Robert Bryant, fr Orkney to NY 30
May 1755; fr Orkney to NY 6 Jan.1758; fr Orkney to NY 19
Sep.1759. [E504.26.3]

HANNIBAL,Thomas Workman, fr. GK to NFD in May 1783.
[E504.15.38]

HANOVER OF IRVINE, William Hunter, fr. Irvine to VA in
1728. [AC10/136]

HAPPY BETTY, John Grant fr. Leith to VA 13 June 1765.
[E504.22.12]

HAPPY JANET OF DUNBAR, Robert Beattie, fr Dunbar to
Charleston 6 Feb.1773, arr. in Charleston, SC, in Apr. 1773;
Andrew Petticrow fr Dunbar to Charleston 11 Dec.1773, arr.
in Charleston in Mar. 1774; fr Dunbar to Charleston 14
Dec.1774, arr. in Charleston in Dec.1774. [EA#20/333;
22/288] [SCGaz:30.4.1773/7.3.1774/11.12.1774][E504.10.5]

HARMONY OF MONTREAL, 280 tons, John Wilson, fr. GK to
Quebec 1 Aug.1814; N. Coverdale, fr. GK *with 4 passengers*
to Quebec 18 Aug.1815; W Abrams fr. GK *with 136
passengers* to Quebec and Montreal 14 May 1817; Norrison
Coverdale, fr. GK *with 10 passengers* to Charleston and
Savannahh 22 Nov.1817. [E504.15.105/109/114/116]

HARMONY OF GREENOCK, Charles Spence, fr. GK to NY 27
May 1818; fr GK to Charleston 11 Dec.1819; fr GK to NY 6
May 1820, arr. NY 15 July 1820 *with passengers* fr. GK; fr

GK to Charleston 27 Oct.1820.[E504.15.120/126/129/132]
[USNA.M237]

HARRIETT OF BATH, 261 tons, James Reid, fr GK to NY 29
Mar.1820 .[E504.15.128]

HARRIET, J. Bull, arr. in NY *with passengers* fr. Scotland in
1820. [pa]

HARRIET NEWALL OF ST JOHN, NB, 191 tons, Robert Thain,
fr GK to Boston 13 Mar.1820. [E504.15.128]

HARRIOT, a 180 ton brigantine, fr. Leith via NY to Cape Fear,
NC, in July 1774. [CM#8201]

HARRY OF GLASGOW, Dugald Shannon, fr. GK to MD in Sept.
1771, [E504.15.20]

HARRY OF NEW PROVIDENCE, 113 tons, James Ferguson, fr.
GK to NFD 27 Aug.1814. [E504.15.105]

HAWK OF GLASGOW, a brigantine, William McCunn, fr. GK to
Boston in Aug. 1750; William Heastie, fr. GK to MD in Apr.
1751; fr. GK to MD in Mar. 1752; arr. in Roanoke fr. Glasgow,
5 Apr. 1768; Robert Neil, fr GK to SC May 1772; Archibald
Weir, fr. GK *with passengers* to Cape Fear and Edenton, NC,
25 Aug. 1773; John Hastie, fr. GK to Charleston in Nov. 1779;
fr. GK *with passengers* to Charleston in Nov. 1780; fr. GK to
Charleston on 24 Jan. 1781; Archibald Paterson, fr. GK to
Quebec on 17 Apr. 1781. [NCSA/PC67/21][EEC:21.8.1773]
[GJ:12.8.1773][GC#343]
[504.15.4/5/21/23/32/33][GM#III.343;IV.38/126]

HAWK, Capt. Ryder, arr. in NY fr. Argyll in Sept. 1786.
[Penn.Herald#174]

HAWK OF GREENOCK, 173 tons, Alexander McLea, fr. GK to
NFD in Jan.1806; Robert Muir, fr. GK to NFD 4 Oct.1817.
[E504.15.77/117]

HAWTHORNE, a snow, Hugh Wyllie, arr. in Charleston, SC, in
Mar. 1755 fr. Glasgow. [SCGaz#1083]

HAZARD OF AYR, 184 tons, James Hannah, fr. GK *with 26
passengers* to Philadelphia 6 June 1817; fr. GK to Philadelphia
12 Feb.1818. [E504.15.116/119]

HEARTS OF OAK OF CHEPSTOW, 196 tons, Samuel Wills, fr.
GK to NFD 10 Apr.1819. [E504.15.124]

HEBE OF GREENOCK, 96 tons, Hugh Montgomery, fr. GK to
NFD in June 1795; fr. GK to NFD in Apr. 1796.
[E504.15.68/71/72]

HECTOR OF GREENOCK, John Spier, fr. Leith via Greenock to Pictou, NS, and Boston & Falmouth, NE, in Mar. 1773. [EA#19/1151][E504.15.22]

HECTOR OF DUNDEE, 192 tons, James Webster, fr Dundee *with passengers* to Miramachi 1816; fr Dundee *with passengers* to Miramachi Apr.1817; fr Dundee *with passengers* to Quebec 1 Apr.1819; fr Dundee *with passengers* to NY 4 May 1820; fr Dundee 16 Jan.1821 to NY, arr. NY 16 May 1821 *with passengers* fr. Dundee; fr Dundee 11 Feb.1822 to NY, arr. NY 18 July 1822 *with passengers* fr. Dundee; Cap. Ritchie, fr Dundee to NY Feb.1823; fr Dundee to NY Jan.1824; Cap. Mitchell fr Dundee to NY Jan.1825; D. S. Ogden, arr. NY 18 Apr.1825 *with passengers* fr. GK; Joseph E. Delano, arr. NY 17 Aug.1825 *with passengers* fr. GK. [E504.11.20/21/22/23][USNA.M237][CE70.1.14/15]

HELEN OF LEITH, 45 ton snow, James Seaman, fr. Leith to Charleston, SC, in 1734, arr. via London and Winyaw in Charleston on 11 Nov. 1734. [AC9/1960] [PRO.CO5.509]

HELEN, Donald Edie, arr. in Charleston, SC, in Dec. 1756 fr. Leith; fr. SC to Leith in 1758, captured by the French and taken to Louisbourg. [SCGaz#1175][SM#20.50]

HELEN OF NEW YORK, John Montgomery, fr. GK to NY in Aug. 1768 [E504.15.16]

HELEN OF IRVINE, 130 tons, Hugh Dunlop, arr. in Port Brunswick, NC, on 3 May 1785 fr. Port Glasgow, [NCSA.S8.112]

HELEN, John Mathie, fr. Campbeltown to Cape Fear, NC, on 31 July 1769. [E504.8.4]

HELEN, 210 tons, William Douglas, fr. Port Glasgow *with passengers* to Charleston, SC, in Sept. 1792, [GCr#163]

HELEN OF GREENOCK, 218 tons, John Carlyle, fr. GK to NY 28 Oct.1815. [E504.15.109]

HELEN OF ABERDEEN, 94 tons, John Jamieson, fr. Inverness to Pictou, NS, 17 July 1815; George Legertwood, fr. Aberdeen *with 11 passengers* to Quebec, 24 June 1816; George King, fr Aberdeen to Quebec 17 June 1822. [E504.17.8; E504.1.26/29]

HELEN OF ABERDEEN, 185 tons, Joseph Moore, fr. Aberdeen to St Johns 22 Apr. 1816; fr. GK to Charleston 17 July 1817; G. W. Legertwood, fr Aberdeen to Miramachi 10 May 1819. [E504.1.26/28; E504.15.117]

HELEN OF NORTH SHIELDS, 'Laves'?, fr Leith *with 40 passengers* to NY, 1 May 1817. [E504.22.77]

HELEN OF DUNDEE, Thomas Erskine, fr Dundee *with passengers* to Quebec/Montreal 19 Apr.1820; fr Dundee to Quebec/Montreal 22 Feb.1821; fr Dundee to NY 21 Jan.1822, arr. NY 13 May 1822 *with passengers* fr. Dundee; fr Dundee to Quebec/Montreal Mar.1823; fr Dundee to Charleston and Savannah Sep.1823; fr Dundee to Quebec Apr.1824 [USNA.M237][E504.11.22/23][CE70.1.16]

HELEN DOUGLAS, fr. Dumfries to NB in 1826; Alexander Forrest, fr. Annan to Richibucto, NB, in 1830. [DWJ: 11.4.1826][DCr:2.3.1830]

HELENA, James Seaman, arr. in Charleston in Oct. 1734 fr. Scotland. [SCGaz.12.10.1734]

HELENA, Daniel Crawford, fr. GK to VA on 22 Apr. 1786; fr. GK *with passengers* to the James River, VA, on 15 Sept. 1786. [E504.15.43][GM#IX.434.134/271/279/302]

HELENA, a brig, Hugh Dunlop, fr. Port Glasgow *with passengers* to Petersburg, VA, on 1 June 1786. [GM#IX.436.151/182]

HELMSLEY OF SUNDERLAND, 211 tons, Lancelot Hudson, fr. Inverness to Pictou, NS, 16 Aug. 1815. [E504.17.8]

HENDERSON, William Hamilton, fr. GK to MD in June 1761 [E504.15.10]

HENRIETTA, 90 tons, Alexander Buchanan, fr. GK to MD and Boston in Feb. 1758; James Kerr, fr. GK to Halifax on 20 Feb. 1781. [E504.15.8/33] [GM#IV/62]

HENRY OF GLASGOW, Alexander Dundas, fr. GK to MD in Feb. 1750. [E504.15.4]

HENRY OF NORTH SHIELDS, 303 tons, John Chaplain, fr. Fort William *with a family of 8 passengers* to Miramachi, NB, 26 June 1817. [E504.12.6]

HENRY OF WITHERSFIELD, Peter Edgar, fr. GK to NY 5 Aug.1818. [E504.15.122]

HENRY CLAY OF NEW BEDFORD, 224 tons, Peleg Barker, fr. GK *with 16 passengers* to NY 12 Sep.1815; Peter G.Fosdick, fr GK to NY 7 Feb.1822, arr. NY 25 Apr.1822 *with passengers* fr. GK.[E504.15.109/139] [USNA.M237]

HERALD OF GREENOCK, 189 tons, William McKessock, fr. GK to NFD 1 March 1815; David Hogg, fr. GK to Boston 19 Sept.1816; fr. GK *with 4 passengers* to Quebec 15 Aug.1817;

Alexander Shand, from GK to NFD July 1818; fr. GK to NFD
4 July 1818; fr. GK to NFD 28 June 1819
[E504.15.107/113/117/120/121/124]

HERALD OF WHITBY, 336 tons, John Snowden, fr. GK to St
John, N.B., 7 May 1817. [E504.15.116]

HERCULES OF AYR, John McGowan, fr. Ayr to NFD in May
1769; William Thomson, fr. Ayr to NFD in June 1771; fr. Ayr
to NFD in June 1774; fr. Ayr to St Johns, NFD, in Apr. 1775.
[E504.4.5/6]

HERCULES OF GREENOCK, James McArthur, fr. GK to St
Augustine, Fla., and NY, in Apr. 1779; fr. the Clyde to NY in
May 1780; Daniel Crawford, fr. GK *with passengers* to the
James River, VA, in Apr. 1786.[E504.15.32]
[GM#III.198;IX.89]

HERCULES OF ABERDEEN, 200 tons, James Dunlop, fr.
Aberdeen to Halifax and NY in June 1777; John Dunlop, fr.
Aberdeen to Philadelphia. [E504.1.13]

HERCULES OF AYR, 242 tons, Hugh Hunter, fr. GK to St John,
NB, 3 Aug.1818; fr. GK to Miramachi and St John 30
Apr.1819. [E504.15.122/123/124]

HERCULES OF DUNDEE, David Boyack, fr Dundee *with
passengers* to Quebec/Montreal Apr.1816; James Birnie, arr.
NY 6 Oct. 1825 *with passengers* fr. Dundee. [CE70.1.14]
[USNA.M237]

HERO OF AYR, John Johnston, fr. Ayr to NY in Oct. 1771; fr.
Ayr via Antigua to VA 17 Nov. 1772; fr GK to Quebec
Apr.1774 [E504.4.5/6; E540.15.23]

HERO OF NORFOLK, James Thomson, fr GK to VA Feb.1774.
[E504.15.23]

HERO OF GREENOCK, James Morrice, fr GK to St John's, NFD,
Apr.1779. [E504.15.31]

HERO, a brigantine, Capt. Kerr, fr. the Clyde to NFD on 10 Aug.
1780; John Gordon, fr. the Clyde *with 40/50 men including
passengers* NY on 11 Sept. 1781; Francis Roxburgh, fr. GK
with passengers to Wilmington, NC, 29 Feb. 1784; arr. in
Wilmington, NC, fr. GK, in 1784. [CM:28.6.1784]
[E504.15.39] [GM#III.262;#IV.135/160/294]

HERO, James Carnochan, fr. GK *with passengers* to Quebec in
Aug. 1802. [GkAd#62]

HERO, Thomas Potter, fr GK *with passengers* to NY Apr.1828, arr. NY 19 May 1828 *with passengers* fr. GK; fr GK to NY Oct.1828. [USNA.M237][E504.15.163/166]

HERVIE, brigantine, Henry Ninian, arr. in Charleston, SC, on 5 Feb. 1768 fr. Glasgow. [SCGaz:5.2.1768]

HESTER, a brigantine, Captain Johnston, arr. in Charleston, SC, in May 1770 fr. Kirkcudbright. [SCGaz.10.5.1770]

HIBERNIA OF GK, 218 tons, James McEachern, fr. GK to NFD 3 Sept.1814. [E504.15.105]

HIBERNIA OF ABERDEEN, 113 tons, Robert Lamb, fr. Stornaway *with 42 passengers* to Quebec on 5 Aug. 1815. [E504.33.3]

HIGHLAND LAD OF QUEBEC, William Moore, fr, GK to Quebec 19 Mar.1818. [E504.15.119]

HIGHLANDER OF ABERDEEN, 174 tons, Archibald Donald, fr Dundee to Charleston 2 Mar.1818; fr Aberdeen *with 32 passengers* to St John, New Brunswick, 16 Apr.1818; fr. GK to Charleston 10 Aug.1818; fr GK to Charleston 25 Jan.1819; James Laird, fr Aberdeen to Pictou 30 Mar.1820. [E504.11.20; E504.1.27/28; E504.15.122/124]

HINDUSTAN OF CHARLESTON, Benjamin Cozens, fr. GK *with 84 passengers* to NY 16 Aug.1811. [E504.15.93]

HIRAM OF ST JOHN, NB, 155 tons, John Hyndman, fr GK to St John 20 June 1821. [E504.15.136]

HOMER, James Miller, fr. Port Glasgow to VA in Aug. 1772. [E504.28.21]

HOMER OF GREENOCK, 286 tons, William Jeffrey, fr.GK to NFD 24 Aug.1815; James Bell, fr. GK to Savannah 12 March 1817; James Bell, fr. GK to Savannah 22 Aug.1817; fr. GK to St John's 24 Feb.1818; fr. GK to Charleston 3 Aug.1818; R. Kerr, fr GK to Savannah 8 Sep.1819; fr GK to Savannah 6 Mar.1820; fr GK to Savannah 29 Aug.1820; fr GK to Charleston 1 Sep.1821 [E504.15.109/115/117/119/122/125/128/131/137]

HOPE OF INVERKEITHING, 70 ton snow, Charles Greig, arr. in Charleston, SC, on 17 May 1734 fr. Leith, [PRO.CO5.509]

HOPE OF LONDON, 60 ton brigantine, George Urquhart, fr. Leith via Cromarty to SC in Dec. 1736; arr. in Charleston, SC, in July 1737 *with passengers* fr. Inverness, [AC8/599][PRO.CO5.509]

HOPE OF AYR, Hector Armour, fr. GK to VA in Feb. 1769; George Ruddiman, fr. Ayr to VA in Apr. 1771 [E504.15.16; E504.4.5]

HOPE, a brigantine, Hugh Walker, fr. GK to St Augustine in Dec. 1779; John Kelso, fr. GK *with passengers* to St Augustine or Charleston, SC, in Dec. 1780. [E504.15.32][GM#III.367]

HOPE, 300 tons, James Steel, fr. the Clyde *with passengers* to Petersburg, VA, on 18 July 1786; fr. Port Glasgow *with passengers* to the James River, VA, in Jan. 1787 [GM#IX.434.129/230/415]

HOPE, Capt. Kerr, fr. the Clyde to NFD on 19 Apr. 1786. [GM.IX.434.134]

HOPE, Capt. Montgomerie, fr. the Clyde to VA on 23 Oct. 1786. [GM#IX.460.342]

HOPE OF CORK, 300 tons, John Ayre, fr. GK to Baltimore 23 Sept. 1788. [E504.15.49]

HOPE OF CHARLESTON, 164 tons, John Rodick, fr. GK to Charleston or Georgetown, SC, on 21 Apr. 1789. [E504.15.51][GM#XII.586.94/134]

HOPE, a US ship, Capt. Rice, fr. Glasgow to Boston *with passengers* in Feb. 1797. [CM#11765]

HOPE, a brigantine, Hamilton Foster, fr. Port Glasgow *with passengers* to Norfolk, VA, in Mar. 1792; fr. the Clyde to Plymouth, North America, 11 Oct. 1802. [GCr#70] [GkAd#80]

HOPE OF AYR, 117 tons, Robert Muir, fr. Ayr to Pictou, NS, 2 Aug. 1806. [E504.4.11]

HOPE OF GREENOCK, 166 tons, John Banner, fr. GK to NFD 16 Oct. 1810; William McMorland fr. GK to Miramachi 7 March 1816; fr. GK *with 10 passengers* to Miramachi 31 Aug.1816. [E504.15.90/111/113]

HOPE OF GREENOCK, 186 tons, John Duncan, fr. GK to Quebec 12 March 1816; fr. GK to NFD 9 Oct.1816; Capt. Warden fr Oban to Quebec 23 June 1819; J.Duncan fr GK to Quebec 1 June 1820 [E504.15.111.113/129; 25/3]

HOPE OF ST JOHN, NB, 226 tons, John Banner, fr. GK to NFD 20 Feb.1816; fr. GK to NFD 12 July 1817; fr. GK to St John's, NFD, 4 Mar.1818; fr. GK to NFD 8 Aug.1818. [E504.15.111/117/119/122]

HOPE OF LONDON, 190 tons, George Normand, fr. GK *with 149 passengers* to Pictou 8 May 1817. [E504.15.116]

HOPE OF NEWBURYPORT, brig, Enoch Pilsbury, fr Port
    Glasgow to NY 5 Mar.1818; fr Leith to NY 16 Sep.1818.
    [E504.28.100; E504.22.82]

HOPE, Daniel Moore, arr. NY 21 Oct. 1823 *with passengers* fr.
    GK; Peter Tycan, arr. NY 5 Dec.1827 *with passengers* fr.
    Port Glasgow. [USNA.M237]

HOPEWELL OF NEW YORK, snow, Samuel Matthews, fr
    Orkneyto NY 26 Sep.1760. [E504.26.3]

HOPEWELL, William Wallace, fr. Port Glasgow to Quebec in
    Apr. 1773. [E504.28.22]

HOPEWELL OF GREENOCK, 160 tons, John Williamson, fr.
    GK to Charleston, SC, on 29 Oct. 1787; fr. GK to Charleston
    on 13 Aug. 1788, [E504.15.46/48]

HOPKIRK, Colin Campbell, fr. GK via Jamaica to VA in Sept.
    1764 [E504.15.12]

HOPTON OF GLASGOW, Robert Steel, fr. Glasgow to Boston in
    Jan. 1750, [E504.15.4]

HORIZON OF PORTSMOUTH, E.L.Sheafe, fr Leith to NY 17
    Sep.1819. [E504...22.86]

HOUSTOUN, Robert Shannon, fr. GK to NY in May 1759; Robert
    McLeish, fr. Port Glasgow to MD in May 1774; fr. Port
    Glasgow to MD in Oct. 1774 [E504.15.9; E504.28.23/24]

HOWARD, George Fram, fr. GK to NY in July 1802. [GkAd#48]

HOWARDEN CASTLE OF AYR, John Reid, fr. GK to Pictou 16
    June 1818. [E504.15.120]

HUGH CRAWFORD OF GREENOCK, 366 tons, Andrew
    Stewart, fr. GK to Charleston 4 Feb.1817; William Athol, fr.
    GK to Charleston 22 Aug.1817; John Halliday, fr. GK to
    Charleston 5 July 1819; Samuel C Stiles, fr GK to St John,
    NB, 24 July 1821. [E504.15.115/117/124/137]

HUME OF NORFOLK, Peter Bryson, fr. GK to VA in Oct. 1768,
    [E504.15.16]

HUNTER OF SALTCOATS, a 136 ton brig, Abram Hunter, fr.
    Port Glasgow to America in Mar. 1776; John Kinnear, fr. GK
    to Philadelphia in Aug. 1784; arr. in Philadelphia *with 36
    passengers* fr. Glasgow in Apr. 1785; fr. GK to Quebec 12
    Mar. 1786, [GM#IX.428.86] [E504.15.39; E504.28.24]
    [PaGaz#2864]

HUNTER, a 200 ton brigantine, Thomas Orr, fr. GK *with
    passengers* to the York River, VA, in Feb. 1789; John Kinnear,

fr. Port Glasgow to the James River in Aug. 1789; arr. in the
James River, VA, during Oct. 1789 fr. Glasgow.
[Phila.Gaz.#319] [GM#XII.575.6; 575.16; 603.232]
[E504.15.50]

HUNTER OF GREENOCK, 185 tons, James Salmon, fr. GK to
NFD 28 July 1814; fr. GK to NFD 25 July 1816; fr. GK *with 4
passengers* to NFD 9 Aug.1817; fr. GK to NFD July 1818; fr.
GK to NFD 25 June 1819. [E504.15.103/113/117/121/124]

HUNTLY, fr GK to Quebec June 1828. [E504.15.164]

HUSSAR OF GREENOCK, Daniel Campbell, fr. GK to
Charleston, SC, 1 Nov. 1810, [E504.15.90]

HYND OF DUNDEE, Alexander Smith, fr Dundee *with
passengers* to NY 6 June 1818; fr Dundee *with passengers* to
NY/St John, Nbr Mar.1819; fr Dundee to NY/St John, NBr. 3
Feb.1820; John Boyack, fr Dundee *with passengers* to NY 5
Apr.1820, arr. NY 12 July 1820; fr Dundee *with passengers* to
NY Sep.1820; fr Dundee to NY 18 Jan.1821; fr Dundee to NY
20 Aug.1821; Robert Mawer, fr Dundee to NY 27 June 1822;
fr Dundee to NY Jan.1823, arr. NY 12 May 1823 *with
passengers* fr. Dundee.
[E504.11.20/21/22/23][USNA.M237][CE70.1.15/16]

INDEPENDENCE OF CHARLESTON, 349 tons, Edward
Walker, fr. GK *with 6 passengers* to Charleston in Dec. 1805;
Job B. Thomas, fr. GK *with 8 passengers* to NY 25 Mar.1815;
R. Frisbie, fr GK to Charleston 23 Sep.1819.
[E504.15.75/107/125]

INDEPENDENCE OF NEW YORK, 326 tons, Job B. Thomas,
fr. GK *with 5 passengers* to NY 11 Dec.1815; fr. GK *with 52
passengers* to NY 20 Aug.1816; fr. GK *with 26 passengers* to
Charleston 19 Mar.1817; fr. GK to NY 13 Aug.1817; fr. GK to
NY 24 Feb. 1818; T. McMaster, fr. GK to NY July 1818; fr.
GK to NY 12 Apr.1819
[E504.15.109/113/115/117/119/121/123/124]

INDIANA OF GREENOCK, 111 tons, John Potter, fr. GK to
NFD 4 Feb.1813. [E504.15.99]

INDUSTRY OF LEITH, Andrew Cowan jr., fr. Leith to Carolina
in 1748; arr. in Charleston, SC, in Mar.1749 fr. Leith; arr. in
Charleston in Jan.1750 fr. Leith; arr. in Charleston in Dec.
1750 fr. Leith; arr. in Charleston in Feb. 1752 fr. Leith; arr. in
Charleston on 25 Jan.1753 fr. Leith; arr. in Charleston *with*

tradesmen in Nov. 1753 fr. Leith; arr. in Charleston in
Nov.1754 fr. Leith; arr. in Charleston in Dec.1755 fr. Leith; arr.
in Charleston in June 1756 fr. Leith; arr. in Charleston in
Jan.1757 fr. Leith. [SRO.AC8/723] [PRO.CO5.509]
[SCGaz#778/924/972/1013/1067/1179;11.12.1755; 22.6.1756]

INDUSTRY OF BO'NESS, 100 tons, W. Muir, arr. in Charleston,
SC, in Jan. 1758 fr. Bo'ness; Hercules Angus, arr. in
Charleston *with passengers* in Jan. 1759 fr. Bo'ness; arr. in
Charleston fr. Bo'ness on 29 Jan. 1760; fr. SC to Bo'ness and
Holland, captured by a French privateer and wrecked on the
coast of Zealand.
[SCGaz#1270/1329][SM#22.610][PRO.CO5.509]

INDUSTRY OF NEW YORK, brigantine, John Green, fr Orkney
to NY 12 June 1759; fr Orkney to NY 28 June 1760.
[E504.26.3]

INDUSTRY, a snow, Nicol Watson, arr. in Charleston, SC, in Nov.
1759 fr. Cockenzie. [SCGaz#1318]

INDUSTRY OF GREENOCK, a brigantine, William McCunn, fr.
GK to Madeira and SC in Jan. 1750; John Moor, fr. GK *with
passengers* to Norfolk, VA, and the Potomac River in Dec.
1756; John McKirdy, fr. GK to VA 11 Jan. 1758; William
Muir, fr. GK to VA in Mar. 1758; William Lead, fr. GK to
Quebec in Mar. 1766 [E504.15.4/8/13][GJ#795]

INDUSTRY OF GREENOCK, a 133 ton brigantine, John Ritchie,
fr. GK to Port Roseway in Apr. 1785; John Denniston, fr. GK
with passengers to Charleston, SC, on 27 Sept. 1786; fr. GK to
Charleston in July 1787; William Jamieson, fr. GK to Halifax
30 Apr. 1788; John Alexander, fr. GK to NC 11 Nov. 1788; fr.
GK to Wilmington in Oct. 1789, arr. in Port Brunswick, NC,
on 3 Dec. 1789; fr. GK *with passengers* to the Rappahannock
River, VA, in July 1792 [E504.15.41/43/45/48/49/52]
[NCSA.S8.112] [GM#IX.451.271/279/318][GCr#127]

INDUSTRY, a 210 ton US ship, Charles Connor, fr. GK to VA 4
July 1788; fr. Port Glasgow to the James River, VA, *with
passengers* 15 July 1790.[E504.15.48] [GM#XIII.651/199]
[GJ#2613]

INDUSTRY, a 133 ton brig, John Alexander, arr. in Beaufort, NC,
on 27 Mar. 1789 fr. Glasgow. [NCSA.S8.112]

INDUSTRY OF WARREN, a 79 ton US ship, Richard Holbrook,
fr. GK to Wiscasset on 5 Aug. 1790. [E504.15.56]

INDUSTRY OF WISCASSET, 149 tons, David Trask, fr. GK to
    Wiscasset 23 Sept. 1791. [E504.15.60]

INGRAM, John Ritchie, fr. GK to VA in July 1758; Alexander
    Campbell, fr. GK to NFD in June 1759, [E504.15.8/9]

INTREPID OF GREENOCK, Peter Jason, fr GK to NY 22 May
    1822, arr. NY 8 Aug. 1822 *with passengers*.
    [E504.15.140][USNA.M237]

INVERMAY OF VIRGINIA, William Laughton, fr. GK to VA in
    July 1771 [E504.15.19]

IRIS OF NEW YORK, John R. Smith, fr. GK to NY 27 Aug.1818;
    fr Leith to NY 25 Mar.1818; arr. NY 15 June 1822 *with
    passengers* fr. GK. [E504.15.80/122][USNA.M237]

IRVINE OF GREENOCK, 144 tons, James Barclay, fr. GK to
    NFD in Feb. 1806. [E504.15.77]

ISABELLA, James King, fr. GK to VA in Apr. 1760 [E504.15.9]

ISABELLA OF GREENOCK, Hugh Henry, fr GK to Philadelphia
    Apr.1778. [E504.15.29]

ISABELLA, 80 tons, John McAlestar, fr. GK to NY in July 1783;
    Jonathan Taylor, arr. in Port Brunswick, NC, on 14 Dec. 1784
    fr. Port Glasgow, fr. Port Glasgow *with passengers* to the
    James River, VA, on 7 Mar. 1786, arr. in the James River, VA,
    in June 1786, fr. Glasgow; fr. Port Glasgow *with passengers* to
    the James River, VA, on 15 Sept. 1786; Capt. Currie, fr. the
    Clyde to VA on 27 Apr. 1789; Capt. Curry, arr. in Hampton
    Road, VA, fr. GK, in Feb. 1789; Donald McKellar, fr. Port
    Glasgow to the James River, VA, in Aug. 1792. [WSGA,
    #1/48] [GM#IX.418.8; 427.78; 449/263; 455/302; 591.142]
    [E504.15.38][GCr#126][NCSA.S8.112] [PennMerc#96]

ISABELLA, 90 tons, to Wilmington *with passengers* in Feb. 1804;
    Capt. Livingston, fr. GK to SC in 1804, [GC:21.2.1804;
    18.12.1804; 20.12.1804]

ISABELLA OF STRANRAER, 117 tons, Robert Glen, fr. GK to
    NFD 28 June 1815. [E504.15.108]

ISABELLA OF PORT GLASGOW, 279 tons, Isaac Davis, fr.
    Port Glasgow to St John, NB, in Mar. 1820. [E504.28.108]

ISABELLA, fr GK to Halifax Aug.1828.[E504.15.165]

ISABELLA, Thomas Fyfe, arr. NY 5 July 1826 *with passengers*
    fr. Dundee. [USNA.M237]

ISABELLA, J. Dobinson, fr. Tobermory, Mull, *with 24 passengers*
    to NS on 20 Aug. 1827. [E504.35.2]

ISABELLA AND EUPHEMIA OF ABERDEEN, John
Middleton, fr. Stornaway *with 32 passengers* to Quebec on 24
Aug. 1815. [E504.33.3]

ISLE OF SKYE OF ABERDEEN, a 183 ton brigantine, John
Thom, fr. Tobermory, Mull, to P.E.I. 24 July 1806. [E504.35.1]

JACKIE, Dugald Thomson, fr. Port Glasgow to NFD in Aug.
1774; Capt. Bog, fr. the Clyde to Wilmington was captured by
the French and taken to Brest, 1795; to Wilmington 23 Sept.
1794. [E504.28.23][CM#11461][GC: 25.9.1794]

JAMAICA, fr. Port Glasgow to the Potomac River in July 1792.
[GCr#126]

JAMAICA PACKET, a brigantine, Thomas Smith, fr. Burntisland
to Cape Fear on 20 Oct. 1774. "*good encouragement to
tradesmen - coopers in particular - who want to go to
America. NB wanted a few stout young men that are
farmers*" [CM#8262, 17.10.1774]

JAMAICA OF GREENOCK, a 189 ton brigantine, John Baird, fr.
GK to NY in Oct. 1779; fr. GK to NY in Nov. 1780; John
McIver, fr. GK to Charleston, SC, in Aug. 1781; Archibald
Malcolm, fr. GK to Wilmington, NC, on 2 Feb. 1786, arr. in
Port Brunswick, NC, on 22 Apr. 1786; arr. in NC fr. the Clyde
in 1786; Archibald Malcolm, fr. GK *with passengers* to
Charleston in May 1787; Duncan Niven, arr. in Port
Brunswick, NC, on 4 Feb. 1789 fr. GK; Daniel Niven, fr. GK
to Wilmington 26 Nov. 1789; fr. GK to Wilmington 9 July
1791. [GJ#2444][NCSA.S8.112] [GM.6.7.1786]
[E504.15.32/33/42/45/48/49/60]

JAMAICA, fr GK to NO Apr.1828. [E504.15.163]

JAMES OF PRESTONPANS, John Hastings, to VA before Sept.
1707. [John Hasting's will probate 9/1707 PCC]

JAMES, James Melville, fr. Dunbar to VA 1727. [AC9/1016]

JAMES OF DUNDEE, Capt. Traill, to Boston in 1739. [CM#2993]

JAMES, Capt. Orr, taken by the Spanish when to Cape Fear in
1741. [GJ#16]

JAMES OF DUNDEE, fr. Leith to VA in 1748. [AC10/339]

JAMES OF GLASGOW, a brigantine, 100 ton; Robert Shannon,
arr. in Charleston, SC, in Apr. 1745 fr. Glasgow; fr. GK to SC
in Nov. 1745; arr. in Charleston in Apr. 1746; fr. GK to VA in
Oct. 1747; Robert Shannon, fr. GK to VA in June 1749;
Robert Campbell, fr. GK to VA in July 1750; fr. GK to VA in

July 1751; Robert Manderston, fr. GK, in Mar. 1753; William
Warden, fr. GK to MD in Aug. 1766; fr. GK to MD in Apr.
1767; Gabriel Wood, fr. GK to MD in Sept. 1767; fr. GK to
MD in Mar. 1768; fr. GK to MD in Aug. 1768; fr. GK to MD
in Mar. 1769; fr. GK to MD in Sept. 1769; fr. GK to VA in
Aug. 1770; fr. GK to MD in Aug. 1771; fr GK to VA
Feb.1772; fr GK to VA/MD Aug.1772; fr GK to GA/NC in
Mar. 1773; George Steel, fr. Port Glasgow to VA in Dec. 1774
[GJ:4.3.1773][SCGaz#574/628]
[E504.28.24//E504.15.2/4/5/6/13/14/15/16/17/18/20/21/22]

JAMES OF SALTCOATS, a brigantine, fr. Fort William *with
passengers* to Quebec in Sept. 1802. [GkAd#83]

JAMES OF GREENOCK, 227 tons, William Jack, fr. GK to
Quebec 18 Aug.1814; fr. GK *with 24 passengers* to
Quebec/Montreal 5 June 1817, arr. there on 8 Aug. 1817.
[E504.15.105/116][MG]

JAMES AND AGNES OF GLASGOW, 262 tons, Peter
McDougal, fr. GK *with 40 passengers* to Philadelphia 6
Sept.1816. [E504.15.113]

JAMES AND ELIZABETH, Thomas Buchanan, fr. Glasgow to
Virginia in Mar.1722. [Gar#B10.15.3998/4182/4183]

JAMES AND JOHN OF GREENOCK, a brigantine, Hugh
Purdie, fr. GK to Boston in Feb. 1749; fr. GK to Boston in Oct.
1749; Hugh Wyllie, fr. GK via the Canary Islands to SC in
Oct. 1750; Hugh Wyllie, arr. in Charleston, SC, in Jan. 1751
fr. GK. [E504.15.4/5][SCGaz#869]

JAMES AND MARGARET OF ABERDEEN, 187 tons, James
Moss, fr. Aberdeen to Miramachi, NB, 22 Mar. 1817; Peter
Milne, arr. NY 4 Aug. 1823 *with passengers* fr. Aberdeen; arr.
NY 30 May 1825 *with passengers* fr. Aberdeen; arr. NY 28
June 1826 *with passengers* fr. Aberdeen; arr. NY 17 May
1827 *with passengers* fr. Aberdeen.
[USNA.M237][E504.1.26]

JAMES AND MARY OF NEW YORK, John Moore, fr. GK to
NY in Sept. 1768 [E504.15.16]

JAMES AND MARY OF ST MARY'S, NEWFOUNDLAND,
104 tons, James Cowan, fr. GK via Malaga to NFD 7 March
1815. [E504.15.107]

JAMES DUNLOP OF MONTREAL, 310 tons, William Kerr, fr. GK to Quebec 23 Aug.1814; David Hogg, fr. GK to Quebec 8 Sep.1815. [E504.15.105/109]

JAMES HAMILTON OF ARDROSSAN, 118 tons, Thomas Ross, fr. GK to NFD 30 Apr. 1819. [E504.15.124]

JAMES M OF NEW BEDFORD, 296 tons, master Stephen Braley, fr. GK *with 13 passengers* to Charleston, SC, 28 July 1812. [E504.15.97]

JAMES MONTGOMERY, a brig, Capt. W. Holmes, fr. GK *with 11 passengers* to Quebec, arr. on 11 Aug. 1817. [MG]

JAMES AND JOHN OF GREENOCK, John Young, fr. GK to Boston in May 1748. [E504.15.2]

JAMIESON OF LEITH, 150 tons, John Aitken, arr. in Charleston, SC, on 4 Jan. 1763. [PRO.CO5.509]

JAMIESON AND PEGGY OF KINGHORN, John Aitken, fr. Leith to Boston on 5 June 1765; arr. in Boston on 22 Aug. 1765 *with 15 passengers* fr. Leith; fr. Kirkcaldy to Charleston in Feb. 1772, arr. there in May 1772 fr. Kirkcaldy; fr. Kirkcaldy to Charleston in Nov. 1772; arr. in Charleston in Feb. 1773 fr. Bo'ness.[PAB] [SCGaz:18.5.1772/19.2.1773] [E504.20.8/12]

JANE, a snow, John Lyon, arr. in Charleston, SC, in July 1746 fr. Glasgow. [SCGaz#644]

JANE, a brigantine, John Smith, arr. in Charleston, SC, in Apr. 1765 fr. Dunbar; arr. in Charleston, in Jan. 1766, fr. Leith; arr. in Charleston on 8 Feb. 1768 fr. Leith; arr. in Charleston on 3 Feb. 1769 fr. Leith; arr. in Charleston on 8 Dec.1769 fr. Kirkcaldy; Archibald McQueen, arr. in Charleston in Aug. 1771 fr. Glasgow. [SCGaz:6.4.1765; 28.1.1766/6.2.1768/ 8.12.1769/22.8.1771]

JANE, a brig, Capt. Watson, arr. in Bath, NC, on 10 Dec. 1784, fr. Glasgow. [NCSA/S8/112]

JANE, 200 tons, James Fyfe, fr. GK to Halifax in Mar. 1784; fr. GK *with passengers* to Halifax in July 1786; fr. GK to NFD in July 1786; fr. GK to NFD in Apr. 1787; fr. the Clyde to NFD on 29 Mar. 1789; fr. GK to NFD in Apr. 1790; fr. GK to Quebec in Apr. 1792; Archibald Kelso, fr. GK to NFD in Apr. 1795. [GCr#85] [E504.15.39/43/45/56/68] [GM#IX.441.191; XII.588.110]

JANE OF GREENOCK, 194 tons, George Kinnear, fr. GK to NFD 24 Feb.1813. [E504.15.99]

JANE OF GREENOCK, 240 tons, Douglas McGregor, fr. GK to Quebec 4 Aug.1815; Daniel Cumming, fr GK to Charleston 16 Mar.1819; fr GK to Charleston 25 Mar.1820. [E504.15.109/123/128]

JANE OF GREENOCK, 340 tons, James Rodger, fr. GK *with 7 passengers* to Charleston 19 March 1816; fr. GK *with 16 passengers* to Quebec, 29 Aug.1816; fr. GK to Charleston 17 May 1817; fr. GK to Charleston 5 Dec.1817; fr. GK to Charleston 28 Dec.1818; fr GK to Quebec 18 June 1819; Cap. Cumming, fr GK to Charleston 23 Oct.1819; fr GK to Charleston 6 Sep.1820; fr GK to Charleston 23 Oct.1821. [E504.15.111/113/114/116/122/124/125/313/138]

JANE OF AYR, 193 tons, Peter Craig, fr. GK to Quebec 14 June 1814; James Ross, fr. GK to Montreal 30 Mar.1815; Alexander Murdoch, fr. GK *with 8 passengers* to Quebec 2 Apr. 1816; fr. GK to Quebec 7 Mar.1818; fr. GK to Quebec 11 Aug.1819; fr GK to Quebec 8 Feb.1820. [E504.15.104/107/111/119/125/128]

JANE OF ABERDEEN, 120 tons, James Davidson, fr Dundee to Charleston 3 Aug.1817. [E504.11.20]

JANE OF SUNDERLAND, 340 tons, James Rogers, fr. GK *with passengers* to Canada in July 1818. [PRO.CO226/36]

JANE OF CAMPBELTOWN, 169 tons, Cap. Colville, fr GK to Chaleur Bay 29 Mar.1821. [E504.15.135]

JANE, a snow, Patrick Thorn, arr. in Philadelphia *with passengers* fr. Scotland in 1820. [pa]

JANE MONTGOMERIE OF IRVINE, 166 tons, William Holmes, fr. GK *with 12 passengers* to Quebec 27 June 1817. [E504.15.116]

JANET, Capt. McNeil, to NC in June 1773. [GJ:20.5.1773]

JANET, a brigantine, Capt. McLanahan, fr. GK *with passengers* to GA in Aug. 1780; fr. the Clyde to Charleston, SC, in 1781 when captured and taken to Boston. [GM#III.216] [SM#42.222]

JANET OF GLASGOW, David Kerr, fr. GK to NY in Apr. 1783; John Barclay, fr. GK to Baltimore in Dec. 1783; John Kerr, fr. GK to Baltimore, MD, in Feb. 1784; fr. GK to Philadelphia in Apr. 1785. [E504.15.38/39/41]

JANET OF GREENOCK, a 144 ton brigantine, Francis Ritchie, fr GK to NY and St Augustine Nov.1778; William Chisholm, fr.

GK to VA in Aug. 1784; fr. GK to VA in Mar. 1785; fr. GK to
Hampton, Norfolk, and the James River, VA on 7 Mar. 1786;
arr. in the James River, VA, in June 1786 fr. Glasgow; fr. GK
to Rappahannock, VA on 29 Sept. 1786; James Hanna, fr. GK
to VA 25 Feb. 1788; fr. GK to VA in Jan. 1789;
[E504.15.30/39/40/42/43/46/50] [PennMerc#96]
[GM#IX.418.15; 427.78; 448.247; 449/263; 457.318]

JANET OF IRVINE, 92 tons, William Watson, fr. GK to Halifax
11 July 1814. [E504.15.105]

JANET AND ANN OF ABERDEEN, 100 tons, John Youll, fr.
Aberdeen to Quebec in May 1774. [E504.1.13]

JANET AND MALLY, Capt. Anderson, fr. GK to VA in Apr.
1759. [GJ#922]

JANETS, John Williamson, fr. GK to Charleston in Aug. 1784.
[E504.15.39]

JANET DUNLOP OF GLASGOW, 181 tons, James McKechnie,
fr. GK to Quebec 11 Aug.1814; fr. GK to Montreal 23 June
1815; fr. GK *with 8 passengers* to Montreal 12 March 1816;
Peter Scott, fr. GK *with 26 passengers* to Boston 5 June 1817;
Robert C. Dow, fr. GK to Boston 17 Oct.1817; Peter Scott, fr.
GK to NFD 23 Mar.1818. [E504.15.105/108/111/114/116/119]

JEAN, a 100 ton brigantine, John McArthur, fr GK *with
passengers* to Boston in Aug.1721. [EEC#408]

JEAN OF GLASGOW, 110 tons, Donald McIntosh, fr. GK to NC
in Feb. 1744; John Somerville, fr. GK to VA in Dec. 1749;
John Moderwell, fr. GK to VA in May 1753; Robert Howe, fr.
GK to VA and MD in Feb. 1755; fr. GK to MD in Nov. 1755;
James Corbet, fr. GK to VA in Oct. 1757; James Corbet, fr.
Port Glasgow *with passengers* to NY in Aug. 1759, [GJ#938]
[E504.15.1/4/6/7/8]

JEAN OF PORT GLASGOW, William Butcher, fr. GK to VA in
Mar. 1745; John Lyon, fr. Port Glasgow to SC in May 1746.
[E504.15.2; E504.28.2]

JEAN OF ELY, 105 tons, John Smith, fr. Leith to Charleston, SC,
8 Oct. 1765. [E504.22.12]

JEAN, to Charleston, SC, in Oct. 1768; to SC in Sept. 1769.
[CM#7207][EA#12/142]

JEAN OF AYR, John Smith, fr. Ayr to VA in Apr. 1771.
[E504.4.5]

JEAN, John Ritchie, fr. Port Glasgow to the James River, VA, in
June 1774; James Fulton, fr GK to Halifax, NS, Feb.1776;
John Ritchie, fr Port Glasgow to Halifax/NY Nov.1777;
Patrick Montgomerie, fr GK to NY Mar.1779; Francis
Ritchie, fr. GK to Philadelphia and NY in Aug. 1783; fr. GK to
Newbury, NE, in Apr. 1784; Capt. Taylor, fr. the Clyde to VA
18 July 1786. [E504.28.23/28/30/38/39; E504.15.26]
[GM#IX.446.230]

JEAN, William Dunlop, fr. GK to NY in June 1781. [E504.15.33]

JEAN OF GREENOCK, 201 tons, James Fyffe, fr. GK to NFD in
Mar. 1789; fr. GK to NFD 22 Apr. 1791; fr. the Clyde to
Quebec in Apr. 1792, [GCr#97] [E504.15.50/59]

JEAN, 192 tons, William Anderson, fr. GK to NY in Aug.1802.
[GkAd#58]

JEAN OF ABERDEEN, 280 tons, Thomas Innes, fr. Aberdeen
with 3 passengers to NY, 26 July 1816. [E504.1.26]

JEAN OF DUNDEE, 162 tons, Alexander Brown, fr Dundee to NY
16 Dec.1817; fr Dundee *with passengers* to NY 7 Mar.1818.
[E504.11.20][CE70.1.15]

JEAN OF DYSART, Peter Black, fr Leith *with 3 passengers* to
Quebec 7 Apr.1817. [E504.22.77]

JEAN OF IRVINE, 169 tons, Alexander Anderson, fr GK to
Montreal 10 Mar.1820; fr GK to Montreal 20 Mar.1821; fr
GK to Montreal 15 Mar.1822. [E504.15.128/135/139]

JEAN, William Paton, arr. NY 17 Aug. 1827 *with passengers* fr.
Glasgow. [USNA.M237]

JEAN HASTIE, fr GK to Halifax Aug.1828; James O. Forsyth, arr.
NY 27 July 1829 *with passengers* fr. GK.[E504.15.165]
[USNA.M237]

JEAN AND ELIZABETH OF ABERDEEN, 100 tons, Thomas
Smith, fr. Aberdeen to VA in Apr. 1750. [E504.1.3]

JEAN AND MARY OF BOSTON, James Watson, fr GK *with
passengers* to Boston Aug.1721; James Ferguson, from GK
*with passengers*to Boston 10 Aug.1723. [EEC#408/729]

JEAN AND PEGGY OF GREENOCK, Duncan Baxter, fr. GK to
Philadelphia in June 1784; arr. in Philadelphia during Aug.
1784 fr. Glasgow. [Pa.Merc.#3] [E504.15.39]

JEANIE OF GLASGOW, William Dunlop, fr. GK to VA in Apr.
1745; fr. Port Glasgow to VA in Dec. 1745; fr. Port Glasgow to
VA in Aug. 1746; Alexander Keir, fr. GK to VA in June 1747;

fr. Port Glasgow to VA in Jan. 1748; Robert Douglas, fr. GK
to VA in Oct. 1748; fr. Port Glasgow to VA in July 1749; John
Motherwell, fr. GK to VA in Apr. 1751; fr. GK to NY in May
1756; Archibald Omey, fr. GK to VA in Feb. 1760; fr. GK to
VA in Sept. 1760; fr. GK to VA in Aug. 1761; fr. GK to VA in
Oct. 1762; fr. GK to MD in Aug. 1763; Robert Speir, fr. GK to
NY in Sept. 1764; fr. GK to Philadelphia in May 1765; fr. GK
to Philadelphia in Jan. 1766; fr. GK to VA in Aug. 1766;
Robert Morrison fr. GK to MD in Sept. 1767; fr. GK to MD in
Aug. 1768; fr. GK to MD in Mar. 1769; Archibald Omey fr
GK to VA Aug.1772; John Hastie, fr GK to NC Oct.1774
[E504.15.2/4/5/7/9/10/11/12/13/14/16/21/24; E504.28.2/3/4]
JEANIE, John Steel, fr. Port Glasgow to VA in May 1773; fr. Port
Glasgow to VA in Dec. 1773. [E504.28.22]
JEANIE OF GREENOCK, a 108 ton brigantine, William Hunter,
to NY *with passengers* in July 1768; fr. GK to NY in July
1769; Robert Esson, fr. GK to Charleston, SC, in Sept. 1769;
fr. GK to VA and Charleston in July 1770; Archibald Iver, fr.
GK to SC in June 1771; Robert Esson, fr. GK to SC in July
1771; fr GK to SC Sep.1772; fr. Port Glasgow to Charleston in
July 1773; John Steel, fr. Port Glasgow to VA in Aug. 1774;
John Kirkwood fr GK to Salem Sep.1774; William Dunlop, fr.
GK to NY on 23 July 1781; Alexander Taylor, fr. GK to the
James River, VA, Feb. 1784; fr. GK to VA in Aug. 1784; John
Simpson, fr. GK to VA in Feb. 1786; Alexander Taylor, fr.
GK to Passamaquady, NE, in June 1786; John Simpson, fr.
GK *with passengers* to the James River, VA, in Nov. 1786; fr.
GK to VA on 5 Sept. 1787; fr. the Clyde to VA on 18 Mar.
1789, Angus Martin, fr. GK *with 15 passengers* to NY on 8
Aug. 1790. [E504.15.17/18/19/20/21/22/24/33/39/42/43/45/56]
[GM#IX.456.311][GA#IV.238; VII.347.182]
JEANIE, a 150 ton brigantine, Daniel Martin, fr. GK *with
passengers* to Charleston, SC, 25 Feb. 1786; fr. GK *with
passengers* to Charleston on 19 Dec. 1786; fr. GK to NY in
July 1787; Capt. Martin, arr. in NY on 30 Sept. 1787 fr.
Glasgow; fr. GK *with 60 passengers* to NY in Mar. 1788; fr.
GK to NY on 4 Aug. 1788; fr. GK *with 60 passengers* to NY
on 6 Mar. 1789; fr. GK *with passengers* to NY in Aug. 1789;
Angus Martin, fr. GK *with passengers* to NY in Mar. 1792; fr.
GK *with passengers* to NY in Aug. 1792 [CM#7169/7335]

[Phila.Gaz.#285] [GCr#65/149] [GM#XII.581.55; XII.598.199; 604.240] [GM#IX.420.33; 454.295; 465.382; 469.414] [E504.15.45/46/47/48/50/52/58; E504.28.22/23]

JEANY OF WHITEHAVEN, James Welsh, fr. Kirkcudbright to NY on 2 June 1774. [E504.21.4]

JEANIE, a snow, fr. GK *with passengers* to Savannah, GA, in Feb. 1780. [GM#III/106]

JEANIE, Capt. Wilson, fr. the Clyde to NY in 1781 when captured and taken to Cherbourg. [SM#42.614]

JEANY, Capt. Huskins, fr. GK *with passengers* to Wilmington, NC, 15 July 1784. [CM:5.6.1784]

JEANIE, 250 tons, William Kinnear, fr. Port Glasgow *with passengers* to Quebec in 1781; fr. GK *with passengers* to Quebec in Mar. 1787. [E504.15.44][GM#IV.7; IX.467.399]

JEANIE, Neil Cook, fr. the Clyde to VA on 4 Sept. 1791; fr. GK to the James River, VA, in Dec. 1792; John Cowan, fr. GK *with passengers* to City Point, James River, VA, in June 1802. [GM#XIV.715.294] [GkAd#45][GCr#203]

JEANIE AND SALLY OF GREENOCK, William Drummond, fr GK to Halifax, NS, Feb.1776; fr. GK to Halifax in Oct. 1776, [E504.15.25/26]

JENNY OF IRVINE, a snow, Hugh Patterson, fr. GK to VA in July 1748; arr. in Charleston, SC, in Apr. 1749 fr. Irvine; James Montgomery, fr. GK to MD in May 1750; Robert Patterson, fr. GK to MD in Apr. 1751; arr. in Charleston in Nov. 1751 fr. Irvine; arr. in Charleston in Nov. 1752 fr. Irvine; Robert Caldwell, fr. GK to NY in Sept. 1768, [E504.15.2/4/5/16] [SCGaz#782/914/962]

JENNY OF GLASGOW, a 200 ton snow, Thomas Bogle, fr. GK to VA in Mar. 1744; fr. GK to VA in Mar. 1745; fr. GK to VA in Mar. 1746; captured by the French and taken to Nantes in 1746; William Cunningham, fr. GK to VA via France in May 1750; fr. GK to VA in July 1752; W. Cunningham, arr. in the Rappahannock, VA, on 3 Nov. 1752 fr. Glasgow; John Paterson, fr. GK to VA in Aug. 1753; Alexander McTaggart, fr. GK to MD in Mar. 1754; fr. GK to VA in July 1755; Arthur Tran, fr. Port Glasgow to the Rappahannock and Potomac rivers, VA, 8 Mar. 1757; James Lyon, fr. GK to VA via Cork in Sept. 1757; Donald Hyndman, fr. GK to VA in Jan. 1758; James Orr, fr. GK to Boston in Aug. 1761; fr. GK to Boston in

May 1762; fr. GK to Boston in Apr. 1763; arr. in Boston on 27
June 1763 *with 4 passengers* fr. Scotland; Robert Dawson, fr.
GK to VA in Mar. 1764; Archibald Orr, arr. in Boston on 31
Oct. 1766 *with 12 passengers* fr. Scotland; Hector Orr, fr. GK
to Boston in Apr. 1767; arr. in Boston on 17 Aug. 1767 *with 24
passengers* fr. Glasgow; fr. GK to Boston in Apr. 1768; arr. in
Boston on 1 June 1768 *with 8 passengers* fr. Glasgow.; Capt.
Morrison, fr. the Clyde to VA 30 Aug. 1769; fr. GK to Boston
in July 1769; fr. GK to MD in Mar. 1770; Archibald McLarty,
fr. GK to MD in Mar. 1771; James McLeish, fr. GK to MD in
Sept. 1771; James McLeish, fr GK to Port North Potomac,
MD and VA *with passengers* in July 1773; John Reid, fr Port
Glasgow to Halifax Nov.1776; James Cochrane fr GK to MD
Aug.1774; John Simpson, fr. GK *with passengers* to NY on 6
Feb. 1781; Thomas Logan, fr. GK to NY in May 1787.
[CM:11.8.1746] [VG#97] [PAB] [SM#8.449][E504.28.26]
[E504.15.2/4/5/6/7/8/10/11/12/14/15/17/18/19/20/22/24/33/45]
[GJ: 31.8.1769; 15.7.1773][GM#III.382; IV.8/46][GC#57/67]
[GJ#812]

JENNY, Capt. Smith, fr. VA to Dumfries in 1758, captured by the
French but ransomed for £450. [SM#20.331]

JENNY OF GREENOCK, a 130 ton brigantine, Donald
Hyndman, fr. GK to SC in Nov. 1758, arr. in Charleston on 12
Mar. 1759; arr. in Charleston on 19 Nov. 1759 fr. Glasgow; R.
Esson, fr. GK to SC in Sept. 1767; arr. in Charleston on 14 Jan.
1768 *with passengers* fr. Glasgow; fr. GK to SC in Aug. 1768;
arr. in Charleston on 24 Oct. 1768 fr. Glasgow; to NC in Sept.
1768; Hector Orr, fr. GK to Boston in Apr. 1770; fr. GK to
Boston in Oct. 1770; arr. in Charleston in Nov. 1771 fr.
Glasgow; R. McFerrand, arr. in Charleston in Mar. 1772 fr.
Glasgow; William Thomson, fr. GK to Wilmington, NC, in
July 1786; William Thompson, fr. GK to NC, 29 Apr. 1788,
arr. in Port Brunswick, NC, on 23 July 1788.
[SCA][NCSA.S8.112] [SCGaz#1725] [PRO.CO5.509]
[SCGaz: 14.1.1768/17.11.1771/ 11.3.1772]
[E504.15.14/16/18/19/43/48][GJ:1.9.1768]

JENNY OF BOSTON, 80 ton snow, Capt. Paterson, arr. in
Charleston in Nov. 1752 fr. Irvine; Adam McLeish, arr. in
Charleston in Dec. 1756 fr. Ayr; fr. GK to VA in July 1757;
arr. in Charleston, on 22 Jan. 1759; John Wilson, fr. GK to VA

in June 1760; fr. GK to SC in Mar. 1761; arr. in Charleston on 23 May 1761; fr. GK to VA in July 1761; fr. GK to SC in Nov. 1761; Thomas Wilson, fr. GK to VA in Mar. 1762; fr. GK to VA in Oct. 1762; fr. GK to VA in June 1763, [SCGaz#20.11.1752;1175/1399] [E504.15.8/9/10/11]

JENNY, James Fullerton, fr. Leith to Halifax, NS, in Aug. 1775. [E504.22.20]

JENNY, Robert Kerr, fr. Port Glasgow to the James River, VA, in Nov. 1773. [E504.28.22]

JENNY, William McGill, arr. in Norfolk, VA, on 24 Nov. 1784 *with passengers* fr. Glasgow. [PaGaz#2845][Pa.Merc.#7]

JENNY OF PORT GLASGOW, a brigantine, John Duncan, to NC July 1773; fr. GK to NFD July 1777; William Bell, fr. Port Glasgow to Edenton, Newbern, and Wilmington, NC, *with passengers* in Sept. 1784, arr. at Beaufort, NC, 2 Feb. 1785. [CM:30.8.1784][NCSA/S8.112][GJ:1.7.1773][E504.15.28]

JENNY, William Thomson, fr. GK to VA in Nov. 1785; fr. the Clyde on 31 Aug. 1786 to Wilmington, NC; fr. GK to Wilmington in May 1788, [E504.15.42/48][GM:27.7.1786]

JENNY OF GREENOCK, 110 ton brig, James Fleming, arr. in Port Brunswick, NC, on 23 July 1788 fr. GK; Ninian Rodger, fr. GK to Halifax, NS, in Sept. 1789; John Hunter, fr. GK to NFD on 27 Sept. 1790. [E504.15.52/56] [NCSA.S8.112]

JENNY OF PHILADELPHIA, a 217 ton brig, David Hardy, fr. GK to Philadelphia in July 1791; arr. in Philadelphia in Oct. 1791 fr. GK. [E504.15.60][PIG#1362]

JENNY AND NANCY, John McCunn, fr. GK to VA in Apr. 1758, [E504.15.8]

JERVISWOOD, a snow, master Thomas Baillie, arr. in Charleston in Dec. 1732 fr. Orkney. [SCGaz.30.12.1732]

JESS AND FLORA OF GREENOCK, 258 tons, George Alexander, fr. GK to Quebec 16 March 1814. [E504.15.103]

JESSE, a snow, Colin Campbell, arr. in Charleston, SC, on 17 Jan. 1761 fr. Glasgow; fr. GK to SC in Apr. 1761; arr. in Charleston in June 1761 fr. Glasgow; arr. in Charleston on 16 Dec. 1761 fr. Glasgow. [E504.15.10][SCGaz#1403/1426/1429]

JESSE, a brigantine, William Boyd, arr. in Savannah on 12 Apr. 1774 fr. GK. [GaGaz.30.11.1774]

JESSIE OF GREENOCK, William Boyd, fr GK to MD Aug.1774; fr. GK to NFD in July 1776, [E504.15.24/26]

JESSIE OF GREENOCK, a 100 ton brigantine, John Fleck, fr.
Saltcoats via GK *with passengers* to Charleston, SC, in Sept.
1786; James Rodger, fr. GK to Charleston on 17 Nov. 1787;
fr. GK to VA in Oct.1789.
[E504.15.46/52][GM#IX.451.271/279]

JESSIE OF PORT GLASGOW, a 126 ton brig, John Heartwell,
arr. in Port Brunswick, NC, on 28 June 1787 fr. Glasgow.
[NCSA.S8.112]

JESSIE, John Alexander, fr. GK to Wilmington, NC, in Oct. 1789
[E504.15.52]

JESSIE, a 200 ton brigantine, Thomas Boag, fr. GK *with
passengers* to Quebec 3 Feb. 1802; fr. GK *with passengers* to
Wilmington, NC, in Dec. 1802. [GkAd#16/96]

JESSIE OF NEW PROVIDENCE, 216 tons, John Cuthbertson,
fr. GK to NFD, 3 Oct.1814. [E504.15.105]

JESSY OF GREENOCK, 183 tons, Patrick Duggan, fr. GK to
NFD 8 Apr.1815; Thomas Boag, fr. GK to NFD 25 March
1816; fr. GK to NFD 22 Jan.1817; fr. GK to NFD 17 July
1817; fr. GK to NFD 3 June 1818.
[E504.15.108/111/115/117/120]

JESSIE, a 209 ton brig, fr. Annan and Dumfries to NB in Aug.
1817; arr. in St John *with 70 passengers* fr. Dumfries 1818; fr.
Glencaple *with passengers* to Philadelphia in 1818; fr. the
Carse of Dumfries *with 179 passengers* to P.E.I. on 17 Apr.
1820; Capt. Williams, fr. Glencaple, Dumfries-shire, *with
passengers* to America in 1821; fr. Glencaple to America in
1822; fr. Glencaple *with passengers* to NB in 1823 [DCr:
30.1.1821][CG] [DWJ: 29.7.1817; 24.3.1818; 13.8.1822;
18.3.1823] [Times#10916]

JESSY OF AYR, 213 tons, William Lyon, fr. GK to Savannah 6
Oct.1818; fr GK to Savannah 15 Mar.1819. [E504.15.121/123]

JESSY OF ABERDEEN, a 154 ton brig, James Thompson, fr.
Aberdeen *with 8 passengers* to Quebec, 3 July 1816; fr.
Aberdeen *with 14 passengers* to Quebec, arr. there on 30 July
1817; fr Aberdeen *with 21 passengers* to Quebec 9 May 1818.
[E504.1.26/27][MG]

JESSIES OF AYR, 177 tons, John Patterson, fr. GK *with 10
passengers* to Montreal and Quebec in Mar. 1796.
[E504.15.71]

JEVON OF NEW YORK, William Heysham, fr Orkney to NY 25 July 1757. [E504.26.3]

JOANNA OF GLASGOW, 200 tons, David Hunter, fr. GK to Boston in Aug. 1748; Hugh Coulter, fr. GK to Boston in Aug. 1753 [E504.15.2/6]

JOANNA OF PHILADELPHIA, 107 tons, John McShane, fr. GK to Philadelphia on 3 Mar. 1788. [E504.15.46]

JOHN OF LONDON, Thomas Leider, fr. Leith to VA, in Jan. 1680. [AC7/5]

JOHN OF IRVINE, John Francis, fr. Port Glasgow to NY in Oct. 1747. [E504.28.3]

JOHN OF BOSTON, schooner, Alexander Inglis, fr Orkney to Boston 28 Sep.1762. [E504.26.4]

JOHN OF BO'NESS, 130 ton snow, Archibald McMillan, arr. in Charleston, SC, on 11 Feb. 1766 fr. Bo'ness; fr. Leith to VA on 27 July 1767. [E504.22.13] [PRO.CO5.511]

JOHN OF GREENOCK, Archibald Bog, fr GK to Boston Mar.1773; John Hunter, fr GK to Norfolk, VA, Oct.1773. [E504.15.22/23]

JOHN OF GREENOCK, 105 tons, W. Miller, fr. GK to NFD 20 Sep.1815. [E504.15.109]

JOHN OF BO'NESS, T. Mitchell, fr Leith *with 210 passengers* to Quebec 13 May 1817.[E504.22.77]

JOHN OF ABERDEEN, 154 tons, George Allan, fr Aberdeen to St John, NB, 21 Mar.1822. [E504.1.29]

JOHN AND ARCHIBALD OF IRVINE, Robert Glasgow, fr. GK to VA in Sept. 1753, [E504.15.6]

JOHN AND EDWARD OF NEW YORK, 296 tons, C. Giles, fr. GK to NY 11 May 1819; Henry Greenleaf, arr. NY 6 July 1824 *with passengers* fr. Glasgow. [E504.15.124][USNA.M237]

JOHN AND JEAN OF ABERDEEN, 140 tons, Andrew Baxter, fr. Aberdeen to Halifax in Apr. 1774; George Knowles, fr. Aberdeen to Quebec in July 1774. [E504.1.12]

JOHN AND MARGERY, John Sangster, arr. in Charleston, SC, in Aug. 1740 fr. Montrose. [SCGaz#337]

JOHN AND ROBERT OF GOUROCK, Robert Scott, fr. Glasgow to Charleston, SC, in Nov. 1726, arr. there in 1727. [PRO.CO5.509]

JOHN AND SAMUEL OF LIVERPOOL, 188 tons, Finlay Cook, fr. Stornaway *with 82 passengers* bound to Quebec on 31 Aug. 1815. [E504.33.3]

JOHN DICKENSON, Samuel Burras, arr. NY 12 Aug. 1824 *with passengers* fr. GK. [USNA.M237]

JOHN MURPHY OF GREENOCK, 137 tons, Johnstone Howie, fr. GK to NFD 3 Oct.1814; fr. GK to NFD 6 May 1816. [E504.15.105/112]

JOHNSON, snow, Robert McCormick, fr Orkney to NY 5 Sep.1759; John McConnall, fr orkney to NY 15 Sep.1763. [E504.26.3]

JOLLY BACHELOR, Edward Young, fr. GK via the West Indies to NC in Sept. 1756; James Barnhill, fr. GK to VA in Dec. 1757 [E504.15.7/8]

JOSEPH, John Montgomerie, fr GK to St John's, NFD, July 1778. [E504.15.30]

JOSEPH OF GREENOCK, 103 tons, Capt. Bennet, fr. the Clyde to Halifax in Apr. 1792; Robert Lang, fr. GK *with 6 passengers* to Quebec in Apr. 1795. [GCr#112][E504.15.68]

JOSEPH AND ANN, a snow, to VA, 1745(?). [AC8/659]

JOSEPH HUME, Henry Rattray, arr. NY 26 Oct. 1829 *with passengers* fr. GK. [USNA.M237]

JUBILEE OF GREENOCK, 258 tons, Thomas Buchanan, fr. GK *with passengers* to Halifax, 25 Mar.1812; John Morrison, fr. GK to Halifax 13 Feb. 1813; fr. GK to Halifax 27 July 1813; fr. GK to St John, NB. 23 Feb.1814; fr. GK to Halifax 29 Aug.1814. [E504.15.95/99/101/103/105]

JUBILEE, John Nichols, arr. NY 13 Sep. 1827 *with passengers* fr. 'Galaway'. [USNA.M237]

JUDITH, John Sedgwick, fr. Port Glasgow *with passengers* to the Patuxent River, MD, in Nov. 1755, [GJ#742]

JUDITH, a brig, James Black, fr. GK *with passengers* bound via Cork to NY in Oct. 1781. [E504.15.35][GM#IV.296]

JULIET OF BATH, 250 tons, S. Swanston, fr. GK to NY 16 July 1819. [E504.15.125]

JUNE OF GREENOCK, David Cumming, fr. GK to Charleston 10 Oct.1818. [E504.15.121]

JUNO OF GREENOCK, a brigantine, John McCunn, fr. GK to NC in Oct. 1769; arr. in Charleston, SC, in Jan. 1770 *with passengers* fr. Glasgow to Cape Fear, NC; fr. GK *with*

passengers to NC on 25 July 1771; fr GK to VA Jan.1772;
James Paton, fr GK to NC Aug.1772; John McCunn, fr GK to
VA Feb.1774; fr GK to VA Aug.1774; George Orr fr GK to
Halifax Mar.1776; fr GK to Quebec Feb.1779
[SCGaz:18.1.1770] [GJ:27.6.1771; 27.8.1772]
[E504.15.17/20/21/23/24/26/30][CM#7711]

JUNO, Thomas Ritchie, fr. GK to Charleston, SC, in Dec. 1785;
Capt. McAlister, fr. the Clyde to NC in Aug. 1792; Capt.
McKie, fr. GK to Quebec 20 Mar. 1802; fr. GK to Quebec in
Aug. 1802.[GCr#150] [GC:14.8.1792] [GkAd#22/58]
[E504.15.42]

JUNO OF ABERDEEN, 150 tons, John Henderson, fr. Aberdeen
via Dundee to Quebec, 11 Mar. 1817; fr Dundee to
Quebec/Montreal 21 Mar.1818; fr Aberdeen to St John, NB. 12
Mar.1822 [E504.1.26/29; E504.11.20]

JUPITER OF STRANRAER, 152 ton brig, James McMurray, arr.
in Port Brunswick, NC, on 13 Feb. 1788 fr. Stranraer,
[NCSA.S8.112]

KATE, James Anderson, fr Dundee to NY 18 June 1821; arr. NY
2 Oct. 1827 *with passengers* fr. Dundee. [E504.11.22]
[USNA.M237]

KATHERINE OF WHITEHAVEN, John Stenhouse, fr. GK to
VA in 1722. [AC9/849]

KATY OF BOSTON, brigantine, Isaac Coleman, fr Orkney to
Boston 11 July 1764. [E504.26.4]

KATTY, James Morrison, fr. GK to NFD in Aug. 1783; fr. GK to
Boston in May 1784; fr. GK to Philadelphia in Jan. 1785; fr.
GK to NY in July 1785. [E504.15.38/39/40/41]

KATTY, John McClenehan, fr. GK to NFD in Sept. 1783.
[E504.15.38]

KATTY, Capt. McRobb, to NC 5 Apr. 1786. [GM:6.4.1786]

KEATTIE OF GREENOCK/PORT GLASGOW, John Paterson,
fr. GK to VA in Feb. 1764; James Clark, fr. GK to VA in
Feb. 1768; fr. GK to VA in Aug. 1768; fr. GK to VA in Sept.
1769; fr. GK to VA in May 1770; fr. GK to VA in Oct. 1770;
fr. GK to VA in Mar. 1771; fr. GK to VA in Aug. 1771; fr
GK to VA Mar.1772; fr GK to VA Aug.1772; fr GK to VA
Mar.1773; fr GK to James River, VA, Sep.1773; William
Harvie, fr. Port Glasgow to Salem and Boston, NE, in Apr.
1775; fr. GK to Halifax in Dec. 1776; fr Port Glasgow to NY

May 1777; fr Port Glasgow to NY May 1778; John Wilson
  fr GK to NFD Aug.1778; fr Port Glasgow to NY Mar.1779;
  Moses Crawford, fr. GK to VA in Aug. 1785 [E504.28/24/27
  /28/30;E504.15.12/15/16/17/18/19/20/21/22/23/27/30/41

KEITH, a snow, W. Miller, fr. Port Glasgow *with passengers* to the
  James River, VA, 10 July 1759, arr. in Charleston, SC, fr.
  Glasgow, on 12 May 1761. [SCGaz#1398] [GJ#931]

KENNEDY, J. Montgomery, fr. GK to Quebec in June 1767.
  [E504.15.14]

KENT OF WHITEHAVEN, J. Kilsick, fr GK to VA 5 Apr.1721.
  [EEC#365]

KENT OF IRVINE, 193 tons, J. Stirling, fr. GK to Quebec 4 Sep.
  1815; fr GK to Quebec 25 Apr.1821. [E504.15.109/136]

KERELAW, J. Stevenson, fr. GK to Halifax, NS, in Apr. 1785.
  [E504.15.41]

KING GEORGE, brigantine, John Shand, fr Orkney to NY 26
  Aug.1761. [E504.26.3]

KING'S COVE, fr GK to NFD Apr.1828. [E504.15.164]

KING OF PRUSSIA, W. Corbet, fr. GK to NC in Jan. 1758;
  James Howie, fr. GK to VA in Aug. 1760; James Glassford, fr.
  GK to VA in May 1761 [E504.15.8/9/10]

KINMONT, a snow, A. Alexander, arr. in Charleston, SC, in May
  1768 fr. Leith. [SCGaz;30.5.1768]

KINNOUL OF BO'NESS/LEITH, a 100 ton snow, A. Alexander,
  arr. in Charleston, SC, on 5 May 1766 fr. Leith via St Eustatia;
  fr. Leith to Charleston, SC, 24 Sept. 1766; arr. in Charleston on
  8 Jan. 1767 fr. Leith; fr. Leith to Charleston in Mar. 1768; fr.
  Leith to SC in Sept. 1768; arr. in Charleston, on 21 Nov. 1768
  fr. Leith *with 11 passengers*; fr. Leith to Charleston, SC, 17
  July 1769; Andrew Clunes, fr. Leith to Charleston in Jan.
  1771; arr. in Charleston in May 1771 fr. Leith.
  [SCGaz:1640/1729/21.11.1768/2.5.1771][CM#7106/7194]
  [EA#9/86] [E504.22.12/14/15/16] [PRO.CO5.511]

KITTY OF IRVINE, 100 ton snow, Peter Montgomerie, arr. in
  Charleston, SC, on 5 Feb. 1766 fr. GK, [PRO.CO5.511]

KITTY OF GREENOCK, 169 tons, Robert Love, fr. GK to NFD
  17 Feb. 1813; Robert McLea, fr. GK to Quebec 6 Apr. 1814;
  Archibald Currie, fr. GK to NFD 5 Oct.1814; Archibald
  Currie, fr. GK to NFD 9 Apr. 1816; fr. GK to NFD 19
  Oct.1817. [E504.15.99/104/105/111/114]

LADY FORBES OF LEITH, J. Marjorybanks, fr Leith *with 22 passengers* to NY/Jamaica 8 Sep.1817.[E504.22.78]

LADY MARGARET OF GLASGOW, James Kippen, fr. GK to VA in Jan. 1770; William Noble, fr GK to MD Apr.1773; fr GK to Patuxent River, MD, Oct.1773; fr. GK to Halifax Aug. 1777; Capt. Huie, fr. the Clyde to NY on 26 May 1780, captured at sea.[E504.15.17/22/23/28] [GM#III/174][SM#42.715]

LADY MONTGOMERY OF SALTCOATS, 84 tons, Adam Bell, fr. GK to NFD on 15 Feb. 1788. [E504.15.46]

LADY OF THE LAKE OF MONTREAL, 118 tons, David Priose, fr. GK *with 27 passengers* to Montreal 6 July 1816. [E504.15.113]

LADY WALLACE, William Fleck, fr GK to Quebec July 1779; fr. the Clyde to Quebec was wrecked off the coast of NFD in 1780. [E504.15.31][GM#111/109]

LAMB, John Price, to Carolina in 1753. [AC7/46/212]

LANCASTER OF WORKINGTON, 76 tons, John Thompson, fr. GK to Miramachi 13 Apr. 1816. [E504.15.112]

LANGDON CHEVIS OF CHARLESTON, 205 tons, James Moderen, fr. GK *with 26 passengers* to NY 3 June 1816. [E504.15.112]

LANGRISHE OF GREENOCK, John Forgie, fr. GK to NFD 13 Nov. 1810, [E504.15.90]

LARK OF PHILADELPHIA, brigantine, fr Orkney to Philadelphia 27Aug.1763 [E504.26.4]

LARK, John Kennedy, fr. Port Glasgow via Waterford to NFD in Apr. 1773; Alexander Ferguson, fr. Port Glasgow to NFD in May 1775; Capt. Whiteford, fr. the Clyde to Charleston, SC, on 22 July 1780. [GM#III.238] [E504.28.22/24]

LARK OF PETERHEAD, 120 tons, John Will, fr Aberdeen to Quebec 7 Apr.1818. [E504.1.27]

LATONA OF DUNDEE, Alexander Craig, fr Dundee *with passengers* to Quebec Apr.1817. [E504.11.20][CE70.1.14]

LAUTORA OF CHARLESTON, 249 tons, Benjamin Mathews, fr. GK *with 34 passengers* to Charleston 6 Aug.1817. [E504.15.117]

LAVINIA OF GREENOCK, 212 tons, Thomas Connell, fr. GK to NFD 29 Jan. 1813; Thomas Boag, fr. GK to NFD 10 Feb.1814; fr. GK to NFD 9 Feb.1815. [E504.15.99/103/107]

LAWRIE OF GREENOCK, Thomas Ramsay, fr GK *with troops* to North America Apr.1778. [E504.15.29]

LEAH OF GLASGOW, a brigantine, John Bain, fr. Port Glasgow to VA in Oct.1743; William Andrew, fr. Port Glasgow to VA in Dec. 1744; arr. in Hampton, (VA?), on 9 Mar.1745 fr.Glasgow. [E504.28.1/2] [PaGaz:25.4.1745]

LEATHLY OF ABERDEEN, 70 tons, John Lickly, fr. Aberdeen to MD in June 1749; arr. in MD during Sept.1749 fr. Aberdeen; fr. Aberdeen to MD in Mar. 1751 arr. in MD during July 1751 fr. Aberdeen; arr. in MD during Sept. 1754 fr. Aberdeen; arr. in MD during June 1756 fr. Aberdeen. [E504.1.3][MdGaz#230/323/488/581]

LEDA, James Lyall, arr. NY 30 Aug. 1828 *with passengers* fr. Dundee. [USNA.M237]

LEGAL TENDER OF GREENOCK, 116 tons, William Service, fr. GK to NFD 20 June 1814. [E504.15.104]

LEITH, W. Miller, arr. in Charleston, SC, in Apr. 1761 fr. Glasgow. [SCGaz#1398]

LEOPOLD OF LEITH, John Wilson, fr Leith to Halifax/Quebec 18 May 1819. [E504.22.85]

LEVANT OF BREMEN, 185 tons, Cap.Sandborn, fr GK to NY 5 July 1820. [E504.15.129]

LIBERTY OF GREENOCK, a brigantine, Hugh Smith, fr. GK to NC in Oct. 1764; Hugh Smellie, arr. at Cape Fear before Apr. 1765; fr. GK *with passengers* to NC and Charleston, SC, in Sept. 1765; arr. in Charleston, SC, in Nov. 1765, fr. Glasgow; Capt. Smillie, to NC 15 Nov. 1770; Capt. Wright, fr. the Clyde to NC in Aug. 1771, arr. in NC by Feb. 1772; Francis Rosburgh, arr. in Port Brunswick on 4 May 1775; William Walker, fr. GK *with 28 passengers* to NY in June 1784. [AC7/60][E504.15.12/13/39] [SCGaz:27.11.1765][GJ: 11.4.1765; 1.8.1765; 29.11.1770; 27.6.1771; 27.2.1772] [CM#7711][NCSA.S8.112];

LIBERTY AND PROPERTY, John Martin, fr. Port Glasgow to Charleston, SC, in Sept. 1773. [E504.28.22][GC#346]

LILLIAS, Hercules Angus, arr. in Charleston SC, on 27 Oct. 1768 fr. Bo'ness; arr. in Charleston on 28 Nov. 1769 fr. Bo'ness; arr. in Charleston in Oct. 1771 fr. Bo'ness; arr. in Charleston in Dec. 1772 fr. Bo'ness; arr. in Charleston in Nov. 1773 fr. Bo'ness; arr. in Charleston in Nov. 1774 fr. Bo'ness.

[SCGaz#1726/1785; 26.10.1771/16.12.1772/
6.11.1773/15.11.1774]

LILLY OF GLASGOW, a snow, James Baylie, fr. Port Glasgow
and GK to VA in Apr. 1743; Hugh Wallace, fr. Port Glasgow
and GK to VA in Apr. 1744; fr. Port Glasgow to VA in Apr.
1745; William Andrews, arr. in Charleston in May 1746 fr.
Glasgow; James Noble, fr. GK to Philadelphia in Oct. 1770
[E504.15.1/18; E504.28.1; E504.28.2] [SCGaz. 5.5.1746]

LILLY, Capt. Wallace, fr. Glasgow to VA in 1747, captured by the
French and taken to St Malo. [SM#9.97]

LILLY OF DUMFRIES, D. Blair, arr. at Port South Potomac,
VA, via France, on 10 Aug. 1752. [VG#94]

LILLY, 85 tons, James Sommerville, fr. GK via Bordeaux to VA
in Apr. 1754; fr. GK *with passengers* to VA in July 1756; fr.
GK to VA in May 1757 [E504.15.6/7/8][GJ#777]

LILLY, 150 tons, Henry White, fr. GK to VA in July 1757; fr. GK
to MD in Apr. 1758; [E504.15.8]

LILLY, Capt. Roy, fr. Glasgow to NC in 1766. [GJ:31.7.1766]

LILLY OF BO'NESS, Hercules Angus, arr. in Charleston, SC, on
18 Nov. 1767 fr. Bo'ness; fr. Bo'ness *with passengers* to
Charleston in July 1768; arr. in Charleston in Oct. 1768 fr.
Bo'ness. fr. Leith to Charleston in Sept. 1769; fr. Leith to
Charleston in Sept. 1770, arr. in Nov. 1770; fr. Bo'ness/Leith to
Charleston in July 1771; fr. Bo'ness/Leith *with passengers* to
Charleston in Aug. 1772; fr Bo'ness to Charleston 11
Aug.1773; fr.Bo'ness/ Leith to Charleston 19 July 1774,
[EA#10/37;12/175;14/134; 16/32; 18/62; 18/78; 22/47;]
[CM#7175/7365][GC#78/80] [SCGaz:18.11.1767/27.10.1768;
29.11.1770][E504.6.9]

LILLY, Thomas Bog, arr. in NC fr. the Clyde in 1764; fr. Port
Glasgow *with passengers* to Carolina in 1765; fr. the Clyde to
NC in Spring 1767; fr. the Clyde to NC on 25 Dec. 1767, arr.
in Roanoke, NC, fr. Glasgow via Tenneriffe on 28 Mar. 1768;
to NC in Aug. 1768; arr. in Roanake 22 Oct. 1768 fr. Glasgow;
arr. in Roanake 30 Sept. 1769 fr. Glasgow; arr. in Roanoke fr.
Glasgow 7 May 1770; William Dunlop, fr. Port Glasgow to
NC in July 1772; fr. Port Glasgow *with passengers* to Edenton,
NC, in Mar. 1774; James Muir (David Wyllie?), *'with troops'*
fr. Port Glasgow/Greenock to America in Mar. 1776;
Alexander Keith, fr Port Glasgow to NY Aug.1777; fr Port

Glasgow to St Augustine/NY Jan.1779 [GC:6.1.1768]
[CM#7091/8172] [GC#50] [NCSA/PC67/21][GJ:27.12.1764;
14.2.1765; 9.4.1767; 25.8.1768; 17.3.1774]
[E504.28.21/23/24/28/30; 15.26]

LILLY OF GREENOCK, Thomas Cochrane, fr GK to NY
Nov.1774; fr GK *'with troops'* to North America, Mar.1776; fr.
GK to Halifax and NY in May 1777; fr GK to NY and St
Augustine Oct.1777; William Drummond, fr GK to NY and St
Augustine Aug.1778; Hugh Smith, fr. GK to Halifax in May
1786 [E504.15.24/25/27/28/30/43]

LILLY, a 150 ton brig, Robert Sharp, fr. GK to Halifax, NS, in
Mar. 1785; fr. GK *with passengers* to Halifax in May 1786.
[GM#IX.432.119][E504.15.40]

LILLY'S PRIZE OF GLASGOW, William Andrew, fr. GK to
VA in Aug. 1744; fr. Port Glasgow to VA in Apr. 1745; fr. Port
Glasgow to SC in Feb. 1746, captured by the Spanish and taken
to St Augustine. [SM#8.449][E504.15.1; E504.28.2]

LION, Edward Drew, fr. GK to NY in Jan. 1780; Colin Campbell,
fr. Port Glasgow to the Potomac River, VA, in Feb. 1786.
[GM#IX.467.399] [E504.15.32]

LION OF ABERDEEN, 178 tons, Thomas Leask, fr. Aberdeen to
Pictou, NS, 2 Apr. 1816; fr. Aberdeen to NY, 15 Mar. 1817.
[E504.1.26]

LITTLE CHERUB OF PHILADELPHIA, 246 tons, M. H.
Parkinson, fr. GK *with 20 passengers* to Philadelphia 28 June
1815; fr. GK to Philadelphia 4 March 1816. [E504.15.108/111]

LITTLE DONALD OF LEITH, 70 ton brigantine, John Morrison,
arr. in Charleston, SC, on 9 Sept. 1759 fr. Glasgow/GK.
[SCGaz#1308] [PRO.CO5.509]

LITTLE JAMES, James Morrison, fr. GK to Charleston, SC, on
10 Sept. 1781. [E504.15.33][GM#IV.294]

LITTLEJOHN, a US brigantine, Capt. Patterson, fr. GK to Boston
in Aug. 1802. [GkAd#66]

LITTLEPAGE OF GLASGOW, Thomas Hyndman, fr GK to VA
13 Apr.1720; fr GK to VA 5 Apr.1721; fr. Glasgow to VA in
Mar.1722. [EEC#211/365][GAr/B10/15/3998, 4182, 4183]

LIVELY, William Shafto, fr. GK to VA in Mar. 1759, [E504.15.9]

LIVELY OF MARYPORT, Nicholas Martindale, fr. Ayr to St
Johns, NFD, in Sept. 1776. [E504.4.6]

LIVELY, Capt. Telford, fr. the Clyde to NY in 1780 when captured
and taken to Newry, NE. [SM#42.561]

LIVELY, James McCunn, fr. GK to VA in Feb. 1785; Thomas
Codner, fr. GK to Montreal in Mar. 1793.
[E504.15.40][GCr#249]

LIVERPOOL PACKET, a US ship, Isaac Waite, fr. GK *with
passengers* to NY in Sept. 1802. [GkAd#67]

LIVERPOOL TRADER, Robert Henry, arr. NY 24 Oct. 1825
with passengers fr. GK. [USNA.M237]

LOCKHART, James Coats, fr. GK to VA in July 1762; fr. GK to
VA in Apr. 1763; fr. GK to VA in Dec. 1764; fr. GK to VA in
Aug. 1765; fr. GK to VA in Dec. 1766; fr. Port Glasgow *with
passengers* to Charleston, SC, and Cape Fear, NC, in
1767.[E504.15.11/13/14] [GJ: 29.1.1767]

LOCKHART OF TARBERT, Archibald McAlester, fr.GK to
NFD in Mar.1768. [E504.15.15]

LONDON, David Denny, fr. GK to Charleston, SC, in Jan. 1787.
[E504.15.44]

LORD ANKERVILLE, David Ross, fr. GK *with passengers* to
Quebec on 27 May 1786.[E504.15.43][GM#IX.431.111;174]

LORD COLLINGWOOD, Peter McLachlan, fr. GK *with 34
passengers* to Pictou on 18 July 1812. [E504.15.97]

LORD DUNLUCE OF LARNE, Robert Shutter, fr. Campbeltown
to Wilmington, NC, on 4 Aug. 1775, with *"300 chests and
100 casks or barrels containing used bed clothes, body
clothes, bed, body and table linen and household furniture
belonging to the passengers"*. [E504.8.5]

LORD FREDERICK OF GREENOCK, a 160 ton snow,
Archibald Corbet, fr. GK to NC in Sept. 1762; Peter Speir, fr.
GK to NFD in Apr. 1767; fr. GK to NFD in Apr. 1769; fr. GK
with passengers to Charleston on 20 Nov. 1780; Thomas
Mitchell, fr. GK to Charleston and NY in Jan. 1781
[E504.15.11/14/16/33][GM#III/335; IV/7]

LORD GARDINER OF GREENOCK/AYR, 307 tons, Robert
Mackie, fr. GK to Miramachi 2 Sept.1814; fr. GK *with 31
passengers* to Halifax 28 Feb.1815; fr. GK *with 11
passengers* to Halifax and Pictou 2 Sept.1815; John Brown,
fr. GK *with 29 passengers* to Halifax and Pictou 9 March
1816; fr. GK *with 12 passengers* to Halifax and Pictou 14

Aug.1816; Robert Cuthbert, fr. GK to Miramachi 19
Apr.1817. [E504.15.105/107/109/111/113/115]

LORD HOWE OF GREENOCK, Alexander McLarty, fr. GK to
St Augustine in May 1777 [E504.15.27]

LORD KEITH, fr. GK to Quebec in Feb.1802. [GkAd#9] *"Wanted
a young man as house servant to a gentleman in the vicinity
of Niagara. He must indent for 4 years, his employment will
be easy and his encouragement liberal, and none need apply
but such as can be well recommended."*

LORD MONTGOMERY OF GLASGOW, 80 tons, Thomas
Clark, arr. in Charleston, SC, in Jan. 1732 fr. Scotland.
[SCGaz.22.1.1732] [PRO.CO5/506]

LORD MIDDLETON, G. Kerr, fr. Leith *with 130/300 passengers*
to Quebec 14 May 1817, arr. there on 20 July 1817.
[MG][E504.22.77]

LORD SHEFFIELD OF GREENOCK, 220 tons, Andrew
Ramsay, fr. GK to VA 4 Sept. 1788; fr. the Clyde to VA on 28
Mar. 1789; arr. at Norfolk, VA, *with passengers* fr. Glasgow,
in Nov. 1789; fr. GK to the James River, VA, in Mar. 1792.
[PIG#1216][GM#XII.588.110][GCr#65][E504.15.48]

LORD STONEFIELD OF TARBERT, Robert Sinclair, fr. GK to
NFD in Mar. 1767; James McNeil, fr. GK to NFD in Mar.
1768 [E504.15.14/15]

LORD WELLINGTON OF ABERDEEN, 285 tons, James
Mitchell, fr Aberdeen to St John, NB, 7 Apr.1821.[E504.1.29]

LOUDOUN OF GLASGOW, 140 tons, James Crawford, arr. in
Charleston, SC, in Nov. 1759 fr. Glasgow; arr. in Charleston on
22 May 1761 fr. Glasgow; Andrew Lyon, fr. GK to SC in Jan.
1763; Andrew Lyon, arr. in Charleston on 2 Apr. 1763 fr.
Glasgow; Capt. McRobb, fr. Glasgow via Cork to America,
captured by a French privateer on 23 June 1780 and taken to
L'Orient. [PRO.CO5.510][GM#III.230] [SCGaz#17.11.1759;
1399/1493] [E504.15.11]

LOUISA OF GREENOCK, 36 tons, William Wilson, fr. GK to
NFD in Sept. 1796. [E504.15.73]

LOUISA OF ABERDEEN, 213 tons, James Oswald, fr. Aberdeen
with 36 passengers to Halifax, NS, 25 Mar. 1816; fr. Aberdeen
with 13 passengers to Halifax, 26 Sept. 1816; fr. Aberdeen
with 65 passengers to Halifax, 25 Feb. 1817; fr Aberdeen to
Halifax 11 Feb.1819; fr. Tobermory *with 120 passengers* to

Pictou, NS, on 26 July 1819; fr Aberdeen to Halifax 17
Feb.1820; fr Aberdeen to Pictou 4 Aug.1821; fr Aberdeen to
Halifax 5 Mar.1822. [E504.1.26/28/29; E504.35.2]

LOUISA OF GLASGOW, Thomas Pollock, fr. GK to Charleston
17 June 1818. [E504.15.120]

LOUISIANA, James Oswald, fr Aberdeen to Halifax
Apr.1816.[E504.1.26]

LOUISIANA, C.R.Dean, arr. NY 3 Nov.1827 *with passengers* fr.
Glasgow. [USNA.M237]

LOVELY ANN, a brigantine, James Taylor, fr. Port Glasgow *with
passengers* to the Potomac River, VA, on 22 June 1789.
[GM#XII.592.143/206]

LOVELY BETSY, a schooner, William Hayman, fr. GK to Boston
in May 1766; arr. in Boston on 7 Aug. 1766 *with 6 passengers*
fr. Scotland. [PAB] [E504.15.13]

LOVELY MARY, fr. Annan, Dumfries-shire, to Miramachi, NB, in
1817. [DWJ: 8.4.1817]

LOYAL SUBJECT OF GLASGOW, Andrew Lyon, fr. GK to
New York Aug. 1777. [E504.15.28]

LOYALTY OF GLASGOW, Mungo Graham, fr. the Clyde to
Guinea and VA, but captured by pirates before 1720.
[AC9/718]

LUCEA, Robert Hunter, fr. GK to Philadelphia in Sept. 1785; arr.
in Philadelphia in Nov. 1785 fr. Glasgow. [E504.15.41]
[PaGaz#2895]

LUCEAS OF NEW YORK, 288 tons, Edward Russell, fr. GK
with 2 passengers to N.O. 11 Sep.1815. [E504.15.109]

LUCITANIA OF BOSTON, John Blany, fr. GK via Cork to
Boston in Apr. 1743. [E504.15.1]

LUCRETIA OF GREENOCK, 231 tons, James Wilson, fr GK to
North America *with troops* May 1778; Theo Tyre, fr. GK to
NFD 22 Apr. 1789; James Kerr, fr. GK to Boston in Sept.
1789. [E504.15.29/51/52][GM#XII.591.142]

LUCY OF GREENOCK, 133 tons, James Laurie, fr. GK to NFD
in Mar. 1783; Archibald Cambridge, fr. GK to Halifax in
May 1784; fr. GK to Halifax in May 1785; fr. GK to NFD in
Feb. 1786; James Robertson, fr. GK to Halifax on 14 Apr.
1788; fr. GK to Halifax on 11 May 1789; fr. GK to Halifax in
May 1790; Neil Kennedy, fr. GK to St John, NB, in Apr.
1795; James Robertson, fr. GK *with 16 passengers* to St

John, NB, in July 1796. [GM#IX.426.70; XII.594.158]
[E504.15.37/39/41/42/45/48/50/55/68/71/73]

LUCY OF AYR, 130 tons, John Goldie, fr. GK *with 6 passengers*
to Montreal in Apr. 1795; George Finlay, fr. Ayr to Pictou,
NS, 2 July 1806. [E504.15.68; E504.4.11]

LYDIA, Thomas Watson, arr. fr. Port Glasgow on 27 Aug. 1785 fr.
GK. [NCSA.S8.112]

LYDIA OF WISCASSET, 170 tons, Spencer Finkham, fr. GK to
Boston 15 Mar. 1791; Henry Tredwell, fr. GK to NY in
Nov.1802. [GkAd#82][E504.15.58]

LYDIA OF BATH, Joseph Reid, fr. GK to NY 8 June 1818.
[E504.15.120]

LYON OF LEITH, 130 tons, Robert Mudie, fr. Leith to VA 24
May 1766; fr. Leith to VA 4 Apr. 1767. [E504.22.12/13]

LYON, Capt. Drew, fr. the Clyde to NY and St Augustine in
Feb.1780. [GM#III/110,112]

MAC, W. F. Hill, fr. GK *with passengers* to Charleston, SC, on 2
Mar. 1802. [GkAd#5]

MACCLESFIELD OF POOLE, Thomas Pevans, fr. GK to NFD
July 1818. [E504.15.121]

MACDOWAL, James Wallace, fr. GK to VA in Sept. 1763.
[E504.15.11]

MAGDALENE, William Carse, fr. Leith *with passengers* to
Charleston, SC in 1743, arr. there on 29 Aug. 1743; John
MacKenzie, arr. in Charleston in May 1746 fr. Leith; arr. in
Charleston fr. Leith in June 1747; fr. Stromness to the
Carolinas in 1748, arr. in Charleston in March 1748 fr. Leith.
[SCGaz#492/632/686][AC10/323] [CM:14.4.1743; 29.2.1748]

MAGDALENE OF DUNBAR, 110 ton snow, Robert Beattie, arr.
in Charleston, SC, on 20 Nov. 1764 fr. Dunbar; arr. in
Charleston in Nov. 1765 fr. Dunbar; arr. in Charleston on 22
Nov.1766 fr. Glasgow; arr. in Charleston on 6 Dec. 1767 fr.
Dunbar; to Charleston in Sept. 1768; arr. in Charleston on 16
Dec. 1768 fr. Dunbar; arr. in Charleston during Feb. 1770 fr.
Dunbar; fr Dunbar to Charleston 1 Nov.1770, arr. in Charleston
during Jan. 1771; fr Dunbar to Charleston 2 Nov.1771; John
Dick, arr. in Charleston in Jan. 1773 fr. Dunbar.
[PRO.CO5.511][SCGaz:14.11.1765/ 6.12.1767/ 16.12.1768/
3.2.1770/ 17.1.1771/12.1.1773]
[SCGaz#1633][CM#7192][E504.10.5]

MAGDALENE OF GLASGOW, James Wallace, fr. GK to
Philadelphia in July 1771; fr GK to Philadelphia Aug.1772; fr
GK to Philadelphia Aug.1773; fr GK to Philadelphia
Aug.1774. [E504.15.20/21/22/24]

MAGDALENE OF GLASGOW, wrecked off Savannahh,
Georgia, 8 Sept. 1804. [ChCr#220]

MAGNET, Thomas Mitchell, arr. NY 22 Aug.1822 *with
passengers* fr. Leith. [USNA.M237]

MAID OF THE MILL OF PORT GLASGOW, John Bell, fr Port
Glasgow to St John, NBr. 6 Apr.1818.[E504.28.101]

MAJESTIC, Alexander Lawson, arr. NY 27 July 1829 *with
passengers* fr. Aberdeen and Dundee. [USNA.M237]

MALAY OF GREENOCK, John Young, fr. GK to St John, NB,
16 Sep.1818. [E504.15.122]

MALLY, a brig, master Joseph Tucker, fr. Port Glasgow *with
passengers* to the James River in Dec. 1756. [GJ#797]

MALLY OF GLASGOW, 150 tons, Alexander Butcher, fr. GK to
VA in Mar. 1743; fr. GK to SC in Feb. 1746; arr. in Charleston
in May 1746 fr. Glasgow; Robert Bennet, fr. GK to VA in Dec.
1767; Robert Peacock, fr. Leith to MD in Sept. 1769;
Alexander Alexander, arr. in Charleston in May 1771 fr.
Glasgow. [SCGaz:#632; 2.5.1771] [E504.15.1/2/15; E504.28.1;
E504.22.15]

MALLY, David Starret, fr. Port Glasgow to Port North Potomac,
MD, in July 1773; fr. Port Glasgow to Port North Potomac,
MD, in June 1774; John Lusk, fr Port Glasgow to Philadelphia
Apr.1778;. [E504.28.22/23/30]

MALLY, John Lamont, fr. Port Glasgow to MD in Apr. 1774.
[E504.28.23]

MALLY OF CRAWFORDSDYKE, James Colquhoun, fr. GK to
VA in Apr. 1743, fr. GK via the Isle of May to VA in Feb.
1745; fr. GK to VA in Mar. 1746. [E504.15.1/2]

MALLY, Robert How, fr. GK to VA in Aug. 1762. [E504.15.11]

MALLY OF GREENOCK, Alan Stevenson, fr. GK to VA in June
1762; Robert Bennet, fr. GK to VA in Sept. 1766; Thomas
Pollock, fr. GK to VA in June 1767; Robert Bennet, fr. GK to
NY in Dec. 1767; Archibald Orr, fr. GK to Casco Bay in Apr.
1770; fr. GK to SC in Feb. 1771 [E504.15.11/13/14/15/18/19]

MALLY, a brigantine, Capt. Hunter, fr. the Clyde to NY 19 Dec.
1767; Thomas Archdeacon, fr. GK to Edenton, NC, Feb. 1774;

fr. Port Glasgow to SC in Nov. 1774.
[GC#50][GJ:3.2.1774][E504.28.24]

MALLY, a 200 ton brigantine, John Ritchie, fr. GK to St John,
NFD, in July 1781; John Ferguson, fr. GK to St Johns, NFD,
in Mar. 1782; Robert Wyllie, fr. GK to Halifax in Apr. 1784;
Robert Wyllie, fr. GK to NC in Sept. 1785, arr. in Port
Brunswick, NC, on 20 Dec. 1785 fr. GK; fr. GK *with
passengers* to Charleston, SC, in Feb. 1789; fr. GK *with
passengers* to NY in Aug. 1789.[NCSA.S8.112]
[E504.15.33/35/39/41] [GM#XII.578.40/223/232]

MALLY OF ISLAY, John Sprott, fr. GK to NC in July 1769
[E504.15.17]

MALLY OF DUMFRIES/KIRKCUDBRIGHT, William
Lowden, fr. Kirkcudbright to Halifax, NS, in Apr. 1776.
[AC7/60][E504.21.4]

MALLY, a 140 ton brig, John Maxwell, fr. Tobermory, Mull, via
Uist, *with 230 passengers* to Cape Breton Island, landed at
Charlottetown, Prince Edward Island, in Sept. 1791; James
Wyllie, fr. GK to Wilmington, NC, 24 Aug. 1790; fr. GK *with
30 passengers* to Quebec, St Johns, and the Carolinas, on 7
June 1791; fr. GK *with passengers* to Wilmington, NC, in
Sept. 1792. [Royal Gazette#5/1]
[GC:11.8.1792][GCr#149/162][E504.15.56/59]

MALVINA, Capt. Fullarton, fr. the Clyde to NFD in Mar. 1792.
[GCr#85]

MANCHESTER OF LEITH, J.Hutchinson. fr Leith to Halifax 4
Apr.1820. [E504.22.89]

MARCIA OF PROVIDENCE, P.H.Briggs, fr Leith to NY 7
Oct.1819. [E504.22.86]

MARGARET OF GLASGOW, 120 tons, William McCunn, fr.
GK to VA in Mar. 1748; James Crawford, fr. GK to VA in Jan.
1752; fr. GK to VA in Aug. 1752; arr. in Port South Potomac,
VA, on 8 Nov. 1752 fr. GK; fr. GK to VA in Mar. 1753; fr. GK
to VA in Mar. 1754; Robert Gordon, fr. GK to VA in Mar.
1755; fr. GK to VA in Aug. 1754; fr. GK to VA in Aug. 1755;
fr. Port Glasgow *with passengers* to the Rappahannock River,
VA, May 1756; fr. GK to VA in Dec. 1756; Charles Robertson,
fr. GK to VA in Apr. 1759; fr. GK to VA in Jan. 1760; fr. GK
to VA in Mar. 1761; fr. GK to VA in Nov. 1761.[GJ#764/923]
[E504.15.2/5/6/7/8/9/10] [VG#97]

MARGARET, Robert Speir, to NC, in 1773; fr. Port Glasgow to NY in Aug. 1774. [GJ:19.8.1773][E504.28.23]

MARGARET OF GREENOCK, a 161 ton brigantine, fr. GK *with passengers* to NY and Savannah, GA, on 28 Apr. 1780; captured by a French privateer off Cork on 23 June 1780 and taken to L'Orient; 10 men crew, Archibald Boag, fr. GK to Charleston, SC, in Aug. 1785; Robert Lindsay, fr. GK to VA on 21 June 1786; fr. GK to NY and MD in Mar. 1787; fr. GK to VA 24 Aug. 1787; fr. GK to VA 31 Jan. 1788; William Morrison, fr. GK to VA 13 Jan. 1791; fr. GK to VA 19 July 1791; fr. the Clyde to Charleston in July 1792. [GCr#142] [E504.15.41/43/44/45/46/58/60] [GM#III/117, 143, 230; IX.442.206]

MARGARET OF GREENOCK, 214 tons, John Blain, fr. GK to NY on 28 May 1788; fr. GK to NY 12 Nov. 1788; fr. GK to NY in May 1790; fr. GK to NY 2 Oct. 1790; Alan Harvie, fr. GK to Montreal and Quebec in July 1791; Thomas Bog, fr. GK to St John, NB, in Apr. 1795; fr. GK to NFD in Feb. 1796 [E504.15.48/49/55/56/59/60/68/71]

MARGARET, Robert Millar, fr. Glasgow *with passengers* to Halifax, NS, 3 Mar. 1802. [GkAd#7]

MARGARET OF GLASGOW, 246 tons, William McClimment, fr. GK to Quebec 28 July 1813. [E504.15.101]

MARGARET OF GREENOCK, 81 tons, Thomas Simson, fr. GK to NFD 3 Oct.1815. [E504.15.109]

MARGARET OF PETERHEAD, 200 tons, John Will, fr. Aberdeen to Quebec, 8 Apr. 1816; Andrew McIntosh, fr Leith *with 72 passengers* to Halifax 11 Mar.1817; fr Leith to Halifax 6 Oct.1817. [E504.1.26; E504.22.76/78]

MARGARET OF WORKINGTON, Joseph Creeks, fr. GK to NFD 18 Mar.1818; fr. GK to NFD 18 Mar, 1818. [E504.15.119]

MARGARET OF KIRKCALDY, 217 tons, D. Oliphant, fr leith to Quebec 17 May 1820; fr GK to Quebec 23 Mar.1821; Cap. Craig, fr GK to NY/VA 13 Apr.1822. [E504.22.90;15.135/140]

MARGARET OF CAMPBELTOWN, Cap.McGill, fr GK to Chaleur Bay 11 May 1822. [E504.15.140]

MARGARET, Cap.Ferguson, fr Dundee to NY Aug.1822. [E504.11.22]

MARGARET, Alexander Craig, arr. NY 3 June 1822 *with passengers* fr. GK. [USNA.M237]

MARGARET AND MARION, Capt. Moodie, to Wilmington 30 July 1797. [GC:10.8.1797]

MARGARET BOGLE, John Porter, arr. NY 11 June 1824 *with passengers* fr. GK. [USNA.M237]

MARINER OF GRANGEMOUTH, 308 tons, Thomas Callendar, fr. Port Glasgow to Miramachi in Apr. 1820. [E504.28.108]

MARIA OF GLASGOW, David Wallace, fr. GK to Halifax 5 Aug.1818. [E504.15.122]

MARIAN OF NEW YORK, James Greenhill, fr. GK *with 12 passengers* to NY 3 Sept 1811. [E504.15.93]

MARIAN OF GREENOCK, 341 tons, John McFarlane, fr. GK to St Andrews, NB., 31 Mar.1817; fr. GK to St John, NB., 28 Aug.1817; Daniel Thomson, fr. GK to St Andrews, NB, 4 Apr.1818; fr GK to St Andrews, NB, 6 Feb.1819; fr GK to St Andrews, NB, 22 Mar.1822. [E504.15.115/117/119/123/128]

MARIAN, Cap.Briggs, fr Dundee to Quebec Apr.1823. [E504.11.23]

MARINER OF GRANGEMOUTH, Alexander Adams, fr port Glasgow to Miramachi 6 Apr. 1818; fr Port Glasgow to Miramachi 20 July 1818; fr GK to Chaleur bay Apr.1828. [E504.28.101/102/163]

MARION OF GOUROCK, 70 ton brigantine, William McCunn, fr. GK *with passengers* to Boston in Mar. 1743; fr. GK to Boston in Aug. 1743; fr. GK to Boston in Mar. 1744; fr. GK to Boston in Feb. 1745; John Morison, fr. GK to Boston in Sep. 1745; William McCunn, fr. GK to Boston in Mar. 1746; fr. GK to Boston in Aug. 1746; fr. GK to Boston in Apr. 1747; fr. GK to Boston in Oct. 1747. [E504.15.1/2][GJ#76]

MARQUIS OF WELLINGTON OF GREENOCK, 208 tons, James Nilvig, fr. GK to NFD 9 Oct.1815; James Killing, fr. GK to N.O. 26 Dec.1817. [E504.15.109/118]

MARS OF GREENOCK, William Motherwell, fr. GK to Savannahh, GA, 10 Nov. 1810, [E504.15.90]

MARS OF ABERDEEN, 145 tons, Alexander Kenn, fr. GK to Quebec 11 May 1813. [E504.15.100]

MARS OF PORT GLASGOW, 303 tons, Richard Brown, fr. Tobermory to Quebec and Pictou 20 July 1818. [E504.35.2]

MARS OF GLASGOW, Cap.Burnside, fr GK to NO 18 Oct.1821. [E504.15.138]

MARSHAL KEITH, 170 tons, Andrew Gibson, fr. Port Glasgow *with passengers* to the Rappahannock and Potomac Rivers, VA, in Apr. 1759. [GJ#919]

MARTHA, a snow, Thomas Knox, fr. Port Glasgow *with passengers* to the James River, VA, in Aug. 1759; John Wilson, fr. GK to Charleston, SC, in Nov. 1779; fr. GK *with passengers* to Charleston on 15 Nov. 1780. [E504.15.32][GM#III/336,400][GJ#935]

MARTHA OF LONDON, 183 tons, Ebenezer Newman, fr. GK to N.O. 19 Aug.1817. [E504.15.117]

MARTHA, a brig, fr. Dumfries to Quebec and Montreal in 1820. [DWJ: 30.5.1820]

MARTHA OF GLASGOW, 263 tons, Roger Martin, fr Port Glasgow to Miramachi 1 Apr.1818; fr Port Glasgow to Miramachi 29 July 1818; John Martin, fr. Port Glasgow to Miramachi in Apr. 1820. [E504.28.100/102/109]

MARY OF INVERNESS, David Tolmie, fr. Inverness to VA before 1729; a 70 ton brigantine, Alexander Johnston, arr. in Charleston, SC, via Bristol on 5 June 1764, [AC10/151][PRO.CO5.511]

MARY OF GLASGOW, 200 tons, Andrew Turner, fr. GK to VA in Mar. 1743; fr. GK to VA in Nov. 1743; John Orr, fr. GK to VA in Feb. 1745; Alexander Dundas, fr. GK to MD in May 1748; Robert Jaffrey, fr. GK to VA in Mar. 1750; Robert Shannon, fr. GK to VA in Mar. 1753; Alexander Dundas, fr. GK to MD in Aug. 1753; fr. GK to VA in Apr. 1754; Archibald McLarty, fr. Glasgow via Islay/Jura *with passengers* to Philadelphia then Cape Fear then the West Indies and return in summer 1754; Robert Shannon, fr. GK to VA in Apr.1755 [E504.15.1/2/4/6/7][AC20.2.14, 14]

MARY OF NEW YORK, sloop, Jacob Moris, fr Orkney to NY 11 Aug.1760. [E504.25.3]

MARY OF LEITH, 100 tons, Philip Walsh, fr. Leith to NFD 15 Apr. 1765; fr. Leith to NFD 10 May 1766, [E504.22.12]

MARY OF CARRON, 100 tons, Andrew Stewart, fr. Leith to Philadelphia 1 Oct. 1766. [E504.22.12]

MARY, a snow, Alexander Ritchie, arr. in Charleston, SC, in Dec.1753 fr. Burntisland; Samuel Corrie, fr. Leith to Cape

Fear on 12 Sept. 1765; arr. in NC in Feb. 1766 fr. Leith.
[SCGaz.17.12.1753][E504.22.12][NCGaz#70, 12.2.1766]

MARY, Alexander Pearson, arr. in Charleston, SC, on 22 Nov.
1769 fr. 'Burrow Firth'. [SCGaz#1784]

MARY OF GLASGOW, 203 tons, Thomas Edgar, fr. GK to VA
25 June 1788, [E504.15.48]

MARY OF GREENOCK, a 100 ton snow, Archibald Hamilton,
fr. GK to VA in Apr. 1753; Donald Hyndman, fr. GK *with
passengers* to Boston in Mar. 1756; James Scott, fr. GK *with
passengers* to the Potomac River in Mar.1757
[E504.15.6/7/8][GJ#749/809]

MARY, John Lusk, fr. GK to Passmaquidy, NE, in Mar. 1786.
[E504.15.42] [GM#IX.431.118]

MARY OF GREENOCK, 148 tons, Abram Hunter, fr. GK to
Halifax, NS, on 5 Sept. 1787; fr. GK to Halifax on 19 June
1788; fr. GK to Halifax on 12 Apr. 1789.
[E504.15.45/48/50][GM#XII.590.126]

MARY OF GREENOCK, 165 tons, John Kerr, fr. GK to NFD 18
July 1788; William Milnes, fr. GK to Halifax in May 1790;
John Kerr, fr. GK to Charleston, SC, on 21 Sept. 1790; fr. GK
to Quebec 12 Apr. 1791 [E504.15.48/56/59]

MARY OF GREENOCK, 236 tons, John Marquis, fr. GK to St
Andrews, NS, in Sept. 1789. [E504.15.52]

MARY OF ANTIGUA, 129 tons, Finlay McKinlay, fr. GK to
NFD in July 1789. [E504.15.52]

MARY, a 160 ton brigantine, fr. GK *with passengers* to Halifax,
NS, on 10 Feb. 1786. [GM#IX.418.6]

MARY, a snow, William Welchman, fr. GK to Boston in Mar.
1767; arr. in Boston on 30 May 1767 *with 31 passengers* fr.
Glasgow; fr. GK to Boston in Sept. 1767. [E504.15.14][PAB]

MARY, Capt. Kinnear, fr. the Clyde to NY in 1781 when captured
and sent to Philadelphia. [SM#43.555][GM#IV.245]

MARY, a brigantine, arr. in Shelbourne *with 70 passengers, mainly
mechanics* fr. Glasgow, on 10 Sept. 1785. [Times#270]

MARY, a brigantine, William Reid, fr. GK *with passengers* to the
James River, VA, on 19 Oct. 1786. fr. the Clyde *with
passengers* to the Potomac River, VA and MD, in June 1792;
James Taylor, fr. Port Glasgow *with passengers* to the Potomac
River in Nov. 1792. [GCr#91/180] [GM#IX.460.311/342]

MARY, Robert Wilson, fr. GK to Philadelphia in July 1786; arr. in Philadelphia in Oct. 1786 fr. Glasgow. [E504.15.43] [PaMerc#114]

MARY, John McIver, fr. GK to Charleston, SC, in May 1783; fr. GK to Charleston in Nov. 1783. [E504.15.38]

MARY OF GREENOCK, 116 tons, Robert Roxburgh, fr. GK to NY in July 1784; Francis Telford, fr. GK to NY in June 1785; fr. GK to NY in Apr. 1790. [E504.15.39/41/55]

MARY, Peter Speirs, fr. GK to VA in July 1785. [E504.15.41]

MARY, fr. the Clyde to Charleston, SC, on 16 Feb. 1798. [AC7/71]

MARY OF CHARLESTON, 268 tons, John Johnston, fr. GK *with passengers* to Charleston in May 1795; Benjamin Parson, fr. GK *with 12 passengers* to Charleston in Jan. 1796; Thomas Tait, fr. GK *with 30 passengers* to Charleston in June 1796; Cap. Hunter, fr GK to Charleston, captured by the French 6 Mar.1799. [NAS.CS22.779.22] [E504.15.68/71/72]

MARY, J. Kelso, fr. GK *with passengers* to City Point, on the James River, VA, in Mar. 1802. [GkAd#14]

MARY, 200 tons, W. H. Nichols, fr. GK *with passengers* to NY in Mar. 1802. [GkAd#16]

MARY, a 120 ton brig, T. Jones, fr. GK *with passengers* to Halifax, NS, and St Johns, NB, in Aug. 1802. [GkAd#52]

MARY OF LEITH, Daniel Munro, fr. GK to Savannahh, GA, 20 Oct. 1810; fr. GK *with 6 passengers* to Pictou 26 Mar.1817; fr Leith to Quebec 24 Mar.1819. [E504.15.90/115; E504.22.84]

MARY OF GREENOCK, Alexander Harvey, fr. GK *with 31 passengers* to Montreal 29 Mar. 1811, [E504.15.91]

MARY OF KIRKCALDY, 130 tons, Adam Drysdale, fr. GK to NFD 29 Jan. 1813. [E504.15.99]

MARY OF ABERDEEN, 139 tons, James Oswald, fr. Inverness to Pictou, NS, 1 Sept. 1815; James Clayton, fr. Aberdeen *with 20 passengers* to Miramachi, NB, 27 Mar. 1816; John Innes, fr. Aberdeen to Quebec, 1 Apr. 1817. [E504.1.26; E504.17.8]

MARY OF DARTMOUTH, 167 tons, Thomas Wakeham, fr GK to Labrador 25 June 1819.[E504.15.124]

MARY OF LEITH, David Monro, fr Leith to Pictou 20 Mar.1820. [E504.22.89]

MARY OF STORNAWAY, Capt. Mackenzie, fr. Stornaway to Cape Breton 24 June 1826. [E504.33.4]

MARY OF GREENOCK, 270 tons, Alexander Harvey, fr. GK *with 31 passengers* to Montreal, 7 Mar.1812; fr. GK *with 9 passengers* to Montreal 31.3.1813; Archibald Moore, fr. GK to Quebec 24 Feb.1814; fr. GK to Quebec 28 July 1815; fr. GK *with 15 passengers* to Quebec 2 Apr. 1816; fr. GK to Quebec 1 Aug.1816; fr. GK *with 35 passengers* to Quebec 11 Apr.1817. [E504.15.95/99/103/109/111/113/115]

MARY OF NEWFOUNDLAND, 73 tons, Patrick Murphy, fr. GK to St John's, NFD, 4 May 1815. [E504.15.108]

MARY OF ABERDEEN, James Clayton, fr Aberdeen *with 6 passengers* to Miramachi in Mar.1817. [E504.1.26]

MARY OF WHITEHAVEN, Joseph Penrice, fr. GK to Quebec 13 Mar.1818. [E504.15.119]

MARY, fr GK to Quebec Apr.1828. [E504.15.166]

MARY AND BELL OF GREENOCK, 147 tons, Charles McDonald, fr. GK to Quebec 27 Mar.1815; D. Cunningham, fr. GK to St John, N.B., 8 Oct. 1817. [E504.15.107/117]

MARY AND BETSY, John Young, fr. GK to Charleston, SC, in June 1783. [E504.15.38]

MARY AND HENRY OF CHARLESTON, 364 tons, John Watt, fr. GK to Charleston 19 June 1816; fr. GK to Charleston 20 Dec.1817. [E504.15.112/114]

MARY AND JEAN OF GREENOCK, Daniel Rodger, to NC but wrecked on South Uist on 6 Feb. 1741. [CM:19.3.1741]

MARY AND JEAN, 200 tons, Archibald Boag, fr. GK to the Cape Fear River, NC, on 4 Apr. 1786, *with passengers.* arr. at Port Brunswick, NC, on 29 May 1786; fr. GK to Baltimore, MD, in Mar. 1787. [GM:2.3.1786][NCSA.S8.112][E504.15.42/44]

MARY AND JUNE OF STRANRAER, 153 tons, David Wither, fr. GK to NFD 23 Sept.1817. [E504.15.117]

MARY AND SUSAN OF BOSTON, 379 tons, Cap. Curtis, fr GK to Charleston 10 Apr.1820; Edward Candler, fr GK to NY June 1828, arr. NY 5 Aug. 1828 *with passengers* fr. GK. [E504.15.129/164] [USNA.M237]

MARY ANNE, a brig, Capt. Rankin, arr. in Norfolk on 31 Oct. 1787 fr. Glasgow. [Phila.Gaz.#298]

MARY ANN OF GREENOCK, 77 ton brig, Robert Boyd, fr. GK to Wilmington, NC, on 12 Apr. 1789, arr. Port Brunswick, NC, on 15 June 1789.
[E504.15.51][GM#XII.590.126][NCSA.S8.112]

MARY ANN OF GREENOCK, 226 tons, Hugh Smith, fr. GK to
VA 27 Mar. 1791. [E504.15.58]

MARY ANN OF PORT GLASGOW, 172 tons, James Service, fr.
GK to NY 3 Apr.1815. [E504.15.107]

MARIANNA OF GREENOCK, a new 200 ton brig, John Rankin,
fr. Port Glasgow *with passengers* to Norfolk, Hampton and
the James River, VA, on 3 Aug. 1786; John Young, fr. GK
with 50 passengers to VA 20 July 1791; fr. Shuna Bay in
Appin, Argyllshire, *with 600 passengers* to Wilmington, NC,
on 28 Aug. 1791; fr. the Clyde to Boston in Aug. 1792.
[GM#IX.436.152; 449.254; XIV.715.293]
[GCr#152][E504.15.60]

MARY ANN, a US brig, James Horton, to N.C. in 1792; fr. Port
Glasgow *with passengers* to the James River, VA, or NC, on
5 Sept. 1793.[GC: 25.9.1792; 8.1793;7.9.1793]

MARY ANN OF CHARLESTON, 303 tons, Nathaniel Inglis, fr.
GK to Charleston, SC, 29 Apr. 1802; fr. GK *with 3
passengers* to Charleston in Dec. 1805.
[GkAd#34][E504.15.75]

MARY ANN OF ABERDEEN, 220 tons, Joseph Moore, fr
Aberdeen to Halifax 21 Jan.1819; fr Aberdeen to Quebec 17
Aug.1821. [E504.1.28/29]

MARY AUGUSTA OF NEW YORK, 247 tons, Nicholas Becker,
fr. GK to NY 30 Apr.1818; fr. GK to NY 5 June 1818; fr. GK
to NY 17 May 1819. [E504.15.120/122/124]

MARY HOPE, Cap.Farmer, fr Dundee to NY Mar.1824.
[E504.11.23]

MATILDA OF GREENOCK, a 212 ton snow, Thomas Connell,
fr. GK to NFD 16 Sept.1814; fr. GK to NFD 10 Aug.1816; fr.
GK to NFD 23 Feb.1818. [E504.15.105/113/119]

MATTY OF GLASGOW, a brigantine, James Hume, fr. Port
Glasgow to VA in Feb. 1743; fr. Port Glasgow to VA in Feb.
1744; John Gray, fr. Port Glasgow to VA in Mar. 1745; fr. GK
to VA in Feb. 1749; fr. Port Glasgow to VA in Jan. 1750;
William Hunter, fr. GK to NFD in Apr. 1766; John Mathie, fr.
GK to Boston in June 1767; William Dunlop, arr. in
Charleston, SC, on 3 Dec. 1767 fr. Glasgow; James Moodie,
fr. GK to Charleston, SC, in Aug. 1769; arr. in Charleston on 8
Nov. 1769 fr. Glasgow; Thomas Cochrane, fr GK to
Philadelphia Mar.1773; to Boston and Edenton, NC, in Aug.

1773; fr GK to NY May 1774; Abram Hunter, fr. GK to
Bermuda in Mar. 1783; John Service, fr. GK to Bermuda in
Oct. 1783. [SCGaz:3.12.1767/9.11.1769] [GJ:29.7.1773]
[E504.15.4/13/14/17/22/23/24/37/38/39; E504.28.1/2/4]

MATTY OF WORKINGTON, a brigantine, Christopher Cragg, fr.
Orkney to Philadelphia in Sept. 1774. [E504.26.5]

MATTY, Robert Peacock, fr. Port Glasgow to Oxford, MD, in Sept.
1773. [E504.28.22]

MAY OF GLASGOW, John Orr, fr. GK to VA in Oct. 1745; fr.
GK to VA in July 1746; fr. GK to VA in Mar. 1747; John
Gray, fr. Port Glasgow to VA in July 1747; John Scott, fr. GK
to VA in Dec. 1747; Alexander Dundas, fr. GK to MD in Apr.
1749; Robert Shannan, fr. GK to VA in Mar. 1752
[E504.15.2/4/5; E504.28.3]

MAYFLOWER OF LONDON, John Spurrill, arrived in Barbados
with 108 servants from Scotland, 5 December 1698.
[PRO.CO3/13]

MCDONALD, Capt. Stephenson, fr. the Clyde *with passengers* to
Quebec in Apr. 1786. [GM#IX.449.261]

MEAD OF GREENOCK, Thomas Archdeacon, fr GK to Halifax
Feb.1779. [NAS/E504.15.30]

MECHETABLE, 100 tons, Hugh Coulter, fr. GK to NY, in May
1756. [E504.15.7]

MENIE OF GLASGOW, a snow, Ninian Stewart, fr. GK to
Philadelphia in Aug. 1749; Alexander Montgomery, fr. GK to
VA in June 1752; John Thomson, fr. GK to VA in Mar. 1753;
Arthur Tran, fr. GK *with passengers* to the Rappahannock
River, VA, in Apr. 1755; James Gammell, fr. GK to SC in
Apr. 1756; arr. in Charleston in June 1756 fr. Glasgow;
Archibald Bayne, fr. GK to SC in Oct. 1761; arr. in Charleston
in Jan. 1762 fr. Glasgow. [SCGaz#1145/1432/1435][GJ#710]
[E504.15.4/5/6/7/10]

MENIE, Daniel McKellar,fr Port Glasgow via Uist *with 274
passengers* to St Johns on the St Lawrence 27 June 1802.
[GkAd#48][RH4.188.1/2.531]

MENTOR OF ALEXANDRIA, W. Macklay, fr Leith to
Alexandria, Georgetown and Washington, 21 Sep.1818.
[E504.22.82]

MENTOR, John Laughton, fr. GK to NY in Dec. 1783.
[E504.15.38]

MENTOR OF ABERDEEN, 105 tons, John Logan, fr Aberdeen *with 5 passengers* to Halifax, NS, 8 Apr.1818. [E504.1.27]

MENTOR, Josiah L. Wilson, arr. NY 21 Sep.1824 *with passengers* fr. GK; arr. NY 21 Mar.1828 *with passengers* fr. GK. [USNA.M237]

MEIOPE, fr GK to Quebec July 1828. [E504.15.164]

MERCATOR OF GREENOCK, 283 tons, Alexander Rankine, fr. GK *with 6 passengers* to Charleston, SC, 9 Oct.1816. [E504.15.113]

MERCATOR, David Patten, arr. NY 19 Mar.1828 *with passengers* fr. GK; fr GK to Halifax May 1828. [USNA.M237][E504.15.164]

MERCURY, a snow, James Strachan, arr. in Charleston, SC, in Nov.1753 fr. Dundee; arr. in Charleston in Sept.1754 fr. Leith; arr. in Charleston in Nov.1754 fr. Leith; fr. Dundee in Sept. 1756 *with carpenters, joiners, smiths, shoemakers, tailors, laborers, and others that will indent ;* arr. in Charleston in Dec. 1756 fr. Dundee; arr. in Charleston, SC, in Sept. 1758 fr. Leith; fr. Dundee to Carolina in 1758, captured by the French and taken to Rochelle; Robert Stirling, arr. in Charleston in Nov.1759 fr. Dundee; arr. in Charleston in Jan. 1762 fr. Dundee. [EEC, 26.8.1756] [SCGaz#16.11.1753; 19 Sept.1754; 21.11.1754; 1057/1173/1435; 17.11.1759] [SM#20.50]

MERCURY OF BO'NESS, 110 ton brigantine, William Robertson, arr. in Charleston, SC, on 16 Aug. 1762 fr. Bo'ness; William Robertson, arr. in Charleston on 31 Jan. 1763, [PRO.CO5.509]

MERCURY, a brigantine, W. Gavin, arr. in Charleston, SC, in May 1772 fr. Leith. [SCGaz:22.5.1772]

MERCURY OF GLASGOW, Henry Laird, fr. Port Glasgow to VA in Dec. 1745. [E504.28.2]

MERCURY OF GLASGOW, William Scott fr GK to VA Aug.1772; fr GK to VA Mar.1773; Robert Holmes, fr Port Glasgow to St John's, NFD, Aug.1777. [E504.15.21/22; 28/27]

MERCURY, Michael Beath, fr. Glasgow *with passengers* to NY on 6 Mar. 1802. [GkAd#6]

MERCURY OF GREENOCK, 156 tons, John Irving, fr. GK to NFD 23 Feb. 1813; fr. GK to NFD 27 Apr. 1814; fr. GK to NFD 11 Mar.1815. [E504.15.99/104/107]

MERMAID OF GREENOCK, Alexander Campbell, fr. GK to NFD in Mar. 1755; fr. GK to NFD in Apr. 1756; fr. GK to

NFD in Apr. 1757; James Laurie fr GK to Quebec Apr.1773; fr GK to Quebec Apr.1774; fr GK to Quebec Apr.1775; James Cochrane, fr GK *'with troops'* to North America Mar.1776; [E504.15.7/8/22/23/25/26]

MERMAID OF BOSTON, a brigantine, Ebenezer Gorham, fr. Kirkwall, Orkney Islands, *with 1 passenger* to Boston, 3 Sep.1764, arr. there on 24 Nov. 1764. [PAB][E504.26.4]

MERMAID, Robert Hunter, fr. Port Glasgow *with passengers* to the James River, VA, on 1 Aug. 1786; fr. Port Glasgow *with passengers* to the James River, VA, on 2 Mar. 1789; fr. the Clyde to VA on 2 Aug. 1789; arr. in Norfolk, VA, in Oct. 1789 fr. Port Glasgow. [GM#IX.433.127; 448.246; 584.78; 575.8; 606.254] [PIG#1213]

MESSENGER, fr. the Clyde to Boston in June 1754. [EEC#22611]

METHVINE, 100 tons, Robert Boyd, fr. GK via Hamburg to Boston in July 1753, [E504.15.6]

MINERVA OF DUNDEE, 400 tons, James Rea, arr. in Charleston, SC, on 21 Aug. 1765 fr. Dundee; arr. in Charleston on 22 Aug. 1766 fr. Dundee. [SCGaz#1598][PRO.CO5.511]

MINERVA OF AYR, Alexander McClure, fr. Ayr via Waterford to NFD in May 1770; fr. Ayr to NFD via Waterford in May 1771; John McIlwraith, fr. Ayr to NFD in July 1772, [E504.4.5]

MINERVA OF BO'NESS/LEITH, 80 tons, Robert Alexander, fr. Leith to Charleston in Apr. 1771; arr. in Charleston, SC, in June 1771 fr. Leith; Robert Grindlay, fr Bo'ness to Charleston 23 Aug.1773, arr. in Charleston in Nov. 1773 fr. Bo'ness; fr. Bo'ness to Charleston 22 July 1774, arr. in Charleston in Nov. 1774 fr. Bo'ness. [EA#15/150; 22/53] [SCGaz:13.6.1771/30.11.1773/15.11.1774][E504.22.16; 6/9]

MINERVA, 160 tons, Samuel Eccles, fr. Ayr *with passengers* to St Andrews, NS, in Apr. 1789. [GM#XII.590.128]

MINERVA OF GREENOCK, James Rankin, fr. Ayr to VA in Oct. 1768; fr. GK to VA in Aug. 1770; fr. GK to VA in July 1771; Edward Morrison, fr GK to Boston Mar.1773; fr GK to Boston Aug.1773; fr GK to Boston Mar.1774; fr GK to NY and St Augustine Mar.1779; fr. GK *with passengers* to Savannah, GA, in Mar. 1780; John Boyd, fr. GK to Philadelphia in July 1783; fr. GK to Norfolk, VA, in Sept. 1784; John Hastie, fr. GK to Quebec 11 Apr. 1789; Capt. Gibson, fr. the Clyde to

MD in Jan. 1792; Robert Dunn, fr. GK to NFD 25 May 1814;
John Lynes, fr. GK to NFD 6 June 1816; fr. GK to NFD 20
Mar.1817; fr. GK to NFD 13 Oct.1818; Peter Fisher, fr GK to
Halifax 23 feb.1822 [GCr#49] GM#III/105; XII.590.126]
[E504.15.18/19/22/23/30/38/39/51/104/112/115/121/139;
E504.15.4.6]

MINERVA OF WISCASSET, an 250 ton US brig, to Norfolk,
VA, or Wilmington, NC, *with passengers* in Spring 1804;
Capt. Carrick, arr. in Wilmington fr. Glasgow before
Sept. 1804; T.F. Eastman, fr. Glasgow *with passengers* to
Boston on 26 Apr. 1805; Capt. Barridge, fr. GK to Charleston,
SC, *with 6 passengers* on 16 Nov. 1805. [CCA#10,30.10.1805]
[E504.15.75][CM#13040] [GC: 24.3.1804/ 27.9.1804]

MINERVA OF GREENOCK, 209 tons, Archibald Currie, fr. GK
to Miramachi 8 Apr. 1813; fr. GK to Pictou 6 Aug. 1813; Peter
Fisher, fr GK to Halifax 6 Aug.1821. [E504.15.100/101/137]

MINERVA OF ABERDEEN, 202 tons, William Strachan, fr. Fort
William *with 26 passengers* to Halifax, NS, 21 June 1817.
[E504.12.6]

MINERVA OF ST JOHN, NB, Charles Kean, fr. GK to Halifax
11 September 1818. [E504.15.122]

MINERVA OF ANSTRUTHER, m165 tons, Cap. Williamson, fr
GK to Quebec 10 Apr.1820. [E504.15.129]

MINERVA OF GREENOCK, 134 tons, Cap. Fisher, fr GK to
Halifax 20 Feb.1821. [E504.15.135]

MINERVA, Andrew Anderson, arr. NY 29 Oct. 1822 *with
passengers* fr. GK; John Charles Mayell, arr. NY 8 Oct. 1824
with passengers fr. GK; George H. Wallace, arr. NY 18
Mar.1827 *with passengers* fr. Glasgow. [USNA.M237]

MISSISSIPPI OF BRISTOL, 242 tons, James Drummond, fr. GK
with 10 passengers to Savannahh in Nov. 1805. [E504.15.75]

MISSISSIPPI, fr. GK *with passengers* to Charleston, arr. there on
15 Mar. 1810. [ANY#2.29]

MISSOURI OF PHILADELPHIA, 152 tons, Peter Bell, fr. GK
with 80 passengers to Philadelphia in May 1795. [E504.15.68]

MISSOURI OF PHILADELPHIA, 195 tons, Joseph Baush, fr
GK to Philadelphia 20 Oct.1820, arr. NY 10 Apr.1821 *with
passengers* fr. GK. [E504.15.132][USNA.M237]

MOBILE, Samuel W. Dickenson, arr. NY 21 Aug. 1827 *with
passengers* fr. Glasgow. [USNA.M237]

MOLLY OF CRAWFORDDYKE, John Aitken, fr. GK to VA in
   Apr. 1748; John Crawford, fr. GK to Boston in Sept. 1751;
   Henry Rothery, fr. GK to VA in Feb. 1765 [E504.15.2/5]
MOLLY OF DUNBAR, 40 ton brigantine, John Middlemass, arr.
   in Charleston, SC, on 13 May 1758 fr. Leith, [PRO.CO5.509]
MOLLY OF THE POTOMAC, 140 tons, Alexander Smith, arr.
   in Charleston, SC, on 8 Nov. 1763 fr. Glasgow.
   [SCGaz#1530][PRO.CO5.510]
MOLLY OF VIRGINIA, James Barron, fr. GK to VA in Sept.
   1769 [E504.15.17]
MOLLY, a brig, Thomas Archdeacon, arr. in Charleston, SC, in
   Dec. 1774 fr. Glasgow. [SCGaz:30.12.1774]
MOLLY, 80 tons, John Service, arr. in Port Roanoke, NC, on 9
   Feb. 1785. [NCSA.S8.112]
MOLLY, Capt. John Maxwell, fr. Uist *with 230 passengers* bound
   to Prince Edward Island, arr. in Charlottetown on 8 Sept. 1791.
   [Royal Gaz.#V/I]
MONARCH OF GLASGOW, 375 tons, Dougald Campbell, fr.
   GK to New Orleans 11 Sept.1816; Cap.Burnside, fr GK to
   Charleston 19 Oct.1821. [E504.15.113/138]
MONARCH OF ALLOA, 355 tons, A. McDougall, fr. GK to
   Miramachi 9 Aug.1819; fr Leith to Miramachi 16 Aug.1820.
   [E504.15.125; E504.22.91]
MONARCH OF ABERDEEN, 216 tons, Alexander Martin, fr
   Aberdeen to St John, NB, 20 Mar.1820. [E504.1.28]
MONARCH OF GREENOCK, fr. Campbeltown *with passengers*
   to America in Sept. 1820, [AD14.70.112]
MONIMIA OF GREENOCK, Edward Morrison, fr GK to NY
   Oct.1774; fr. GK *with passengers* to NY in June 1775; fr GK
   'with troops' to North America Mar.1776. [CM#8339,
   15.4.1775] [EA#8362][E504.15.24/26]
MONTAGUE OF ABERDEEN, 70 tons, Alexander Blews, fr.
   Aberdeen to St John, NB, in Apr. 1776. [E504.1.13]
MONTEZUMA, Thomas Morgan, fr. GK *with passengers* to
   Charleston, SC, in Aug. 1802. [GkAd#58]
MONTGOMERY OF IRVINE, David Dunlop, fr. GK to VA in
   Feb. 1748. [E504.15.2]
MONTGOMERY OF GLASGOW, 80 ton snow, John Wilson,
   arr. in Charleston, SC, on 29 Mar. 1760 fr. Irvine,
   [PRO.CO5.509]

MONTGOMERY, a snow, Alexander Montgomery, fr. GK *with passengers* to the James, Potomac, and Patuxent Rivers, VA, in June 1759; arr. in Annapolis, MD, in Dec. 1759, fr. Glasgow; fr. GK to MD in Apr. 1760; fr. GK to MD in Dec. 1760; arr. in Patuxent, MD, on 22 Mar. 1761 fr. Glasgow; George Buchanan, arr. in Charleston, SC, in Dec. 1761 fr. Glasgow; fr. GK to MD in Apr. 1762; fr. GK to MD in Dec. 1762; fr. GK to VA in May 1765; William Hamilton, fr. GK to MD in Mar. 1766; fr. GK to MD in Sept. 1766 [MdGaz#761/829] [SCGaz#1426] [E504.15.9/10/11/12/13][GJ#926]

MONTGOMERY, a snow, James Boyd, arr. in Charleston, SC, in Nov. 1758 fr. Glasgow; John Wilson, arr. in Charleston in Nov. 1758 fr. Glasgow; arr. at North Edisto in Mar.1760 fr. Glasgow; George Buchanan, arr. in Charleston on 25 Nov. 1761 fr. Glasgow, [SCGaz#1259/1336/1426; 24.11.1758]

MONTREAL OF GLASGOW, 307 tons, Robert Allan, fr. GK *with 29 passengers* to Quebec and Montreal 6 Apr. 1814; William Rayside, fr. GK *with 8 passengers* to Quebec 22 March 1816; fr. GK *with 8 passengers* to Montreal 7 March 1817. [E504.15.104/111/115]

MONTREAL OF LONDON, James Service, fr. GK to Quebec 18 Mar.1818. [E504.15.119]

MONTROSE OF MONTROSE, James Mudie, arr. in VA *with 4 passengers* on 10 Oct. 1752. [VaGaz#90]

MOORE OF GLASGOW, Archibald McLarty, fr. Port Glasgow to Port Rappahannock, VA, in Nov. 1773; James McLeish, fr GK to Falmouth, NE, July 1774. [E504.28.22/25]

MORNING STAR OF CHARLESTON, 222 tons, John McIntyre, fr. GK to Charleston 10 July 1815; Tim Stevens, arr. NY 25 June 1822 *with passengers* fr. GK. [E504.15.109][USNA.M237]

MORNINGFIELD OF ABERDEEN, 141 ton brig, James Pirie, fr. Stornaway *with 63 passengers* to Quebec on 5 Aug. 1815; Capt. Laing, fr. Tobermory *with 64 passengers* to Pictou, NS, 26 July 1819. [E504.33.3//35.2]

MOSES GILL, Capt. Paterson, fr. GK to NY on 10 May 1802. [GkAd#36]

MOSES MYRES, Richard Owens, fr. Leith to the James River, VA, in 1798. [CM#11901, 28.12.1797]

MUNRO, John Glassford, fr. GK to SC in May 1758, arr. in
Charleston in July 1758. [E504.15.8][SCGaz.7.7.1758]

MURDOCH OF GLASGOW, 100 tons, Robert Hamilton, fr. GK
to VA in May 1750; fr. GK to VA in June 1752; fr. GK to VA
in Mar. 1754; fr. GK to VA in Feb. 1757; John McCunn, fr.
GK to VA in Jan. 1758; fr. GK to VA in Aug. 1758; fr. GK to
VA in July 1759; fr. GK to VA in May 1760; John
Cunningham, fr. GK to VA in May 1761; John McCunn, fr.
GK to VA in Aug. 1763; fr. GK to VA in May 1765; fr. GK to
VA in Jan. 1766; Archibald Orr, fr. GK to VA in July 1767; fr.
GK to VA in Feb. 1768; fr. GK to VA in Sept. 1768; fr. GK to
VA in May 1769 Capt. Orr, fr. VA to the Clyde, wrecked on
Ailsa Craig on 29 Apr. 1769.
[E504.15.4/5/6/8/9/10/11/12/13/14/15/16] [SM#31.670]

NANCY OF ABERDEEN, 65 tons, James Park, fr. Aberdeen to
MD in Aug. 1746. [E504.1.2]

NANCY OF GLASGOW, 120 ton snow, John McLeish, fr. Port
Glasgow to MD in Jan. 1750; fr. Port Glasgow to MD in June
1750; Finlay Gray, fr. GK to VA via Rotterdam in Mar. 1751;
fr. GK to MD in Apr. 1752; John Morrison, fr. GK to Boston
in Apr. 1754; William Hastie, fr. GK *with passengers* to
Boston in Apr. 1755; fr. GK to Boston in Nov. 1755; fr. GK
with passengers to Boston in Aug. 1756; fr. GK to Boston in
July 1757; Archibald McCall, fr. GK to VA in July 1758;
John Morrison, fr. GK *with passengers* to Charleston, SC, in
May 1759; James Kippen fr. GK to VA in Nov. 1768; James
Orr, fr. GK to Boston in Aug. 1769; Thomas Hastie, fr. GK to
St Aug.ine, Fla., in Oct. 1779; Abram Hunter, fr. GK to
Bermuda in Sept. 1782; William Drummond, fr. GK to NY in
Jan. 1784. [E504.28.4; E504.15.5/6/7/8/9/16/17/32/36/39]
[GJ#736/737/780/922]

NANCY OF IRVINE, 70 ton snow, William Hamilton, arr. in
Charleston, SC, in Dec.1756 fr. Glasgow; Hugh Brown, arr. in
Charleston on 7 Aug. 1758 fr. Glasgow; arr. in Charleston on 7
May 1759 fr. Glasgow; Henry Brown, arr. in Charleston on 7
May 1760 fr. Orkney. [SCGaz#1176/1343][PRO.CO5.509]

NANCY, a brig, John Aiken, fr. GK to NC in Apr. 1762, arr. in
Charleston, SC, in June 1762 fr. Glasgow.
[E504.15.10][SCGaz#1465]

NANCY OF GREENOCK, Andrew Pearson, fr. GK to Boston in
July 1767; James Moody, fr. GK to Boston in Oct. 1768; fr.
GK to Boston in Apr. 1769 [E504.15.16]; arr. in Boston on 1
May 1769 *with 3 passengers* fr. Glasgow; David Hunter, fr GK
to Quebec and St Augustine Feb.1779. [PAB] [E504.15.13/30]

NANCY, 140 tons, Robert Service, fr. Port Glasgow to the James
River and Potomac, VA, in Jan. 1768. [GC#46]

NANCY, William Drummond, fr. GK to NY in Dec. 1783;
Thomas Silk, fr. GK to NY in Oct. 1784; Robert Stevenson, fr.
GK to NY in Jan. 1785; James Lawrie, fr. the Clyde to NY on
17 Mar. 1787, arr. there on 20 May 1787.
[Phila.Gaz.#242][E504.15.38/40/44]

NANCY, David Hunter, fr Port Glasgow to Quebec Mar.1779; John
Hastie, fr GK to GA, St Augustine and Quebec Aug.1779; fr.
Glasgow to Georgia in May 1780; James Young, fr. GK to
NFD in Aug. 1784; James Reeve, fr. GK to NFD in Mar. 1784;
John Robertson, fr. GK to Baltimore in Mar. 1785; fr. GK to
Halifax, NS, in Oct. 1785;
[E504.28.30;15.31/39/40/42][GM#III/173]

NANCY OF GREENOCK, a 183 ton brigantine, Patrick Kelso, fr.
GK to VA in Apr. 1785; fr. GK to VA in Oct. 1785; fr. GK
with passengers to VA in Aug. 1786; James Hamilton, fr. GK
to VA 11 Apr. 1788; fr. GK to VA in Mar. 1789; fr. GK to VA
in Aug. 1789; arr. at Bermuda Hundred in Nov. 1789 fr.
Glasgow; fr. GK to Charleston, SC, 17 Sept. 1790; Robert
Hamilton, fr. GK to Charleston, 2 Mar. 1791.
[E504.15.40/41/42/43/48/50/52/56/58]
[PIG#1221][GM#IX.439.175; 452/278]

NANCY OF GREENOCK, 172 tons, Charles Rogers, fr. GK to
NFD in May 1796. [E504.15.72]

NANCY OF GREENOCK, 124 tons, David Weir, fr. GK to
Philadelphia *with 30 passengers* on 9 May 1788, [E504.15.48]

NANCY OF GREENOCK, a 110 ton brigantine, William
Cochrane, fr. GK *with passengers* to Charleston, SC, in July
1786; fr. GK to Quebec 1 Apr. 1788; fr. GK *with passengers*
to Quebec in Apr. 1789; fr. GK to Montreal 24 Mar. 1791; fr.
GK *with passengers* to Montreal on 25 Mar. 1792.
[GCr#64/70] [E504.15.47/58][GM#IX.440.183;XII.578.32]

NANCY, a brigantine, Robert Jamieson, fr. Port Glasgow *with passengers* to the Potomac River, VA, on 2 July 1789. [GM#XII.594.207; 601.214]

NANCY OF NANTUCKET, schooner, fr.the Clyde toWilmington or Washington, NC, in 1793. [CM#11245][GC:27.7.1793]

NANCY, 346 tons, Nicol Baine, fr. GK *with passengers* to Quebec in Mar. 1802. [GkAd#8]

NANCY OF GREENOCK, 162 tons, fr. GK *with 21 passengers* to Quebec 30 Mar.1815; Robert Love, fr. GK to NFD 23 Apr. 1816; fr. GK to NFD 22 Aug.1816; fr. GK to NFD 20 Apr.1818. [E504.15.107/112/113/120]

NANCY OF ST JOHN'S, NEWFOUNDLAND, 145 tons, Thomas Walker, fr. GK to NFD 21 Apr.1817. [E504.15.116]

NANCY OF SOUTH SHIELDS, Richard Allan, fr Leith *with 200 passengers* to Halifax and Quebec 10 Apr.1817.[E504.22.77]

NANCY, a brig, Joseph Kirk, fr. Glencaple, Dumfries-shire, *with 15 passengers* to America in 1821. [DCr:3.4.1821]

NANCY AND JEAN OF GREENOCK, John McKinlay, fr. GK to Wilmington, NC, in Feb. 1785, arr. in Port Brunswick, NC, on 10 May 1785 fr. Glasgow. [E505.15.40][NCSA.S8.112]

NANCY AND KEATTY, John Tran, fr. GK to VA and MD in July 1758, [E504.15.8]

NANINO, fr. the Clyde to SC before Nov. 1728. [AC7/34/697]

NANNY OF PORT GLASGOW, 70 tons, John Lyon, arr. in Charleston, SC, during 1727 fr. Glasgow. [PRO.CO5/509]

NANNIE OF GLASGOW, Patrick Carnegy, fr. Port Glasgow to VA in Nov. 1747, [E504.28.3]

NANNIE AND JENNY, possibly fr. Dumfries *with passengers* to VA in 1752. [CS96.2161]

NATCHEZ OF NEW YORK, 282 tons, . William D. Cook, fr GK to NY 10 Feb.1822; fr GK to NY 8 June 1822; arr. NY 17 Aug. 1822 *with passengers* fr. GK; arr. NY 22 Apr. 1827 *with passengers* fr. GK. [USNA.M237][E504.15.139/140]

NATIVE OF BATH, Jacob Drummond, from GK to Charleston July 1815; fr. GK to Charleston 11 June 1818. [E504.15.120/121]

NELLY OF GLASGOW, a schooner, James Baylie, fr. Port Glasgow to VA in Mar. 1745; fr. Port Glasgow to Boston in Jan. 1746, [E504.28.2]

NELLY OF GLASGOW, 190 tons, Archibald Galbraith, fr. GK to VA in Feb. 1750; fr. GK to VA in Mar. 1751; fr. GK to VA in June 1753; fr. GK to VA in Apr. 1754; fr. GK to NY in May 1756; Alexander Kerr, fr. GK to VA in Feb. 1757; James Dunlop, fr. GK to VA in Aug. 1757; fr. GK to VA in Feb. 1758; Malcolm Crawford, fr. GK to VA via the Isle of May in Mar. 1759; fr. GK to VA in Mar. 1761; fr. GK to VA in Jan. 1761; Daniel McKirdy, fr. GK to VA in Jan. 1764; Hugh Kerr, fr. GK to VA in May 1765; James Cuthbert, fr. GK to VA in Feb. 1766; fr. GK to VA in Aug. 1766; fr. GK to VA in Apr. 1767; Hugh Brown, fr. GK to VA in July 1771 [E504.15.4/5/6/7/8/9/10/12/13/14/20]

NELLY OF LEITH, 100 ton brig, James Crawford, fr. Leith *with passengers* to Cape Fear, NC, in Sept. 1773, arr. in Port Brunswick, NC, on 21 Mar. 1774 fr. Leith; Duncan McRob, arr. in Port Brunswick, NC, on 20 Mar. 1787 fr. Glasgow. [EEC:8.9.1773][E504.22.18] [NCSA.S8.112]

NELLY OF GREENOCK, Robert McLarty, fr GK to VA Feb.1774; Neil McMillan, fr. GK to Halifax, NS, in May 1776; Duncan McNaught, fr. GK to St Augustine in May 1777; Robert Borland fr GK to St Augustine Oct.1777; fr GK to St John's, NFD, Sep.1779. [E504.15.23/26/27/31]

NELLY, John Blaine, fr. GK *with husbandmen to settle at Albany* to NY, in Mar. 1787; arr. there on 20 May 1787. [Phila.Gaz.#243][E504.15.44]

NELLY AND PEGGY, William McIntyre, fr. GK to Charleston, SC, in Mar. 1785; fr. GK to Charleston, SC, in Nov. 1785; Capt. Provand, fr. the Clyde to Wilmington, NC, 22 May 1804. [GC#26.5.1804][E504.15.40/42]

NEPTUNE, fr. Glasgow to Boston in 1728. [CS228/a3/19]

NEPTUNE, fr. Glasgow to Virginia in Mar.1741. [GAr.B10.15.5442]

NEPTUNE OF DUMFRIES, 90 tons, Archibald Graham arr. in Charleston, SC, on 24 Nov. 1735 via Bristol; captured by the Spanish when to VA in 1742. [PRO.CO5.509][GJ#42]

NEPTUNE OF GREENOCK, a 204 ton brigantine, Thomas Allan, fr. GK to Boston in Jan. 1755; Patrick McKinlay, arr. in Charleston, SC, in Jan. 1766 fr. Glasgow; damaged at sea 90 leagues off Charleston on 27 Jan. 1768, [SCGaz#1711]; arr. in Roanoke, NC, fr. Glasgow, 2 Oct. 1770, [NCSA/PC67.21];

John McNeil, fr. Campbeltown *with passengers* to NC in Mar.
1770; John Wilson, fr. GK toVA and Edenton, NC, *with
passengers* on 15 Oct. 1771; fr GK to VA Jan.1772; Robert
Omand, fr GK to Boston and NC July 1772; John Wilson fr
GK to SC Nov.1772; James Butcher fr GK to VA Mar.1774;
Hugh Morris, fr. Port Glasgow to the James River, VA, in July
1774; Alexander Alexander, fr GK to St John's, NFD, May
1776; Thomas Lang fr GK to NY Feb.1778; Ninian Rodger, fr.
GK to St Augustine, Fla., in Oct. 1779; William Bell, fr. GK to
Petersburg, VA, in June 1784; fr. Port Glasgow *with
passengers* to Petersburg, VA, 18 Feb. 1786; Archibald
Cambridge, fr. GK to Halifax *with 60 passengers* on 23 July
1788; fr. the Clyde to NFD on 24 Apr. 1789; fr. GK *with
passengers* to Halifax, NS, in Aug. 1789; Charles Rodger, fr.
GK *with 12 passengers* to Halifax on 8 Oct. 1790; James
Patterson, fr. GK via Jamaica to VA 28 Sept. 1791; fr. GK *with
passengers* to Halifax in Sept. 1792; John Simpson, fr. GK to
Halifax in Apr. 1795. [GJ#2613] [GJ:3.10.1771]
[SCGaz:28.1.1766][PRO.CO5.511]
[E504.15.7/20/21/22/23/26/31/32/39/48/52/56/57/60/68;
E504.28.23] [GCr#151/163][GM#IX.418.8; 425.62;
XII.591.134; 602.224] [EEC: 21.2.1770]

NEPTUNE, Capt. McKinlay, fr. Glasgow to SC, foundered on 27
Jan. 1768 when 90 leagues off SC. [CM#7139]

NEPTUNE, Atkin Brown, fr GK to NFD *with troops* May 1778.
[E504.15.29]

NEPTUNE OF LINCOLN/POWNLBRO, 90 ton brigantine,
Samuel Hall, fr. GK to Boston 8 Nov. 1787; fr. GK to Boston 6
Oct. 1788; fr. GK *with passengers* to Boston 12 June 1789;
Alexander Askins, fr. GK to Boston in Sept. 1791.
[E504.15.46/48/51/60] [GM#XII.593.152; 598.183]

NEPTUNE OF GREENOCK, 204 tons, John Simpson, fr. GK
with 10 passengers to Halifax, NS, in July 1796; John Smyth,
fr. GK *with 10 passengers* to NS 29 Apr. 1811.
[E504.15.73/92]

NEPTUNE OF AYR, 168 tons, James Neil, fr. GK *with
passengers* bound to Quebec Apr. 1802; fr. GK to Halifax, NS,
in Feb. 1806; James Neil, fr. GK *with 11 passengers* to
Quebec and Montreal, 11 Apr. 1812; fr. GK to Quebec and
Montreal 27 March 1813; fr. GK to Quebec 25 March 1814; fr.

GK to Quebec 30 Mar.1815; fr. GK to Quebec 26 March 1816;
fr. GK *with 22 passengers* to Quebec 15 Apr.1817; fr. GK *with
30 passengers* to Quebec 11 Aug.1817.
[E504.15.77/96/99/103/107/111/115/117][GkAd#22]

NEPTUNE OF GREENOCK, 302 tons, William Athol, fr. GK to
NFD 9 Aug.1814. [E504.15.105]

NEPTUNE OF PORT GLASGOW, 400 tons, James Ritchie, fr.
GK to Quebec 2 March 1815. [E504.15.107]

NEPTUNE OF KINCARDINE, a 169 ton brig, William Clark, fr.
GK *with 6 passengers*bound to Montreal 22 Apr. 1816; fr.
Glasgow on 16 Apr. 1817 *with 5 passengers* to Quebec, arr. 6
June 1817; fr Port Glasgow to Montreal 5 Mar.1818.
[E504.15.112; E504.28.100][MG]

NEPTUNE, William Miller, arr. NY 23 Jan.1826 *with passengers*
fr. GK. [USNA.M237]

NEREA OF GREENOCK, 197 tons, William Orr, fr. GK to N.Br.
23 May 1815. [E504.15.108]

NESTOR OF GREENOCK, John Harrison, fr GK to SC
Dec.1772, arr. in Charleston, SC, in Mar. 1773 fr. Glasgow.
[E504.15.22][SCGaz:19.3.1773]

NESTOR, fr. Portree, Skye, *with passengers* to America in Sept.
1773. [TGSI#55.328]

NESTOR OF GREENOCK, James Robertson, fr GK to St
Augustine and NY Apr.1778; fr. GK to VA on 26 Apr. 1786;
Lewis Colquhoun, fr. GK *with passengers* to NY in Mar. 1792.
[E504.15.29/43][GM#IX.435.142] [GCr#82]

NESTOR OF PHILADELPHIA, 122 tons, William Smith, fr.
Aberdeen to Quebec, 19 Apr. 1816. [E504.1.26]

NESTOR OF ABERDEEN, 362 tons, George Thom, fr Aberdeen
to Quebec 14 Mar.1822. [E504.1.29]

NETHERWOOD, Archibald McCall, fr. GK to VA in Mar. 1760;
fr. GK to VA in Jan. 1761; fr. GK to VA in Oct. 1761; fr. GK
to VA in June 1762 [E504.15.9/10/11]

NETTY, Hugh Kerr, fr. GK to VA in Mar. 1763 [E504.15.11]

NEWALL OF MARYLAND, Walter Smith, fr. GK to MD in
Nov. 1751; arr. in the Patuxent during Mar. 1752 *with
passengers* fr. Scotland. [E504.15.5][MdGaz#359]

NEW BUMPER, Duncan Brown, fr. Glasgow to NY in Aug. 1762.
[E504.15.11]

NEW PACKET OF PORTSMOUTH, USA, A. Bodfish, fr. Stornaway to NY 23 June 1824. [E504.33.4]

NEW SNOW, a brig, fr. Dumfries to Boston in 1817. [DWJ:13.5.1817]

NEW YORK, fr. Port Glasgow *with passengers* via Cork to NY in Mar. 1780; William Farley, fr. GK to NY and Philadelphia in July 1783; fr. the Clyde to NY in Sept. 1783, wrecked on Cape May. [GM#III/111][AC7/61] [CM:12.11.1783] [E504.15.38]

NIAGARA OF PORTSMOUTH, 336 tons, James Lombard, fr. GK to NY 25 May 1818; Cap.Gookin, fr GK to Philadelphia 19 June 1820. [E504.15.120/129]

NIAGARA, fr. GK *with 84 passengers* to Quebec, arr. there on 27 May 1825. [MacNab, London, 1938]

NILE, a brigantine, fr. Dumfries to Miramachi, NB, in 1817; arr. in St John during 1818 *with passengers* fr. Dumfries.[DWJ: 1.4.1817][CG]

NIOD, William Allan, arr. NY 9 July 1827 *with passengers* fr. GK. [USNA.M237]

NISBET, Hugh Wyllie, fr. GK to MD in Apr. 1758, [E504.15.8]

NORFOLK, George Jamieson, fr. GK to VA in Jan. 1785. [E504.15.40]

NORTH CAROLINA, 80 tons, Neil McNeil, fr. GK to Philadelphia and Wilmington, NC, *with passengers* on 15 Aug. 1784, arr. in Port Brunswick, NC, on 3 Dec. 1784; Hugh Smith, fr. GK to Wilmington in Aug. 1785, arr. in Port Brunswick on 25 Oct. 1785; fr. the Clyde to Wilmington in 1786. [GM: 9.2.1786] [E504.15.39/41][NCSA.S8.112] [CM:5.7.1784]

NORTH STAR, fr. Leith via GK to Pictou, NS, *with passengers* in 1804; a schooner, fr. Urr, Dumfries-shire, to North America in 1817. [CS96.3355][DWJ:18.2.1817]

NORTHERN FRIENDS OF GREENOCK, master James Lang, fr. GK to Wilmington in Aug. 1803. [AC7.77]

NORVAL OF GREENOCK, 163 tons, Thomas Work, fr. GK to St Andrews, NB, on 12 May 1791; T. J. Motely, fr. GK to NFD, 4 March 1814; fr. GK *with 2 passengers* to NFD 18 May 1815; John Irving, fr. GK to NFD 25 Mar.1817; fr GK to NFD May 1828. [E504.15.59/103/108/115/164]

NORVAL OF GLASGOW, a 250 ton brigantine, John Wyllie, to NC in 1792; to Wilmington and Orecacke, NC, *with*

passengers in Feb. 1793, ship foundered 25 Mar. 1793.
[CM#11182][GC: 12.4.1792; 4.12.1792; 9.2.1793]

NORVAL OF GREENOCK, 197 tons, Thomas Motley, fr. GK to
NFD 8 March 1816; John Irving, fr. GK to NFD 16 June 1818.
[E504.15.111/120]

NORVAL OF DUNDEE, Alexander Allan, fr Dundee *with*
passengers to Norfolk, VA, 1816. [CE70.1.14]

NYMPH OF ABERDEEN, 121 tons, James Hutcheon, fr. Fort
William *with 51 passengers* to Pictou, NS, 19 Aug. 1816; fr
Aberdeen via Dundee *with passengers* to Charleston Apr.1817.
[E504.12.6; E504.1.26; E504.20][CE70.1.14]

OCEAN, John Ewing, fr. Port Glasgow to VA in July 1772; fr. Port
Glasgow to Hampton, VA, in Aug. 1773; fr. Port Glasgow to
VA in Apr. 1774; Archibald Boag, fr. GK to Quebec in Apr.
1783; William Kinneir, fr. GK *with passengers* to Quebec on
20 Mar. 1786 [E504.28.21/22/23; E504.15.37/42]
[GM#IX.418.8]

OCEAN OF AYR, 157 tons, David Wilson, fr. Ayr to Quebec 3
Apr. 1806. [E504.4.11]

OCEAN OF ABERDEEN, 259 tons, Robert Hogg, fr. Aberdeen
with 2 passengers to NY, 21 May 1816. [E504.1.26]

OCEAN, Cap. Bachelor, fr Dundee to St John, NBr. Apr.1823.
[E504.11.23]

OHIO OF NEW YORK, 290 tons, Archibald McLachlan, fr. GK
to NY in Feb. 1796; fr. GK *with 150 passengers* to NY in
July 1796. [E504.15.71/73]

OLIVE OF GLASGOW, Hugh Colquhoun, wrecked on White
Point, Charleston, SC, on 2 Aug. 1728. [NE Wkly Jrnl #83]

OLIVE OF IRVINE, Andrew Gray, fr. GK to Boston in Mar.1746;
James Aitken, fr. Glasgow to Boston in Mar. 1747.
[E504.15.2]

OLIVE, William Breckenridge, fr. GK to VA in Mar. 1757,
[E504.15.8][GJ#805]

OLIVE OF ABERDEEN, 89 tons, Robert Bennet, fr. Aberdeen
with 1 passengers to Miramachi 19 May 1818. [E504.1.27]

OLIVE BRANCH OF CHARLESTON, 254 tons, Thomas
Bennet, fr. GK to Charleston in Jan. 1806. [E504.15.77]

ORANGE OF ABERDEEN, 137 tons, George Paterson, fr.
Aberdeen *with 30 passengers* to NY, 17 June 1816.
[E504.1.26]

ORANGEFIELD OF GLASGOW/AYR, 100 ton brigantine,
Hugh Morris, fr. GK to Quebec in Mar. 1766; arr. in
Charleston, SC, on 3 Nov. 1766 fr. Glasgow; arr. in Charleston
on 4 Nov. 1767 fr. Ayr; arr. in Charleston on 6 Feb. 1768 fr.
Glasgow; James Morris, fr. Ayr via Ireland to Charleston in
Oct. 1768; arr. in Charleston on 18 Jan. 1769 fr. Bo'ness; John
Harrison, fr. GK to Boston in Mar. 1770; fr. GK to Boston in
Sept. 1770; Hugh Rilley, fr. GK to Boston in June 1771;
Hugh Billie, fr GK to Boston Mar.1772; fr. Glasgow to
Pensacola 1777; James Farrie, fr Port Glasgow to St
Augustine/Pensacola Jan.1778; fr Port Glasgow to Pensacola
Feb.1779. [JCTP#84/201] [PRO.CO5.511] [SCGaz:
3.11.1766/6.2.1768/18.1.1769; 1630] [E504.15.13/18/19/21;
E504.4.5; E504.28.28/30]

ORIENT OF NEW YORK, 276 tons, Timothy Bowmond, fr. GK
with 40 passengers to NY 2 May 1815; G.Brown, fr GK to NY
20 May 1819. [E504.15.108/124]

ORION, Thomas Stetson, fr. GK to Boston in Feb. 1796; Benjamin
Leaver, fr. GK *with passengers* to Boston in Dec. 1810.
[E504.15.71/90]

ORION, Thomas Bridges, arr. NY 15 Jan.1827 *with passengers* fr.
Glasgow. [USNA.M237]

ORYZA OF BALTIMORE, Cap.Valangin, fr GK to Baltimore 1
July 1820, arrived in Baltimore by 30 Sep.1820.
[E504.15.129][USNA]

OSCAR OF GLASGOW, 216 tons, George Johnston, fr. GK to
NFD 9 Oct.1815.[E504.15.109]

OSSIAN OF LEITH, John Hill, fr. Inverness to Pictou, NS, in June
1821; Cap.Black, fr GK to NY 16 Nov.1821.
[E504.17.9//E504.15.138]

OSWEGO OF NEW YORK, John Riven, fr Orkney to NY 18
Sep.1756. [E504.26.3]

OTHELLO, John M. Knight, arr. NY 3 Dec. 1828 *with passengers*
fr. Leith. [USNA.M237]

OUGHTON, a snow, Capt. Stewart or McClure?, fr. the Clyde to
Quebec on 12 Apr. 1802; Capt. Stewart, fr. GK *with*
passengers to Charleston, SC, in Nov. 1802; wrecked off
Charleston on 15 May 1803; fr. Loch Boisdale on 20 June 1803
with 200 passengers fr. South Uist to Charlottetown, P.E.I.
[CM#12573][GkAd#18/86][CS96.1238.60]

OWNER'S SUPPLY, Capt. Hooper, fr. SC to the Orkneys in 1760, captured by the French and taken to Bergen. [SM#23.671]

OXFORD, a 130 ton brigantine, John Stewart, fr. Port Glasgow to the Potomac River and Baltimore, MD, in Sept. 1786. [GM#IX.451.271/279]

PACKET OF CHARLESTON, 185 tons, Life Holden, fr. GK *with 1 passenger* to Charleston 31 July 1816. [E504.15.113]

PAGE OF IRVINE, Alexander McKelvie, fr. GK to Boston in Mar. 1747, [E504.15.2]

PAGE OF GLASGOW, John Fairie, fr. Port Glasgow to Boston in Feb. 1748. [E504.28.3]

PAISLEY OF GLASGOW, Michael Hyndman, fr GK to MD Feb.1772; fr GK to MD Sep.1772. [NAS,E504.1.21]

PAISLEY, a brig, Capt. Johnston, fr. GK *with passengers* to NY, arr. there on 6 Oct. 1801. [ANY#1.352]

PALLAS OF GLASGOW, William Noble, fr. Leith to NY and Philadelphia in Sept. 1770; fr GK to North Potomac, MD, Oct.1773; James Bruce, fr GK to North Potomac River, MD June 1774. [EA#14/175][E504.15.23/24]

PALLAS OF AYR, David Johnstone, fr GK to Quebec Feb.1778; fr GK to NY Jan.1779. [E504.15.29/30]

PALLAS OF CHARLESTON, 177 tons, John Hunter, fr. GK *with 20 passengers* to Charleston, SC, in Apr. 1796. [E504.15.71/72]

PALLAS OF ABERDEEN, 178 tons, James Booth, fr. Aberdeen to St Johns, 25 Apr. 1816. [E504.1.26]

PALLAS OF GREENOCK, 632 tons, R Robinson, fr. GK *with 4 passengers* to Miramachi 21 Apr.1817. [E504.15.116]

PALLAS, Capt. Moir, fr. Tobermory *with 27 passengers* to PEI in Sep.1821. [PEIGaz.22.9.1821]

PANDORA OF GREENOCK, 150 tons, Duncan Douglas, fr. GK to NFD in Feb. 1796; Capt. Laing, to Wilmington *with passengers* in Sept. 1804; arr. in Wilmington fr. GK, [E504.15.71] [GC:28.8.1804][GkAdv:22.1.1805]

PANNEL OF KINGSTON, 189 tons, Elisha Ambler, fr. GK to Philadelphia 7 June 1815. [E304.15.108]

PARAGON OF GLASGOW, 383 tons, John McGowan, fr. GK to Boston 8 Aug.1816; fr. GK *with 11 passengers*to Boston 10 July 1817. [E504.15.113/117]

PATRICK AND PEGGY OF STROMNESS, a sloop, Peter
Sinclair, fr. Orkney to NFD in Apr. 1769. [E504.26.5]

PATRIOT OF ABERDEEN, 198 tons, Alexander Anderson, fr.
Aberdeen *with 14 passengers* to Quebec, 7 Mar. 1817; fr. GK
to Quebec 6 Aug.1817; fr Aberdeen to Quebec 7 Mar.1820; fr
Aberdeen to Quebec 6 Mar.1819. [E504.1.26/28; E504.15.117]

PATRIOT PITT, Alexander Witherspoon, fr. GK to VA in June
1760 [E504.15.9]

PATTY OF GLASGOW, Alexander Marquis, fr. GK to NY and
Halifax in Feb. 1777; fr. the Clyde to NY on 18 Aug. 1780,
[GM#III.270] [E504.15.27]

PATTY, a US brigantine, James Hall, fr. GK *with passengers* to
New Orleans in Dec. 1802. [GkAd#99]

PATUXENT, John Shaw, deposition at Elizabeth City 1 June 1742.
[PaGaz:18.6.1742]

PATUXENT OF GLASGOW, Hannibal Lusk, fr GK to VA
Mar.1773; fr GK to St Mary's, Potomac River, MD, Aug.1773;
fr GK to James River, VA, Mar.1774; fr GK to MD July 1774.
Fr GK to NY Feb.1778. [E504.15.22/23/24/29]

PEACE, a 170 ton US brig, Moses Tinny, fr. Port Glasgow *with*
passengers to the Potomac River, VA, on 30 June 1790.
[GM#X111.651.199]

PEACE OF HULL, 185 tons, John Salter, fr. GK *with 85*
passengers to Montreal 28 May 1817. [E504.15.116]

PEACE, Cap.Bruce, fr Dundee to NY Sep.1820. [E504.11.21]

PEARL OF WHITEHAVEN, Thomas Walker, fr. Glasgow to VA
in 1724. [AC9/868]

PEARL OF GLASGOW, 130 ton snow, Robert Jeffrey, fr. Port
Glasgow to VA in June 1747; fr. Port Glasgow to VA in Apr.
1748; Thomas Francis, fr. Port Glasgow to VA in July 1749; fr.
Port Glasgow to VA in July 1750; fr. Port Glasgow *with*
passengers bound to the Potomac River, MD, in May 1755; fr.
Port Glasgow *'any goodtradesmen such as blacksmiths,*
joiners, bricklayers, tailors and weavers that will indent for 4
years' to the Potomac River 20 Mar.1756; fr. GK *with*
passengers to the Potomac River Jan. 1757; John Francis, fr.
GK *with passengers* to the Potomac River, MD, in June 1759;
fr. GK to VA in Apr. 1763; fr. GK to SC in Nov. 1763; arr. in
Charleston on 2 Feb. 1764 fr. Glasgow; Richard Tucker, fr GK
to NC Aug.1772; fr GK to NY July 1773

[GJ#714/756/801/922] [PRO.CO5.511]
[E504.15.9/11/12/21/22; E504.28.3/4] [SCGaz#1541]
PEGGY OF GLASGOW, William Walkinshaw, fr. GK to VA in
Mar. 1745; fr. Port Glasgow to VA in Mar. 1746; Robert
Jeffrey, fr. GK to VA in June 1747; Archibald Yuill, fr. GK to
Boston in June 1752; Robert Boyd, fr. GK to VA in Mar. 1754;
Colin Buchanan, fr. GK to SC in Nov. 1756; bound fr.
Glasgow *with passengers* for Charleston, wrecked off Cape
Romain, SC, 12 Feb. 1757; Boyd, fr. VA to Glasgow in 1757,
captured by the French and taken to Morlaix; William
Morrison, fr. GK to VA in Feb. 1759; fr. GK *with passengers*
to the James River, VA, in Sept. 1759; fr. GK to VA in Apr.
1760; fr. GK to VA in Mar. 1761; fr. GK to VA in Oct. 1761;
fr. GK to VA in May 1762; David Andrew, fr. GK to VA in
Jan. 1763; fr. GK to VA in July 1763; fr. GK to VA in Mar.
1764; fr. GK to VA in Aug. 1764; fr. GK to VA in Mar. 1765;
fr. GK to VA in Aug. 1765; fr. GK to VA in Mar. 1766; fr. GK
to VA in Aug. 1766; Thomas Ramsay, fr. GK to VA in Aug.
1767; fr. GK to VA in Jan. 1770; fr. GK to VA in July 1770;
Robert Crawford, fr. Port Glasgow to VA in Feb. 1773; Capt.
Reeve, fr. the Clyde to NFD on 24 May 1780; James McLeish,
fr. GK to NFD in Apr. 1781; James Leisk, fr. GK to NFD in
Feb. 1782; Robert Eason, fr. GK to Halifax in Mar. 1783.
[SCGaz#1184] [E504.28/2/21]
[GM#III/174][GJ#938][SM.20.325]
[E504.15.2/5/6/7/9/10/11/12/13/14/18/33/35/37]
PEGGY, a snow, Colin Buchanan, fr. Glasgow *with passengers* to
Charleston, SC, ashore on Cape Romain in Jan. 1757, arr. in
Charleston in Feb. 1757. [GJ#796] [SCGaz#1183; 17.2.1757]
PEGGY, a snow, Thomas Cochrane, fr. GK to NY in Feb. 1764;
William Craig, fr. GK to Boston in Sept. 1765; arr. in Boston
on 22 Jan. 1766 *with 9 passengers* fr. Glasgow; Hugh Brown,
fr. GK to VA in Mar. 1766; William Craig, fr. GK to SC in
Oct. 1766; arr. in Charleston on 14 Jan. 1767; Hugh Brown, fr.
GK to VA in Feb. 1767; William Morrison, fr. GK via Cork to
Charleston in Oct. 1781 [PAB]
[E504.15.12/13/14/33/35][SCGaz#1641][GM#IV.300]
PEGGY OF LARNE, James Sloan, fr. GK to NFD in May 1759,
[E504.15.9]

PEGGIE, James Ryburn, fr. Campbeltown to NFD in Mar. 1768.
[E504.8.4]

PEGGY OF GREENOCK, 170 tons, Robert Speir, fr. GK to NY
and Philadelphia in Jan. 1767; fr. GK to NY and Philadelphia
in Aug. 1767; fr. GK to NFD and Philadelphia in Apr. 1768; fr.
GK to Philadelphia in Mar. 1769; Thomas Ramsay, fr. GK to
VA in July 1769; William Hastie, fr. GK to Philadelphia in
June 1770; Thomas Ramsay, fr. GK to Boston in Mar. 1771;
William Heastie, fr. GK to Philadelphia in July 1771; Thomas
Workman, fr. GK to SC in Oct. 1771; William Hastie, fr GK
to Philadelphia July 1773; Colin Campbell, fr. Port Glasgow to
Port North Potomac, MD, in May 1774; Robert Bog, fr. GK to
NFD Aug.1777; Donald Hastie, fr. GK to NY in Nov. 1779;
Francis Ritchie, fr. GK to Newbury, NE, in May 1785; fr. GK
to the Potomac River, VA and MD, in July 1787; David
Galbreath, fr. GK to MD on 18 Mar. 1788; Thomas Boyd, fr.
GK to VA 19 Nov.1790; fr. the Clyde to VA in Feb. 1792;
Charles Livingston, fr. GK *with passengers* to Charleston, SC,
in Jan. 1793; John Williamson, fr. GK to Halifax in June 1795.
[GCr#76/206] [CM#7108/7257] [E504.28.23//15/23]
[EA#15/32]
[E504.15.14/15/16/17/18/19/20/28/32/41/45/47/57/68]

PEGGY OF CHARLESTON, Alexander Hardie, fr Bo'ness to
Charleston 19 Aug.1772. [E504.6.9]

PEGGY OF GREENOCK, 86 tons, Capt. McLeish, fr. the Clyde
to NFD on 12 Apr. 1781; Walter Black, fr. GK to NFD in Mar.
1786; Robert Frew, fr. GK to NFD 24 Mar. 1788; fr. GK to
NFD 25 May 1789; fr. GK to NFD in Sept. 1789
[E504.15.42/47/51/52][GM#IV.126; XII.596.174]

PEGGY, a snow, Capt. Pollock, fr. the Clyde to NC in July 1768,
arr. in NC during Oct. 1768 *with passengers* fr. Glasgow; T.
Workman, arr. in Charleston, SC, in Jan. 1772 fr. GK.
[GC:13.7.1768][GJ:14.7.1768][SCGaz:24.10.1768; 7.1.1772]

PEGGY OF KIRKCALDY, 80 tons, James Normand, fr.Kirkcaldy
to Brunswick, NC, in Dec. 1772; James Graham, fr. Kirkcaldy
to Wilmington, NC, in Dec. 1774, arr. in Port Brunswick, NC,
on 20 Mar. 1775 fr. Kirkcaldy. [E504.20.8][NCSA.S8.112]

PEGGY OF BO'NESS, a snow, John Shepherd, fr. Bo'ness, *with
passengers* to the James, York, and Rappahannock Rivers, VA,
in Aug. 1769; Alexander Hardie, to Charleston in July 1772;

arr. in Charleston, SC, during Oct. 1772 *with passengers* fr.
Bo'ness. [SCGaz:29.10.1772][EA#18/48] GJ#31.8.1769]

PEGGY OF LEITH, 100 tons, John Scougall, {William Paton jr?}
fr. Leith *with passengers* to Edenton, NC, on 25 Oct. 1774;
William Patton, arr. in Edenton fr. Leith in Jan. 1775.
[NCGaz,13.1.1775][E504.22.19] [CM#8261]

PEGGY OF WHITBY, Jacob Wilson, fr GK *with troops* to North
America Apr.1778. [E504.15.29]

PEGGY OF GREENOCK, a 170 ton brigantine, Alexander
Taylor, fr. GK *with passengers* to the James River, VA, in May
1787; arr. in Norfolk, VA, during July 1787 fr. Glasgow.
[Phila.Gaz.#266]; fr. GK to VA 24 Mar. 1788; David
Galbreath, fr. GK *with passengers* to the Potomac River, MD,
in Feb. 1789; Charles Livingstone, fr. GK to Charleston, SC,
23 Feb. 1791; Capt. McCunn, fr. GK *with passengers* to
Charleston, SC, in Jan. 1793. [GCr#68/204]
[E504.15.45/47/50/58] [GM#XII.578.83][GJ#2444]

PEGGY OF GREENOCK, 153 tons, Donald Haistie, fr. GK *with
passengers* to NY in Nov. 1780; Robert Frew, fr. GK to St
John, NFD, in Apr. 1781; William Morrison, fr. GK *with
passengers* via Cork to Charleston in Sept. 1781; Robert
Eason, fr. GK to Halifax in Apr. 1783; Walter Black, fr. GK to
NFD in Mar. 1785; fr. the Clyde to NFD on 23 Mar. 1786; fr.
GK to NFD in May 1787; William Milne, fr. GK *with
passengers* to Miramachi, NB, via Casco and Pictou 12 June
1789; John Wilson, fr. GK *with 8 passengers* to Halifax, NS, 2
Mar. 1791; John Williamson, fr. GK to St John's, NB, in Feb.
1792; [E504.15.33/38/40/45/51] [GM#III/303; IV.231;
#IX.430.102; XII.589.120/183]

PEGGY OF ABERDEEN, 40 tons, Daniel Gray, fr. Aberdeen to St
John's, NFD, in Mar. 1777. [E504.1.13]

PEGGY AND BETSY OF CARRON, a snow, Andrew Russell, fr
Bo'ness to Charleston 25 Aug.1773, arr. in Charleston, SC, in
Nov. 1773 fr. Bo'ness. [SCGaz:25.11.1773][E504.6.9]

PEGGY AND ELIZABETH, Capt. Scott, arr. in Charleston, SC, in
Oct.1753 fr. Leith. [SCGaz.15.10.1753]

PEGGY AND NELLY OF GREENOCK, 70 ton snow, Robert
Hogart, fr. GK to SC in Oct. 1757, arr. in Charleston on 30 Jan.
1758; fr. GK to Boston in Sept. 1758.[E504.15.8]
[PRO.CO5.509]

PELHAM OF GLASGOW, George Yuille, fr. GK to VA via the Isle of May in Apr. 1750, [E504.15.4]

PELICAN, a brigantine, Henry Laird, arr. in Charleston, SC, in Aug. 1733 fr. Glasgow. [SCGaz#84]

PEMBROKE, John Boyd, fr Port Glasgow to NY May 1778.[E504.28.29]

PENELOPE OF GREENOCK, 80 ton brig, George Jamieson, fr. the Clyde to Wilmington, NC, in July 1774, arr. at Port Brunswick, NC, on 10 Sept. 1774 fr. GK; fr. the Clyde to NC in Mar. 1775, arr. in Port Brunswick, NC, on 10 May 1775; Alexander Thomson, fr GK to Halifax May 1778. [CM#8321] [NCSA.S8.112][GJ: 14.7.1774] [E504.15.24/29]

PENELOPE OF GLASGOW, 313 tons, George Wood, fr. GK to Halifax 17 Feb. 1813. [E504.15.99]

PENELOPE OF PORT GLASGOW, John Burnett, fr Port Glasgow to Newfoundland 6 Mar.1818.[E504.28.100]

PERCIVAL, John Scott, fr Dundee *with passengers* to NY 4 May 1820; arr. NY 16 May 1821 *with passengers* fr. Dundee. [CE70.1.16][USNA.M237]

PERSEVERANCE, 300 tons, Thomas Sheriff/Robert Chapman?, fr. GK *with passengers* to Halifax, NS, in Sept. 1786. [E504.15.43][GM.IX.449.255]

PERSEVERANCE OF ABERDEEN, 116 tons, John Philip, fr. Stornaway *with 52 passengers* to Quebec on 24 Aug. 1815; fr Dundee to Pictou 9 Sep.1817; John Patterson, fr Aberdeen to Pictou 16 Mar.1819. [E504.33.3; E504.11.20; E504.1.28]

PERSEVERANCE OF ST JOHN'S, NEWFOUNDLAND, 183 tons, David Cowan, fr. GK to NFD 10 May 1815; Peter Fisher, fr. GK to NFD 20 Mar.1817. [E504.15.108/115]

PETER OF GLASGOW, Thomas Lang, fr GK to VA Feb.1773; fr. Port Glasgow to the James River, VA, in July 1773; fr. Port Glasgow to the James River, VA, in Feb. 1774; fr. Port Glasgow to the James River, VA, in July 1774; David Barr, fr. GK to VA in July 1785; [E504.28.22/23; 15.22/23/41]

PHAETON, Cap. Alleyne, arr. in Charleston in Nov. 1758 fr. Orkney. [SCGaz.11.1758]

PHEMIE OF GREENOCK, a 120 ton brigantine, 86 tons, John Sharp, fr. GK *with passengers* to NY in July 1786; fr. GK to NFD 2 Aug. 1787, [E504.15.45][GM#IX.442.207]

PHESDO OF ABERDEEN, 244 tons, Andrew Pennan, fr.
  Aberdeen *with 37 passengers* to Halifax/St Johns, 16 Feb.
  1816; fr. Aberdeen *with 8 passengers* to Halifax, 11 Feb. 1817.
  [E504.1.26]

PHOCIAN, George Duplux, arr. NY 8 May 1824 *with passengers*
  fr. GK. [USNA.M237]

PHOEBE OF KINCARDINE, 257 tons, Andrew Anderson, fr. GK
  to NY 7 Feb.1818; fr. GK to NY July 1818; fr GK to
  Charleston 28 Sep.1819; fr GK to Charleston 4 Mar.1820; fr
  GK to Charleston 12 July 1820; fr GK to Charleston 5
  Feb.1821; fr GK to Charleston 17 July 1821
  [E504.15.119/121/125/128/130/135/139]

PHOENIX OF GREENOCK, John Lamont, fr. Port Glasgow to
  VA in Nov. 1772, James Fife, fr. GK to St John's, NFD,
  Sept.1777; Capt. Cunningham, fr. the Clyde to NFD on 30
  Aug. 1780, [E504.28.21//15.28][GM#III.286]

PHOENIX, fr GK to Chaleur Bay, Apr.1828; fr GK to Chaleur Bay
  Aug.1828. [E504.15.165/166]

PILGRIM, Captain Beveridge, fr Kirkcaldy to Halifax
  Apr.1824.[E504.20.17]

PILOT OF ABERDEEN, 120 tons, James McLean, fr Dundee to
  Halifax and Quebec May 1817; fr Dundee to Quebec 10 May
  1818; John Law, fr Aberdeen to Miramachi 20 Mar.1822.
  [E504.1.27/29; E504.11.20]

PITT OF NEW YORK, sloop, Paul Bascomb, fr Orkney to NY 2
  Sep.1760. [E504.26.3]

PITT, a brigantine, James Harvie/Howie, fr. GK *with passengers* to
  Brunswick and Wilmington, NC, in May 1783; fr. GK *with
  passengers* to Wilmington, NC, 25 Jan. 1785.
  [CM:26.4.1783;11.12.1784][E504.15.38]

PITT OF AYR, 320 tons, John Hamilton, fr. GK *with 35
  passengers* to Quebec 22 July 1817. [E504.15.116]

PLANTER, Hannibal Lusk, fr. GK to VA in Feb. 1765
  [E504.15.12]

PLOUGHMAN OF ABERDEEN, 165 tons, A.Duncan, fr.
  Aberdeen *with 7 passengers* to Halifax, NS, 22 Apr. 1816.
  [E504.1.26]

POLLY OF NEW YORK, brigantine, Isaac Sheldon, fr Orkney to
  NY 22 Sep.1759; fr Orkney to NY 24 June 1760; Robert
  McCormick, fr orkney to NY 20 Sep.1764. [E504.26.3/4]

POLLY, James Gammell, fr. GK to MD in Oct. 1760; fr. VA to Loch Ryan, captured by French privateers on 12 May 1761, 80 leagues west of Torry and ransomed for 1230 guineas. [E504.15.9][SM#23.335]; James Langmuir, fr. Port Glasgow *with passengers* to the Choptante River, Eastern Shore of MD, July 1767, *'any tradesmen that are willing to indent may apply'*. [GC#19]

POLLY OF NORTH CAROLINA, 85 tons, Robert Loughead, fr. GK to Bath, NC, 7 July 1787; E L Deering, fr. GK *with passengers* to Wilmington on 20 Aug. 1793. [E504.15.45][GC:25.7.1793]

POLLY, a brigantine, Patrick McArthur, fr. Port Glasgow to MD in May 1773; fr. GK *with passengers* to Quebec in Aug. 1781; John Wilson fr. GK to VA in Sept. 1783. [E504.28.22; E504.15.38][GM#IV.264]

POLLY OF BOSTON, 181 tons, Samuel Chessman, fr. GK *with 100 passengers*_to NY in June 1796. [E504.15.72]

POLLY OF WISCASSET, 139 tons, Peter Cassidy, fr. GK to Boston in Aug. 1796. [E504.15.73]

POMONA OF GREENOCK, 152 tons, William Markland, fr. GK to NFD in Mar. 1806; John McAlpine, fr GK to Antigonish 22 May 1819. [E504.15.77/124]

POPPET OF BOSTON, schooner, Thomas Davis, fr Orkney to Boston 9 July 1764. [E504.26.4]

PORT GLASGOW, Archibald Yuill, arr. in Charleston, SC, in Feb. 1766, fr. Glasgow. [SCGaz: 11.2.1766]

POSTBOY OF ST JOHN, NEW BRUNSWICK, 170 tons, James Ireland, fr. GK to Halifax 14 Oct. 1814. [E504.15.106]

POTOMAC OF GLASGOW, John Thomson, fr. GK to MD in July 1759; fr. GK to VA in Mar. 1760; fr. GK to MD in Feb. 1761; fr. GK to VA in Nov. 1761; Robert How, fr. GK to MD in Mar. 1768; James Bruce, fr GK to MD Aug.1772; James Gibson, fr GK to MD Aug.1774 [E504.15.9/10/15/21/24]

POTOMAC, a brigantine, Thomas Todd, fr. Port Glasgow *with passengers* to NY in Aug. 1792. [GCr#146]

PRESIDENT OF GLASGOW, fr. Glasgow to VA before 1750. [AC9/1746]

PRESTONGRANGE, James Dunlop, fr. GK to VA in Apr. 1759; fr. GK to VA in Jan. 1761; Colin Campbell, fr. GK to VA in Dec. 1761; fr. GK to VA in May 1763; fr. GK to VA in Dec.

1763; fr. GK to VA in Mar. 1766; fr. GK to VA in Apr. 1767;
fr. GK to VA in Jan. 1768; fr. GK to VA in Mar. 1769
[E504.15.9/10/11/12/13/15/16][GJ#922]

PRETTY JENNY OF GREENOCK, Alexander Malcolm, fr. GK
to Boston in May 1748. [E504.15.2]

PRINCE FERDINAND OF GREENOCK, 70 ton snow, John
Ryburn, fr. GK to SC in Nov. 1759, arr. in Charleston, SC, on
9 Feb. 1760 [E504.15.9][PRO.CO5.509]

PRINCE GEORGE OF GLASGOW, Hugh Coulter, fr. GK on 21
May 1743 to Carolina; arr. in Charleston on 5 Sept. 1743 fr.
Leith; fr. GK to Boston in Mar. 1744; fr. GK to VA in Mar.
1745; fr. Glasgow to VA in 1746, captured by the French or
Spanish off the Capes of VA in Mar. 1747.[SM#8.549]
[PaGaz:24.3.1747] [SCGaz#493] [MdGaz#99][E504.28.1;
E504.15.1/2] [CM:26.5.1743]

PRINCE GEORGE, a snow, Richard Askew, arr. in Charleston,
SC, *with passengers* in Jan. 1767 fr. Galloway to NY; arr. in
Charleston in Feb. 1768 fr. Galloway. [SCGaz:
5.1.1767/5.2.1768]

PRINCE GEORGE OF ST PETERSBURGH, William Williams,
fr Leith *with 10 passengers* to NY 22 Jan.1817. [E504.22.76]

PRINCE MADOC OF NEW YORK, 298 tons, Thomas Choat, fr.
GK to NY 24 Apr.1819; fr GK to NY 18 Feb.1820;   James
Watson, fr GK to NY 5 July 1820, arr. NY 28 Aug. 1820 *with
passengers*; Nicholas Sullivan, fr GK to NY 21 July 1821, arr.
NY 24 Sep. 1821 *with passengers* fr GK
[E504.15.124/128/129/137] [USNA.M237]

PRINCE OF ORANGE OF GLASGOW, 40 tons, John Andrew,
to Carolina in 1741;   William Alexander, arr. in Port Roanoke,
NC, in 1741; fr. GK to NC on 31 July 1742; Capt. Adams, fr.
Stromness to the Carolinas on 2 Feb. 1748. [NCSA.S8.112]
[GJ#53] [CM#3276; 26.3.1741; 29.2.1748]

PRINCE OF WALES, Captain Dunbar, arr. in Charleston in March
1736 fr. Inverness. [SCGaz.6.3.1736]

PRINCE OF WALES OF BOSTON, Jonathan Freeman, fr orkney
to Boston 16 June 1760. [E504.26.3]

PRINCE OF WALES OF GREENOCK, George Smith, fr. GK to
VA in Feb. 1764; Andrew Lee, fr. the Clyde to VA 26 Apr.
1768; fr. GK to VA in Sept. 1768; James Chalmers, fr. GK to
VA in Apr. 1769 [E504.15.12/16][GC#67]

PRINCE OF WALES OF LONDON, 340 tons, Henry Hanwell,
fr. Stornaway *with 27 passengers* to Hudson Bay 24 July 1811.
[E504.33.3]

PRINCE WILLIAM OF GLASGOW, 150 tons, Hugh Brown, fr.
Port Glasgow to VA in Dec. 1743; fr. GK to VA in Oct. 1744,
fr. GK to VA in May 1745; Hugh Campbell, fr. GK to VA in
July 1746; Henry Wardrop, fr. GK to VA in June 1747;
William Dunlop, fr. GK via Havre de Grace in France to VA in
Nov. 1753; William Donald, fr. GK to VA in July 1754; fr.
GK to VA in Apr. 1755; fr. GK to VA in Apr. 1756; James
Orr, fr. GK to VA in July 1756; fr. GK to VA in May 1757; fr.
GK to VA in Jan. 1758; fr. GK to VA in Apr. 1759; fr. GK to
VA in Feb. 176O; Hugh Coulter, fr. GK to VA in Jan. 1761;
Capt. Coulter, fr. VA to Glasgow was taken by a 64 gun French
man o'war on 3 July 1761 and ransomed for 2990 guineas.
Archibald Crawford, fr. GK to VA in Sept. 1761; John
Paterson, fr. GK to VA in June 1762; fr. GK to VA in Mar.
1763; fr. GK to VA in Feb. 1765; fr. GK to VA in Aug. 1765;
fr. GK to VA in Apr. 1766; fr. GK to VA in Feb. 1767; John
McCunn, fr. GK to VA in Jan. 1768; fr. GK to VA in July
1768; fr. GK to VA in Jan. 1769; fr. GK to VA in July 1769;
John Bruce, fr. GK to Philadelphia in Feb. 1771; fr GK to GA
Dec.1772 [E504.15.1/2/6/7/8/9/10/11/12/13/14 /15/16/19/22;
E504.28.1] [GJ#923][SM#23.335]

PRINCESS ELIZABETH OF GREENOCK, John Stevenson, fr.
GK *with 3 passengers* to NFD 16 Mar. 1811, [E504.15.90]

PRINCESS LOUISA OF PHILADELPHIA, William Gardner, fr.
GK to Philadelphia in Sept. 1753, [E504.15.6]

PRINCESS MARY OF FALMOUTH, 60 tons, Arthur Howell, fr.
Leith to Falmouth, NE, in Sept. 1772 [E504.22.17]

PROMPT OF MONTREAL, 335 tons, Norrington Coverdale, fr.
GK *with 118 passengers*, to Quebec and Montreal 28
Apr.1817; arr. in Quebec *with 135 passengers* on 6 July 1817;
John Wilson, fr. GK to NO 11 Nov.1818.
[E504.15.116/122][MG]

PROMPT OF BO'NESS, John Kay, fr Leith *with 400 passengers*
to Halifax/Quebec 5 July 1817; fr Leith to Quebec 1 Apr.1818.
[E504.22.77/80]

PROSPERITY OF GLASGOW, 80 tons, James Montier, fr. the
Clyde to VA in 1732; Hugh Crawford, fr. GK to VA in Aug.

1745; Archibald Galbraith, fr. GK to VA in Mar. 1746;
Archibald Galbraith, fr. Aberdeen to VA in Aug. 1747; Robert
Boyd, fr. Port Glasgow to VA in May 1748; William McCunn,
fr. GK to Boston in Mar. 1749; fr. GK to Boston in Oct. 1749,
[E504.15.2/4; E504.1.2; E504.28.3] [AC9/1354]

PROSPERITY, a brigantine, John Smith, fr. GK to Boston in Apr.
1766; arr. in Boston on 21 May 1766 fr. Scotland. [PAB]
[E504.15.13]

PROSPEROUS, a ketch, fr. the Clyde to MD/VA 23 Oct.1693.
[GAr.Shawfield MS4/5]

PROTECTOR OF ST JOHN, NB, 353 tons, Walter Simpson, fr.
GK *with 8 passengers* to St John, NB, and Halifax, 14
Aug.1816; fr. GK *with 25 passengers* to Halifax and St John,
11 Mar.1815; fr. GK to Halifax 25 Aug.1817; fr. GK to St
John, and Halifax 18 Feb.1818; fr GK to St John 29 Feb.1820.
[E504.15.113/115/117/119/128]

PROVIDENCE, James Gardner, fr. GK to Quebec in Mar. 1783;
Richard Brown, fr. GK to Montreal on 1 May 1797.
[CM#11801] [E504.15.37]

PROVIDENCE, fr. Leith *with passengers* to NY, arr. there in
1794. [ANY#2.93]

PROVIDENCE OF QUEBEC, 284 tons, W. Myburn, fr. GK to
NFD 10 Feb.1814. [E504.15.103]

PROVIDENCE, a brig, Capt. Fyffe, fr. Leith *with 1 passenger* to
Quebec, arr. there on 31 July 1817. [MG]

PROVIDENCE OF PERTH, a brigantine, Robert Nicoll, fr
Dundee *with passengers* to NY 3 May 1819.
[E504.11.21][E70.1.15]

PROVIDENCE SUCCESS OF MARYPORT, 240 tons, Daniel
Bowes, fr. GK to St John, NB, 24 Aug.1818; fr GK to St John
24 Feb.1819. [E504.15.122/123]

PSYCHE OF DUNDEE, 146 tons, Thomas Erskine, fr Dundee
with passengers to Quebec/Montreal 1816; fr Dundee *with
passengers* to NY 1816; fr Dundee to NY May 1818; fr
Dundee *with passengers* to Quebec and Montreal 9 Mar.1819;
fr Dundee to Quebec/Montreal 14 Feb.1820; Thomas
McIntosh, fr Dundee to NY 1 Feb.1821, arr. NY 16 May 1821
with passengers; fr Dundee to Quebec/Montreal 27 Feb.1822.
[E504.11.20/21/22][USNA.M237][CE70.1.14/15]

PURPOSE, Richard Woodhouse, fr. GK to VA in Mar. 1759, [E504.15.9]

QUEBEC, Robert Craig, fr. Leith to VA in Oct. 1761. [E504.22.10]

QUEBEC, fr. GK *with passengers* to Quebec in Mar. 1780; Capt. Kerr, fr. the Clyde to Quebec on 17 Mar. 1781. [GM#III/108; IV/94]

QUEBEC PACKET OF ABERDEEN, 196 tons, Alexander Anderson, fr Aberdeen to Quebec 10 Apr.1822. [E504.1.29]

QUEEN CHARLOTTE, a schooner, fr. Glencaple, Dumfries-shire, to NB in 1817. [DWJ: 16.5.1817]

QUEEN OF GREENOCK, 200 ton brig, Robert Workman, fr. GK to Wilmington, NC, in May 1785; William Morrison, fr. GK to SC and Wilmington, 17 Aug. 1787, arr. in Port Brunswick, NC, on 20 Oct. 1787; fr. GK to NC 28 Mar. 1788; arr. in Port Brunswick, NC, on 26 Jan. 1789; fr. GK to Wilmington 27 Nov. 1789; fr. Tobermory, Mull, in July 1790 *with Catholic Highlanders fr. Barra and Uist* to Prince Edward Island, arr. at Pointe de Roche, Savage Harbour, and at Charlottetown, P.E.I. on 20 Sept. 1790; William Morrison, fr. GK *with 40 passengers* to NC 7 June 1791; fr. Tobermory, Mull, and Uist *with 300 passengers* bound to Cape Breton Island, arr. at Charlottetown on 8 Sept. 1791. [Royal Gaz.#V/I] [E504.15.41/45/47/49/59][NCSA.S8.112]

RACHEL, 90 tons, Thomas Pillans, fr. Leith to Wilmington, NC, in May 1775. [E504.22.19]

RACHEL OF GREENOCK, 257 tons, James McAllester, fr. GK to NFD 17 Sept.1814. [E504.15.105]

RAE GALLEY OF GREENOCK, John Baynes, fr. GK to Philadelphia in Apr. 1771; Robert Hunter, fr GK to Philadelphia May 1773. [E504.15.18/22]

RAE GALLEY OF GLASGOW, William Alexander, fr. GK to VA in Dec. 1747; fr. GK to Philadelphia in 1774. [E504.15.2][AC7/55]

RAINBOW OF GREENOCK, William Gordon, fr GK to VA Dec.1774; fr. Port Glasgow and Greenock *'with troops'* to America in Mar. 1776. [E504.28.24; E504.15.24/26]

RAINBOW OF WISCASSET, 125 tons, Robert Wheelwright, fr. GK to Wiscasset, in Aug. 1796. [E504.15.73]

RAMBLER, Thomas Hamilton, arr. in NY *with passengers* fr.
  Scotland in 1820. [pa]

RANGER OF NEW YORK, a sloop, Andrew McLean, fr orkney
  to NY 15 Sep.1756. [E504.6.3]

RANGER OF FALMOUTH, 100 tons, John Curtis, fr. GK to
  Boston 23 Sept. 1788, [E504.15.48]

RANGER, a sloop, Capt. Wallace, arr. in Boston in Feb. 1789 fr.
  GK. [PIG#1252]

RAPID OF GREENOCK, 113 tons, Thomas Dodd, fr. GK to
  NFD 20 June 1814. [E504.15.104]

RAPPAHANNOCK, William Semple, fr. GK to VA in Dec. 1762
  [E504.15.11]

REAPER, J.M.Knight, arr. NY 31 May 1824 *with passengers* fr.
  Glasgow. [USNA.M237]

REBECCA OF BOSTON, William Hamilton, arr. in Charleston,
  SC, on 25 Oct. 1757 fr. GK; James Raeburn, arr. in Charleston,
  SC, on 13 June 1758 fr. Glasgow, [PRO.CO5.509]

REBECCA OF GLASGOW, a snow, 100 tons, William Clerk, fr.
  GK to MD in Apr. 1753; Charles Craig, fr. GK to SC in Jan.
  1754, arr. in Charleston in Mar.1754 fr. Glasgow; fr. GK to
  MD in Apr. 1755; fr. GK *with passengers* to SC in Nov. 1755;
  fr. the Clyde to Carolina in Jan. 1756; arr. in Charleston in May
  1756 fr. Glasgow; William Hamilton, fr. GK to SC in Aug.
  1757; John Ryburn, fr. GK to SC in Apr. 1758, arr. in
  Charleston in June 1758; fr. GK to MD in Feb. 1759; captured
  at sea by a French privateer and taken to Bayonne before May
  1759; Peter Osburn, fr. GK to Philadelphia in Mar. 1767
  [E504.15.6/7/8/9/14] [GJ#741/752/927] [SCGaz#1032/1142;
  16.6.1758]

REBECCA OF GREENOCK, John McCall, fr. GK to Halifax in
  Mar. 1784; Abram Hunter, fr. GK to Halifax in Feb. 1785;
  Capt. Camlyn, fr. the Clyde to NC in Aug. 1792, [GCr#154]
  [E504.15.39/40]

REBECCA, Capt. Folger, arr. in Boston in Feb. 1789 fr. Glasgow.
  [PIG#1252]

REBECCA, Capt. Palmer, to NC 30 Aug. 1793.[GC: 3.9.1793]

REBECCA OF GLASGOW, 305 tons, Thomas McKenzie, fr. GK
  with 10 passengers to Quebec 5 Aug.1816; fr. GK *with 29
  passengers* to Quebec 10 Apr.1817; fr. GK to Quebec 26
  Aug.1817; fr. GK to Quebec 9 Mar.1818; fr. GK to Quebec

July 1818; fr. GK to Quebec 30 July 1819; fr GK to Quebec 2
Mar.1820; Thomas Tait, fr GK to Quebec 14 Aug.1820; fr GK
to Quebec 10 Mar.1821; fr GK to Quebec 17 Aug.1821; fr GK
to Quebec 11 Mar.1822; fr GK to Quebec Apr.1828; fr GK
with passengers to Quebec Aug.1828.
[E504.15.113/115/117/119/121/125/128/131/135/137/139/164/
165]

REBECCA, Wadsworth D. Loring, arr. NY 20 Mar. 1824 *with
passengers* fr. Glasgow. [USNA.M237]

REBECCA AND SARAH OF LEITH, 311 tons, J.Condie, fr.
Leith *with passengers* to Pictou, NS, on 7 May 1805;
fr.Tobermory *with 118 passengers* to P.E.I. 2 Sept. 1806.
[E504.35.1] [CM#13039]

REBECCA COFFIN OF CHARLESTON, 327 tons, John Watt,
from GK to Charleston July 1818; H. Livingston, fr GK to
Charleston 12 Feb.1819; fr GK to Charleston 30 Aug.1819.
[E504.15.121/123]

RECOVERY OF BOSTON, brigantine, James Kirkwood, fr
Orkney to Boston 27 Sep.1763. [E504.26.4]

RECOVERY, a 250 ton brigantine, Daniel Campbell, fr. GK *with
passengers* to NY on 10 Mar. 1802; fr. GK *with passengers* to
NY in Aug. 1802. [GkAd#4/58]

RECOVERY OF GREENOCK, a 169 ton brig, Robert Reid, fr.
GK *with 6 passengers* to Quebec in July 1795; Robert Bog, fr.
GK to Quebec in Apr. 1804. [E504.15.69][CM#12878]

RECOVERY OF GLASGOW, 208 tons, Thomas Hamilton, fr GK
to Halifax 19 July 1820; fr GK to NO 11 Dec.1821; fr GK to
NO 6 July 1822. [E504.15.131/138/141]

RELIEF OF GREENOCK, Dugald. McGregor, fr GK to NC in
Oct.1774. [GJ:17.11.1774][E504.15.24]

RENFREW OF GREENOCK, James Somerville, fr. Port Glasgow
to the James River, VA, in July 1773; fr GK to VA Mar.1774;
fr. the Clyde to VA in Apr. 1775,
[E504.28.22;E504.15.23]][EA#23/1180]

RENOWN OF GREENOCK, 196 tons, Dugald Cameron, fr. GK
to NFD in June 1796. [E504.15.72]

RENOWN OF KIRKCALDY, a brig, James Watt, fr. Leith on 9
Apr. 1817 *with 20 passengers* to Quebec/Montreal, arr. on 9
June 1817; James Abbott, fr Leith to Quebec/Montreal 7
Mar.1818; James Watt, fr Leith to Quebec/Montreal 3

Mar.1819; fr Leith to Quebec/Montreal 11 Mar.1820.
[MG][E504.22.76/80/84/89]

RESIGN OF NEW YORK, Joseph Clements, fr GK to NY 4
Jan.1821;arr. NY 1 May 1822 *with passengers* fr. GK.
[USNA.M237][E504.15.138]

RESOLUTION, a brigantine, John Marquis, fr. GK *with
passengers* to the Rappahannock River, VA, in Nov. 1791.
[GCr#29]

RESOLUTION OF ALLOA, 176 tons, Daniel Crawford, fr. GK
to Quebec in Apr. 1795. [E504.15.68]

RESOLUTION OF KIRKCALDY, 160 tons, John Keir, fr. GK to
Quebec 18 May 1813. [E504.15.100]

RESOLUTION OF NEW BEDFORD, Joseph C. Delano, fr GK
to New Bedford 23 Feb.1822.[E504.15.139]

RETRENCH, fr GK to Charleston May 1828; fr GK *with
passengers* to Charleston Sep.1828. [E504.15.164/165]

RETRIEVE, a schooner, Jacob Hows, arr. in NY *with passengers*
fr. Scotland in 1820. [pa]

REVENGE OF ABERDEEN, 100 tons, Alexander Leslie, fr.
Aberdeen to VA in Aug. 1746. [E504.1.2]

REVENGE, James Allison, fr GK to Quebec Apr.1779; Capt.
Kerr, fr. the Clyde to NFD on 31 May 1780.
[E504.15.31][GM#111.182]

RICHARD OF GLASGOW, Peter Paterson, fr GK to VA May
1773; fr GK to James Rive, VA, Oct.1773; Capt. Robertson, fr.
the Clyde to Charleston, SC, in 1781, when captured.
[E504.15.22/23] [SM#43.109]

RICHMOND OF LEITH, Capt. Hamilton, to Charleston, SC, in
Oct. 1768. [CM#7205]

RICHMOND OF GLASGOW, James Patterson, fr GK to VA
May 1774; fr GK to VA Oct.1774; fr GK to NY, Halifax and
Pensacola Oct.177; fr. GK *with passengers* to Savannah, GA,
in June 1780; Capt. Jamieson, fr. the Clyde to Charleston, SC,
in 1781 when captured; George Jamieson, fr. GK to Quebec in
Feb. 1782. [SM#43.109][E504.15.24/28/35][GM#III/143;
IV.300]

RITCHIE OF GREENOCK, Malcolm Crawford, arr. in
Charleston, SC, on 1 Feb. 1765 fr. Glasgow; arr. in Charleston
in Feb. 1766 fr. Glasgow; fr. GK to VA in Sept. 1769; Angus
McLarty, fr. GK to VA in Jan. 1771 John Guthrie, fr. GK to

NY and St Augustine in June 1777. [E504.15.17/18/27]
[SCGaz:30.1.1766/1565]

RITCHIE OF GLASGOW, Angus McLarty, fr GK to VA
Feb.1772; William Robertson, fr GK to Rappahannock River,
VA, Apr.1774. [E504.15.21/23]

ROANOAK, William P. Bastow, arr. NY 19 Sep.1827 *with
passengers* fr. GK. [USNA.M237]

ROB ROY OF ABERDEEN, 241 tons, William Nairn, fr
Aberdeen to Quebec 16 Feb.1819. [E504.1.28]

ROBERT, to Carolina, arrived by Jan.1688. [GD393.79]

ROBERT OF LONDONDERRY, from the Clyde to Virginia
1691. [GD3.5.805]

ROBERT OF GLASGOW, 150 tons, James Peadie, fr. GK to SC
in Jan. 1745; arr. in Charleston, SC, in Apr. 1745 fr. Glasgow;
fr. GK to SC in Jan. 1746; James Orr, fr. GK to VA in Feb.
1747; fr. GK to VA in Oct. 1747; Thomas Watson, fr. GK to
VA in Mar. 1752; fr. GK to VA in Oct. 1755; fr. GK to VA in
Aug. 1756; fr. GK to VA on 4 Jan. 1758; fr. GK to SC in Oct.
1763; arr. in Charleston on 21 Dec. 1763; fr. GK to VA in Oct.
1764; William Grymes, fr. GK to Quebec in Feb. 1777
[E504.15.2/3/5/7/8/12/27] [SCGaz#575/1536]

ROBERT, Ninian Rodger, fr. GK to NFD in Apr. 1784.
[E504.15.39]

ROBERT OF GREENOCK, a brigantine, 100 tons, Capt. Watson,
fr. GK via the Isle of May to VA in Oct. 1750; Thomas
Watson, fr. GK *with passengers* to the James and Nansemond
Rivers, VA, in Oct. 1755; Thomas Warden, fr. GK to VA in
Mar. 1757; James Boyd, arr. in Charleston, SC, in Nov. 1758
fr. Glasgow; arr. in Charleston on 4 Jan. 1760 *with passengers*
fr. Irvine; Thomas Watson, fr. GK *with passengers* to Boston
in Feb. 1760; James Rankin, fr. GK to Boston in Apr. 1760; fr.
Glasgow to Boston in 1760, captured by the French and
ransomed for 3500 guineas; James Rankin, fr. GK to VA in
May 1761; fr. GK to VA in Sept. 1762; fr. GK to NC in Nov.
1765; arr. in Charleston, SC, in Jan. 1766, fr. Glasgow; arr. in
Charleston on 31 Dec. 1766 fr. Glasgow. [GJ#737/959]
[SCGaz#1259/1324/1639; 28.1.1766]
[E504.15.5/8/9/10/11/13/][SM#22.271]

ROBERT OF IRVINE, 80 ton brigantine, James Boyd, arr. in Charleston, SC, fr. Irvine on 4 Jan. 1760, [SCGaz#1324][PRO.CO5:509]

ROBERT, Robert Cross, fr. GK to NFD in June 1785. [E504.15.41]

ROBERT OF GREENOCK, 67 tons, Archibald McCallum, fr. GK to NFD 26 Sept.1814; James Foster, fr. GK to NFD 2 May 1815. [E504.15.105/108]

ROBERT OF IRVINE, a 181 ton brig, John Neil, fr. GK *with 3 passengers* to Quebec, arr. there on 22 July 1817; fr. GK to Quebec 7 Mar.1818; fr. GK to Quebec 18 Aug.1818; fr. GK to Quebec 17 Aug.1819; fr GK to Quebec 2 Mar.1820; fr GK to Quebec 7 Mar.1821. [MG][E504.15.119/122/125/128/135]

ROBERT, John Whitton, arr. NY 28 Aug. 1829 *with passengers* fr. Dundee. [USNA.M237]

ROBERT AND JAMES, Capt. James Peadie, arr. in Charleston, SC, in Apr. 1746 fr. Glasgow. [SCGaz#630]

ROBERT AND JOHN OF GLASGOW, fr. VA to Glasgow in 1747, captured by the French and taken to St Malo. [SM#9.97]

ROBERT FULTON, Thomas Britten, arr. NY 30 Dec. 1824 *with passengers* fr. GK; arr. NY 18 May 1825 *with passengers* fr. GK; fr GK to NY Dec.1828, arr. NY 14 Mar. 1829 *with passengers* fr. GK. [USNA.M237][E504.15.166]

ROBINA, 80 tons, Hugh Smith, arr. in Port Brunswick, NC, on 25 Oct. 1785 *with 13 passengers* fr. GK. [NCSA.S8.112]

RODNEY, Capt. Gardner, to Charleston on 24 Oct. 1780. [GM#III.341]

ROGERS OF GREENOCK, Hugh Rillie, fr GK to NY Jan.1778. [E504.15.29]

ROGER STEWART OF GREENOCK, 364 tons, John Cooper, fr. GK to Charleston 25 July 1816; fr. GK to Charleston 11 Jan.1817; fr. GK *with 20 passengers* to Charleston 23 July 1817; fr. GK to Charleston 3 Feb.1818; fr. GK to Charleston 14 Sep.1818; fr GK to Charleston 16 Mar. 1819; fr. GK to Charleston 24 Aug.1819; fr GK to Charleston 28 Aug.1820; fr GK to Charleston 4 Oct.1821; fr GK to Charleston 12 Mar. 1822; Peter Kerr, fr GK to NY Apr.1828, arr. NY 9 June 1828 *with passengers* fr. GK; fr GK to Charleston Nov.1828. [USNA.M237]
[E504.15.113/115/117/119/122/123/125/131/137/139/164/166]

ROMULUS OF NEWBURY, Caleb Lufkins, fr. GK to VA 20 Oct. 1810, [E504.15.90]

ROSAMUND, William Cuthel, fr. Glasgow to Charleston, SC, in Nov. 1802. [GkAd#83]

ROSE OF KIRKCALDY, James Beveridge, fr Dundee *with passengers* to Charleston 12 Oct.1818. [E504.11.21][CE70.1.15]

ROSE OF GREENOCK, 100 tons, John Warden, fr. Leith to Cape Fear in Feb. 1771. [E504.22.16]

ROSE OF EAST WEMYSS, 182 tons, James Beveridge, fr. GK to Montreal 27 Apr.1819. [E504.15.124]

ROSEMOUNT, a 150 ton brig, James Service, fr. GK *with passengers* to NY in Mar.1781. [E504.15.33] [GM#IV/80]

ROSINA OF ST JOHN, N.B., 467 tons, Henry Gambles, fr. GK to Halifax 11 March 1815; fr. GK to NB 12 Sep.1815. [E504.15.107/109]

ROSINA, Aaron Lithgow, fr Dundee to Charleston 23 July 1821; fr Dundee to Charleston 13 Mar.1822; arr. NY 12 Aug.1823 *with passengers* fr. GK; arr. NY 27 Feb. 1824 *with passengers* fr. GK; T.C.Butterworth, arr. NY 28 May 1827 *with passengers* fr. GK. [USNA.M237][E504.11.22]

ROTHIEMURCHUS OF LEITH, George Watson, fr Leith *with 99 passengers* to Quebec 27 Mar.1817; fr Leith to Quebec 10 Mar.1818. [E504.22.76/80]

ROWAND OF GLASGOW, 120 tons, Robert Jamieson, fr. GK to NC in Nov. 1755; John Buchanan, fr. GK *with passengers* to the James River in Mar.1757. [E504.15.7/8][GJ#747/803/804]

ROYAL CHARLOTTE, George Smith, fr. GK to Boston in Sept. 1762. [E504.15.11]

ROYAL CHARLOTTE OF GREENOCK, 261 tons, D. McLarty, fr. GK *with 3 passengers* to NFD 15 Oct.1814; fr. GK to NFD 24 July 1815; James Gilchrist, fr. GK to NFD July 1818. [E504.15.106/109/121]

ROYAL WIDOW, 200 tons, Alexander Hutcheson, fr. Port Glasgow *with passengers* to Philadelphia and Kingston, Jamaica, in Aug. 1755; fr. Port Glasgow *with passengers to* Philadelphia and Kingston, Jamaica, 10 Sep. 1756; William Cunningham, fr. Glasgow to Philadelphia and Jamaica in Oct. 1757 [E504.15.8][GJ#729/783]

ROYALIST OF MARYPORT, 250 tons, Peter Asbridge, fr. GK
    to St John, NB, 15 Aug.1817; fr. GK to Miramachi 4
    Aug.1819. [E504.15.117/125]

RUBY OF ABERDEEN, 80 tons, Alexander Gordon, fr. Aberdeen
    to VA in June 1747; fr. Aberdeen to VA in July 1748; fr.
    Aberdeen to VA in Apr. 1750; fr. Aberdeen to VA in Mar.
    1751 [E504.1.2/3]

RUBY OF DUNDEE, 102 ton brig, James Rankin, fr. GK to NY
    and St Augustine, Fla., on 15 Feb. 1780; fr. the Clyde *with
    passengers* to NY on 28 Oct. 1780; to NY *with passengers* in
    July 1781; Edward Morrison, fr. GK to NY on 3 Sept. 1781;
    fr. GK to NY in Sept. 1782; Robert Mavor, arr. in Port
    Brunswick, NC, on 8 Nov. 1788 fr. GK, [NCSA.S8.112]
    [E504.15.32/33/36][GD170] [GM#III/111, 247; III/347;
    IV.152/248/286]

RUBY, 300 tons, Thomas Johnston, fr. Bo'ness *with passengers* to
    Charleston, SC, in Oct. 1786. [GM#IX.454.295]

RUBY OF GREENOCK, a 337 ton brigantine, William
    Robertson, fr. GK to Halifax, NS, in Apr. 1787; fr. GK to
    Halifax in Jan. 1788; Robert Niven, fr. GK to Wilmington 15
    July 1788; Robert Mavor, fr. GK *with passengers* to
    Philadelphia on 12 May 1789; William Robertson, fr. GK to
    Halifax on 7 Aug. 1790.
    [GM#XII.590.126/158][E504.15.45/47/48/50/51/56]

RUBY, John Uday, fr. GK *with passengers* to Halifax, NS, and St
    John, NB, on 2 Mar. 1802. [GkAd#3]

SACHEM OF PHILADELPHIA, Edmond Hennel, fr GK to
    Philadelphia 16 Feb.1822. [E504.15.139]

ST ANDREW, Capt. W, Greig, arr. in Charleston, SC, during Dec.
    1741 fr. Scotland. [SCGaz#407]

ST ANDREW OF ABERDEEN, 80 tons, George Gordon, fr.
    Aberdeen to VA in Oct. 1749; James Cooper, fr. Aberdeen to
    VA in Mar. 1751 [E504.1.3]

ST ANDREW OF GLASGOW, a snow, John Dunlop, arr. in MD
    during Sept. 1745 fr. Glasgow; Thomas Johnstone, fr. GK to
    MD in June 1747; David Blair, fr. GK to MD in Oct. 1748, arr.
    there in Jan.1749. [E504.15.2/4] [MdGaz#23/193]

ST ANDREW OF GREENOCK, Humphrey Warden, fr. GK to
    VA in Feb. 1770; James Bog, fr. GK *with passengers* to NC in
    Sept. 1770; arr. in NC fr. the Clyde before Mar. 1771; fr. GK to

Edenton, NC, 25 May 1771, *with passengers,* arr. before Oct.
1771; Alexander Ritchie fr. GK to Edenton, NC, 25 June
1772; James Morrison, to Edenton, NC, via Boston in Apr.
1773; fr. GK to Boston and Edenton, NC, in Mar. 1774.
[GJ:23.8.1770; 7.3.1771; 9.5.1771; 31.10.1771; 28.5.1772;
8.4.1773; 10.2.1774] [E504.15.18/19/21/22/23]

ST ANDREW, Charles Erskine, fr. Leith to Wilmington in Feb.
1772. [E504.22.17]

ST DAVID OF DYSART, William Jones, fr. Leith to Philadelphia
before 1742. [AC9/1487]

ST DAVID, George Hutchison, arr. in Charleston, SC, in Nov.
1745 fr. Glasgow. [SCGaz#606]

ST GEORGE OF MONTROSE, 100 ton snow, John Dunbar, arr.
in Charleston, SC, on 13 Sept. 1758 fr. Newcastle; arr. in
Charleston in Jan. 1759 fr. Leith.
[PRO.CO5.509][SCGaz#1267]

ST GEORGE, Archibald Fisher, fr. GK to VA in Mar. 1760; fr. GK
to VA in Feb. 1762; Peter Warren, fr. GK to Savannahh,
Georgia, in July 1787 [E504.15.9/10/45]

ST JOHNS, James Laurie, fr. GK to St Johns, NFD, in May 1782.
[E504.15.36]

ST LAWRENCE OF GRANGEMOUTH, 211 tons, Andrew
Love, fr. GK to NFD 26 Jan.1816; fr. GK to NFD 7 March
1817. [E504.15.111/115]

ST LAWRENCE OF GREENOCK, 127 tons, William Cheaplin,
fr. GK to NFD 12 Sept.1817. [E504.15.117]

ST LAWRENCE OF LEITH, Thomas McColl, fr. GK to NFD 5
May 1818. [E504.15.120]

ST NICHOLAS OF ABERDEEN, 180 tons, James Leslie, fr
Aberdeen to St Andrews, NB, 26 Mar.1819; fr Aberdeen to St
Andrews, NB, 27 Mar.1820; Joseph Wilson, fr. Tobermory to
Cape Breton on 21 July 1821. [E504.1.28; E504.35.2]

ST PAUL, a snow, W. Alton, arr. in Charleston, SC, in Aug. 1745
fr. Dundee. [SCGaz#769]

ST PETERSBURGH OF ARCHANGEL, Peter Hoolman, fr Leith
to NY 28 Dec.1818. [E504.22.84]

ST THOMAS, Capt. Wallace, fr. Scotland to VA in 1744, captured
by the French and taken to NFD. [SM#6.440]

SALLY OF NORFOLK, Robert Patterson, fr. GK to VA in Aug.
1747. [E504.15.2]

SALLY, Capt. Montgomery, fr. Glasgow to VA in 1748, captured
by the French or Spanish at sea. [SM#10.651]

SALLY OF BOSTON, brigantine, Alexander Inglis, fr Orkney to
Boston 30 Sep.1763. [E504.6.4]

SALLY, a snow, Samuel Patterson, arr. in Annapolis, MD, *with
passengers* fr. Glasgow on 30 Dec. 1758. [MdGaz#713]

SALLY, William Barbour, fr. GK to Philadelphia in May 1765
[E504.15.12]

SALLY OF LEITH, 100 tons, David Ross, fr. Leith to Cape Fear,
NC, in Sept. 1762; Laurence Fraser, fr. Leith to Boston in June
1769; fr. Leith to Cape Fear in Mar. 1771.
[CM#7302][E504.22.10/15/16]

SALLY OF GLASGOW, Thomas Foster, fr. Port Glasgow to VA
in Apr. 1773; fr. Port Glasgow to VA in Feb. 1774.
[E504.28.21/23]

SALLY OF GREENOCK, 87 tons, George Innes, fr. GK to
Quebec in Mar. 1777; fr GK to NY Dec.1777; fr. GK to NY in
1778, captured by the Wexford, a US privateer on 11 Apr. but
later escaped; John Jamieson, fr GK to St Augustine
Mar.1779; Thomas Seward, fr. GK to NFD in Mar. 1784;
Allan Stevenson, fr. GK to NFD 11 Apr. 1788; Allan
Stevenson, fr. GK to NFD on 26 Mar. 1789; James Spiers, fr.
GK to NFD on 2 Aug. 1789; Capt. Fleck, fr. the Clyde to NFD
in June 1792 [E504.15.27/28/30/39/48/50/52] [GCr#130]
[GM#XII.587.102; 606.254] [AC7/58]

SALLY, a brig, David Scott, fr. GK to Baltimore in Aug. 1784; fr.
GK to NC, in Sept. 1785, arr. in Bath, NC, on 9 Dec. 1785.
[E504.15.39/41] [NCSA/S8/112]

SALLY, Capt. King, arr. in Philadelphia in Feb. 1786 fr. Glasgow.
[PennMerc#79]

SALLY, Capt. Gilkison, fr. the Clyde to VA on 11 Apr. 1786.
[GM#IX.432.118]

SALLY OF PORT GLASGOW, Charles Dow, fr Port Glasgow to
Newfoundland 24 Aug.1818. [E504.28.102]

SALLY OF AYR, Wiliam Cumming, fr GK to Quebec and
Montreal 30 Mar.1820. [E504.15.128]

SALLY OF CHARLESTON, 342 tons, Joseph Callendar, fr GK
to Charleston 30 Mar.1822. [E504.15.139]

SALLY AND MOLLY OF GREENOCK, Charles Robinson, fr.
GK to VA in May 1765; fr. Port Glasgow *with passengers* to

the Rappahannock River, VA, in July 1767; William Dunlop,
  fr. GK to VA in Mar. 1769. [GC#19] [E504.15.12/16]
SALTCOATS OF SALTCOATS, 181 tons, Peter Craig, fr. GK to
  Montreal 29 June 1815. [E504.15.108]
SALTON, 350 tons, John Ramsay, for Pictou, NS, in Apr. 1789.
  *"All kinds of mechanics are wanted at Pictou - ship
  carpenters, joiners, millwrights, coopers, bricklayers, fishers
  and farmers",* [GM#XII.581.56]
SALUS, fr GK to Miramachi Apr.1828; fr GK to Miramachi
  Aug.1828. [E504.15.164/165]
SALUTATION OF STRANRAER, 45 tons, William Whiteside, at
  Hampton, VA, Sept. 1719. [GD180.457]
SAMUEL, a brig, William Jamieson, fr. GK *with passengers* to NY
  on 26 Mar. 1786; arr. in NY in June 1786 fr. Glasgow; fr. GK
  with passengers to Charleston, SC, in May 1787; arr. in
  Charleston during Aug. 1787 fr. GK. [GM#IX.418.14]
  [Phila.Gaz.#274] [GJ#2444] [PennMerc#96] [E504.15.42/45]
SAMUEL OF GREENOCK, a 152 ton brig, Donald Robertson, fr.
  GK to Charleston, SC, on 9 Jan. 1788; fr. GK *with passengers*
  to Charleston in Sept. 1789; arr. in Charleston in Dec. 1789 fr.
  GK; fr. GK *with passengers* to Charleston on 5 Aug. 1790; fr.
  GK to Charleston, SC, 8 Mar. 1791; fr. GK *with passengers* to
  Charleston on 15 Sept. 1791; fr. GK *with passengers* to
  Charleston in June 1792. [E504.15.52/56/58/60] [PIG#1263]
  [GCr#66] [GM#XIV.715.296; XII.606.255][GJ#2613]
SAMUEL OF NEW YORK, David Leger, fr. GK to NY 4
  Sep.1818. [E504.15.122]
SAMUEL ROBERTSON, Thomas Choate, arr. NY 26 Nov.1825
  with passengers fr. GK; arr. NY 9 May 1827 *with passengers*
  fr. GK; arr. NY 5 Oct.1827 *with passengers* fr. GK.
  [USNA.M237]
SARAH OF BOSTON, brigantine, Thomas Potts, fr Orkney to
  Boston 18 Sep.1755; John Mackay, fr Orkney to Boston 8
  Sep.1756; George Smith, fr Orkney to Boston 4 Dec.1759.
  [E504.26.3]
SARAH OF NEW YORK, brigantine, Joseph Smith, fr Orkney to
  NY Oct.1762. [E504.6.4]
SARAH, an American ship, Isaac Elwell, fr. GK *with passengers* to
  Charleston, SC, in Feb. 1802. [GkAd#5]

SARAH OF NEW YORK, a 209 ton brig, Joseph Cole, fr. GK to
     NY 26 March 1816; Joseph Badger, fr. GK to NY 16
     Feb.1818; fr. GK to NY 19 July 1819; fr GK to NY 1
     Feb.1820; fr GK to NY 15 Sep.1820, arr. in NY 9 Nov.1820
     with passengers fr. GK.
     [E504.15.111/119/125/128/131][pa][USNA.M237]
SARAH OF BOSTON, 292 tons, J. H. Hopkins, fr. GK *with 46*
     passengers to NY 22 July 1817. [E504.15.117]
SARAH, fr GK to Richibucto Apr.1828; fr GK to Richibucto
     July1828. [E504.15.164/165]
SARAH AND SUSAN OF PORTSMOUTH, 234 tons, Samuel
     Parker, fr. GK *with 36 passengers* to Philadelphia 28 July
     1817. [E504.15.117]
SAUNDERS OF PHILADELPHIA, 191 tons, James R Garriques,
     fr. GK to R.I. 7 Nov. 1813. [E504.15.102]
SCEPTRE OF BURNTISLAND, Cap. Cowbrough, fr Leith to
     Quebec/Montreal 16 Mar.1819. [E504.22.84]
SCEPTRE, Walter Smith, arr. NY 24 July 1822 *with passengers*
     fr. GK. [USNA.M237]
SCIENCE OF GREENOCK, 329 tons, Daniel Thomson, fr. GK
     with 23 passengers to New York, 17 Feb.1817; Archibald
     Currie, fr. GK *with 4 passengers* to Savannah 1 Oct.1817; fr.
     GK to Savannah 17 Mar.1818; fr. GK to Savannah 9 Sep.1818;
     fr GK to Savannah 12 Mar.1819.
     [E504.15.115/117/119/122/123]
SCIPIO, Andrew Lyon, fr. GK via St Kitts to MD in Feb. 1765
     [E504.15.12]
SCIPIO OF GREENOCK, 232 tons, James Ramsay, fr. GK to
     Boston 11 Aug. 1790; Quintin Leitch, fr. GK to Halifax in
     Aug. 1795; John Gillies, fr. GK to Boston in Oct. 1805.
     [E504.15.56/69/74]
SCIPIO OF GREENOCK, 158 tons, Archibald Montgomerie, fr.
     GK to NFD 7 March 1814; fr. GK *with 6 passengers* to NFD
     22 March 1814; fr. GK *with 2 passengers* to NFD 3 Sept.1814;
     fr. GK to NFD 19 July 1816; fr. GK to NFD 1 Apr.1817; fr.
     GK to NFD 6 June 1818; William Syme, fr. GK to NFD 19
     Apr.1819. [E504.15.103/105/114/115/120/124]
SCIPIO OF WHITEHAVEN, 187 tons, Anthony Madder, fr. GK
     to Halifax 27 July 1814. [E504.15.105]

SCOTIA OF DUNDEE, James Sturrock, fr Dundee *with passengers* to NY Jan.1819. [E504.11.21][CE70.1.15]

SCOTIA OF ABERDEEN, 247 tons, William Robinson, fr Aberdeen to Halifax 10 Mar.1819. [E504.1.28]

SCOTIA, fr GK to NFD Apr.1828; fr GK to NFD July 1828. [E504.15.165/166]

SCOTSMAN, Henry Reid, arr. NY 22 Aug.1828 *with passengers* fr. Dundee. [USNA.M237]

SEAFLOWER OF LONDON, Wallsall Cobby, fr. London to Leith for goods and passengers to NY, NE or New Jersey, charter party dated 1683, arr. in NY on 6 Aug. 1684.[The Dongan Papers, 1683-1688, pt.1, P. R. Christoph, (Syracuse,1994)]

SEA HORSE OF ABERDEEN, 65 tons, John Lickly, fr. Aberdeen to VA on 25 July 1746. [E504.1.2]

SERVANT, G. Sanborn, arr. NY 30 Aug.1820 *with passengers* fr. GK. [USNA.M237]

SHAKESPEARE, a brig, John Goldie, arr. NY 24 July 1828 *with 24 passengers* fr. Glasgow. [USNA.M237.12]

SHANNON OF NY, 70 tons, fr. GK to VA in Jan. 1758; John Orr, fr. GK to MD in Jan. 1760; fr. GK to NY in Mar. 1761; fr. GK to NY in Mar. 1762 [E504.15.8/9/10]

SHARK OF ST JOHN'S, NEWFOUNDLAND, 56 tons, James Benton, fr. GK to NFD 17 Mar.1815. [E504.15.107]

SHARP OF GREENOCK, Robert Speir, fr. GK to Philadelphia and NY in Mar. 1770; Ninian Rodger, fr GK to NY June 1774; James Lawrie, fr. GK to NFD and Grenada in July 1776, [E504.15.18/24/26][EA#13/76]

SHEPHERDESS OF WISCASSET, 185 tons, John McKean, fr. GK to Charleston 11 July 1815. [E504.15.109]

SIBLA OF GREENOCK, John Livingstone, fr. GK to Halifax in July 1784. [E504.15.39]

SILSON OF WHITEHAVEN, 200 tons, Michael Clark, fr. GK to Pictou, NS, 1 Aug.1814. [E504.15.105]

SIMON COCK OF LONDON, John Younger, fr Leith to Pictou 26 Mar.1819. [E504.22.84]

SIMSON, Henry White, fr. GK to MD in July 1761; arr. in Patuxent, MD, on 17 Oct. 1761, *with 1 passenger* fr. Scotland; fr. GK to MD in Mar. 1762; fr. GK to MD in Feb. 1763. [E504.15.10/11] [MdGaz#859]

SIR EDWARD PELLEW OF GLASGOW, 307 tons, Charles
McDonald, fr. GK to NFD on 19 Feb.1813; George Kelly, fr.
GK to Quebec 10 March 1814; fr. GK to NB 29 Oct.1814.
[E504.15.99/103/106]

SIR J.H.CRAIG OF LONDON, James Dease, fr Leith to Quebec
27 Apr.1820. [E504.22.90]

SIR JOHN SHERBROOK OF ST JOHNS, 277 tons, John
Duncan, fr. GK to NFD 23 Feb.1814. [E504.15.103]

SIR WILLIAM ERSKINE OF GLASGOW, John Montgomery,
fr. GK to Halifax July 1777; Duncan McNaught, fr GK to St
Augustine and NY Jan.1779. [E504.15.28/30]

SIR WILLIAM WALLACE OF ABERDEEN, 232 tons, Daniel
Anderson, fr Aberdeen to Miramachi 23 July 1821; fr
Aberdeen to Miramachi 29 Mar.1822. [E504.1.29]

SISTERS, Capt. Morris, arr. in NC fr. the Clyde in 1770; to NC 16
Jan. 1771; James How, fr. Port Glasgow to NC in Dec. 1772;
fr. Port Glasgow to NC in July 1774. [GJ: 9.8.1770; 24.1.1771;
28.7.1774] [E504.28.21/23]

SISTERS OF GREENOCK, 145 tons, James Taylor, fr GK to
Savannah, GA, Nov.1774; Thomas Kerr, fr. GK to NFD in
Mar. 1783; Alan Harvie, fr. GK to NFD in July 1784; Robert
Lusk, fr. GK to NFD in Apr. 1785; fr. GK to NFD in July
1785; fr. GK to NFD on 4 Apr. 1786; fr. GK to NFD on 5 Oct.
1786; fr. GK to NFD 12 Mar. 1788; William Fleck, fr. GK to
NFD 13 Apr. 1791.[GM#IX.432.118; 457.326]
[E504.15.24/37/39/41/42/43/47/50/59]

SISTERS, a 200 ton brigantine, John Grigg, fr. GK *with passengers*
to Philadelphia on 26 Mar. 1789. [GM#XII.578.32; 587.102]

SISTERS OF GREENOCK, Alexander McCall, fr GK to NY and
St Augustine Mar.1778. [E504.15.29]

SISTERS OF KIRKCALDY, John Miller, from Dundee *with 35
passengers* to Philadelphia 1 May 1818; arr. in Philadelphia
with passengers fr. Scotland in 1820. [NAS.CE70.1.15][pa]

SISTERS, fr GK to Quebec/Montreal Apr.1828. [E504.15.164]

SKEEN OF LEITH, James Mason, fr Leith *with 111 passengers* to
NY 31 May 1816; fr Leith *with 100 passengers* to Halifax 11
Mar.1817; fr Leith to Halifax/NY 27 Feb.1818; George Bishop,
fr leith to Halifax/Quebec 12 Mar.1819. [E504.22.73/76/80/84]

SOPHIA, William Walkingshaw, fr. Port Glasgow to Boston in
1740. [CM#3094]

SOPHY OF GREENOCK, 170 tons, Alexander McVicar, fr. GK
to Halifax, in Feb. 1806. [E504.15.77]

SOPHIA OF GREENOCK, 229 tons, John Dunn, fr. GK to NFD
20 Feb.1813; fr. GK to Quebec 10 June 1814; fr. GK to NFD
29 Aug.1815; fr. GK to NFD 10 Aug.1816; fr. GK to
Miramachi 3 May 1817; Alan McLaurin, fr. GK *with 3
passengers* to NFD 23 Sept.1817; Archibald Moore, fr. GK to
Quebec 9 Apr.1818; fr GK *with 106 passengers* to Quebec July
1818; fr GK *with passengers* to Montreal Apr.1828; fr GK
with passengers to Montreal July 1828. [PRO.CO384/3]
[E504.15.99/104/109/113/116/117/120/121/163/165]

SOUTH CAROLINA OF CHARLESTON, 306 tons, George
Easterby, fr. GK *with 23 passengers* to Charleston 29
Aug.1816. [E504.15.113]

SPECULATION OF KINGSTON, 209 tons, John Codd, fr. GK
with 29 passengers to NO 3 July 1817. [E504.15.116]

SPECULATION OF GREENOCK, 205 tons, Cap. Douglas, fr
GK to Quebec 14 Apr. 1820. [E504.15.129]

SPEEDWELL OF GLASGOW, 90 tons, Duncan Graham, fr. the
Clyde to VA/MD 1730; James Colquhoun, arr. in Charleston,
SC, on 18 Jan. 1734; arr. during Jan. 1735 fr. Glasgow.
[PRO.CO5.509]
[SCGaz#2][GAr.B10.15.4711][SCGaz.18.1.1735]

SPEEDWELL OF GREENOCK, a brigantine, Nathaniel Fellows,
fr. GK to Boston in June 1766; William Cochrane, fr. GK
with passengers to Wilmington, NC, in May 1784, arr. in Port
Brunswick, NC, on 24 Aug. 1784.
[CM:17.3.1784][E504.15.13/39][NCSA.S8.112]

SPEIRS, 300 tons, John Lusk, fr. Glasgow to VA in 1768; fr.Port
Glasgow to VAin May 1773; fr. Port Glasgow *with
passengers* to the James River, VA, in Feb. 1786
[CM#7267][E504.28.22][GM#IX.418.7]

SPENCER OF GLASGOW, John Boyd, fr. GK to VA in Mar.
1743; Archibald Riddle, fr. GK to VA in May 1744; fr. GK to
VA in Mar. 1745; Andrew Gray, fr. GK to VA in Mar. 1747;
Ninian Bryce, fr. GK to VA in Nov. 1747. [E504.15.1/2]

SPENCER OF NEWCASTLE, 330 tons, Forster Brown, fr Oban
with 115 passengers to Charlottetown, PEI, 22 July
1806.[E504.25.1]

SPRAY, fr GK to St John, NB, Apr.1828. [E504.15.163]

SPRIGHTLY OF ABERDEEN, 190 tons, Alexander Philip, fr. Aberdeen to Halifax, 18 Feb. 1816; fr. Aberdeen *with 20 passengers* to Halifax, 6 June 1816; fr Aberdeen to Halifax Feb.1817. [E504.1.26]

SPRINGVALE OF SALTCOATS, 118 tons, Andrew Skeoch, fr. GK *with 2 passengers* to Quebec in June 1796. [E504.15.72]

STATIRD, William Patten, arr. NY 26 Aug.1823 *with passengers* fr. Glasgow. [USNA.M237]

STAR OF PETERHEAD, John Kerr fr. Prestonpans, in VA in Oct. 1668. [AC7/4]

STAR OF ABERDEEN, 172 tons, James Mathison, fr Aberdeen to St John, NB, 18 Mar.1819.[E504.1.28]

STEPHEN, J. Potts, fr. Tobermory, Mull, *with 193 passengers* to NB on 7 Aug. 1827. [E504.35.2]

STEPHEN WRIGHT, N. Gibson, fr. Tobermory *with 100 passengers* to Cape Breton 7 Aug. 1827. [E504.35.2]

STEWART, Archibald Williamson, fr. GK to NC in Jan. 1752; Alexander Auld, fr. GK to NY in Feb.1763 [E504.15.5/11]

STIRLING CASTLE, James Colquhoun, fr. GK to Boston in Feb. 1766; Thomas Ramsay, fr. GK to Casco Bay in Aug. 1766; Robert Hunter, fr. GK to Casco Bay in Apr. 1767 [E504.15.13/14]

SUCCESS OF GLASGOW, Andrew Gray, fr. Port Glasgow to VA in Mar. 1744; William McLintock, fr. GK to VA in Feb. 1745; fr. Port Glasgow to VA in Oct. 1745; Jarius Cushing, fr. GK to Philadelphia in Aug. 1763. [E504.15.2/11; E504.28.1/2]

SUCCESS OF RHODE ISLAND, Benjamin Rust, fr Orkney to RI 20 Apr.1758. [E504.26.3]

SUCCESS OF GLASGOW, 70 ton snow, James Robertson, arr. in Charleston, SC, on 13 Sept. 1758 fr. Glasgow, [PRO.CO5.509][SCGaz.15.9.1758]

SUCCESS, a snow, Patrick Ogilvie, arr. in Charleston on 2 Feb. 1767 fr. Dundee. [SCGaz#1643]

SUCCESS, William Dunlop, fr. GK to NFD in Aug. 1784. [E504.15.39]

SUN, Capt. Harton, fr. VA to Scotland in 1761, captured by the French but ransomed for 470 livres. [SM#23.335]

SUPERB OF NEW YORK, John O'Connor, fr GK to NY 5 Apr.1821, arr. NY 28 May 1821 *with passengers* fr. GK; arr.

NY 11 Oct. 1821 *with passengers* fr. GK.[E504.15.135]
[USNA.M237]

SUPERIOR OF MONTROSE, a brigantine, James Birnie, fr
Montrose to Quebec 11 Apr.1820; fr Montrose to Quebec 27
Mar.1825. [E504.24.20]

SUPERIOR, John O'Hara, fr GK to NY July 1828. arr. NY 25
Sep.1828 *with passengers*. [USNA.M237][E504.15.165]

SURREY OF LONDON, 154 tons, Richard Hay, fr. GK *with 23
passengers* to Halifax 21 March 1816. [E504.15.111]

SURREY OF HALIFAX, Edward McKillop, fr. GK to Halifax 18
Mar.1818. [E504.15.119]

SUSANNAH, a 180 ton brigantine, Daniel Cumming, fr. Port
Glasgow *with passengers* to Charleston, SC, on 20 Nov. 1780;
John Stewart, fr. Port Glasgow to Charleston in Apr. 1781;
Charles Cameron, fr. GK to Charleston in Oct. 1784; fr. GK to
Charleston in Aug. 1785; fr. GK *with passengers* to Charleston
in July 1786. [GM#III.336; IV.119; IX.440.183]
[E504.15.40/41]

SUSANNA, Capt. Walker, fr. the Clyde to Pictou, NS, in Apr. 1792.
[GCr#97]

SUSANNA, a US ship, Thomas Bennet, fr. GK *with passengers* to
Charleston, SC, in June 1802. [GkAd#37]

SUSANNAH OF PORT GLASGOW, 297 tons, Peter Jason, fr.
Port Glasgow to Chaleur Bay in Apr.1820. [E504.28.108]

SUSIE OF GLASGOW, James King, fr. GK to VA in Oct.1753;
William Morrison, fr. Port Glasgow *with passengers* to the
James River in Sep 1756; Capt. Gillespie, fr. GK to Boston in
Apr. 1759. [E504.15.6][GJ#784/923]

SWALLOW OF GREENOCK, William Robertson, fr. GK to
Halifax, NS, in June 1783; Robert Steel, fr. GK to
Philadelphia in Apr. 1784; William Robertson, fr. GK to
Halifax in Sept. 1784; fr. GK to NFD in Apr. 1785; Robert
Cross, fr. GK to NFD in 12 Mar. 1786. [GM#IX.428.86]
[E504.15.38/39/41/42]

SWALLOW, fr. Glencaple, Dumfries-shire, to NB in 1822
[DWJ: 9.7.1822]

SWAN OF NEW YORK, a sloop, Nicholas Burger, fr Orkney to
NY 30 July 1755; Le Chevalier Deane, fr Orkney to NY 12
Sep.1757 [E504.26.3]

SWAN, brigantine, James Fairlie, fr Orkney to NY 8 July 1758.

[E504.26.3].

SWIFT OF ST JOHNS, 200 tons, Walter Black, fr. GK to NFD 11 Apr. 1788; Hugh Smith, fr. GK to NFD 9 July 1790; fr. GK to NFD 28 Mar. 1791. [E504.15.47/56/58]

SWIFT OF GREENOCK, 200 tons, Hugh Smith, fr. GK to NFD 25 May 1789. [E504.15.51][GM#XII.596.174]

SYBIL OF CHARLESTON, 346 tons, George Turner, fr. GK *with 10 passengers* to Charleston, SC, 30 Sept.1816. [E504.15.113]

SYBELLA, a 100 ton brigantine, Alexander McKellar, fr GK *with passengers* to Charleston, SC, on 17 July 1786. [E504.15.43][GM#IX.446.230]

TALAVERA OF AMELIA ISLAND, 206 tons, Guillarmo Munro, fr. GK to Amelia Island on 18 Apr. 1814. [E504.15.104]

TARTAR, John Colvin, fr. Campbeltown to NFD in Mar.1768. [E504.8.4]

TARTAR OF GLASGOW, William Drummond, fr. GK to NY in Feb. 1782. [E504.15.35]

TERRY, Thomas Dolson, fr. Port Glasgow to Hampton Roads, VA, 1784. [AC9/3253]

THAMES OF GREENOCK, William Watt, to Carolina in Aug. 1741 [CM#3338]

THETIS OF GLASGOW, 102 ton brig, William Andrews, fr. Port Glasgow to VA in Mar. 1749; John McCall, fr GK to NC Sep.1774; arr. in Port Brunswick on 31 Dec. 1774; Robert Dunlop, fr GK *'with troops'* to North America Mar.1776; John Boyd, fr. Port Glasgow *with passengers* to the Potomac River, MD and VA, on 16 Apr. 1786; fr. Port Glasgow *with passengers* to the Potomac River, VA, on 12 Apr. 1789; Capt. Davis, fr. Port Glasgow *with passengers* to VA in Feb. 1792. [GM#IX.418.15; 430.103; 433.126; XII.584.79; 590.126] [NCSA.S8.112] [GA#VII.347.184][GCr#51.77][E504.28.4; E540.15.24/26]

THETIS OF LERWICK Peter Leslie, fr Leith *with 12 passengers* to Montreal 6 May 1816. [E504.22.73]

THETIS OF GREENOCK, 202 tons, Alexander McLachlan, fr. GK to St John, NB, 11 Mar.1815; John Morrison, fr. GK to Boston 9 Oct.1815; fr. GK to Halifax 17 May 1816; fr. GK to Miramachi 24 Apr.1817; fr. GK to Halifax 9 Aug.1817; fr. GK

to Miramachi 14 Apr.1818; fr. GK to Halifax July 1818; Peter
Fisher, fr GK to Halifax 20 Sep.1819; fr GK to Halifax 10
Mar.1820. [E504.15.107/109/112/116/117/120/121/125/128]

THETIS OF MIRAMACHI, John Charters, fr. GK to Halifax 21
Jan.1818; fr. GK to Miramachi 8 Aug.1818. [E504.15.119/122]

THETIS OF GLASGOW, 327 tons, Cap. Charters, fr GK to
Halifax and Miramachi 26 Jan.1820; fr GK to Miramachi 15
Aug.1820; fr GK to Halifax and Miramachi 23 Feb.1821; fr
GK to Miramachi 23 Aug.1821; fr GK to Pictou Apr.1828; fr
GK *with passengers* to Pictou Aug.1828.
[E504.15.127/131/135/137/163/164]

THISTLE OF AYR, captured off the Capes of VA in 1745.
[SM#8.50]

THISTLE OF SALTCOATS, Robert Brown, fr. Campbeltown to
Cape Fear, NC, in 1739; fr. GK to VA in June 1745.
[CE82.2.79][E504.15.2]

THISTLE, Alexander Marquis, fr. GK to NY in Sept. 1766
[E504.13.15]

THISTLE OF EDINBURGH, John Boyd, fr. GK to VA in Feb.
1750, [E504.15.4]

THISTLE, Hugh Coulter, arr. in MD on 16 July 1752 fr. Glasgow.
[MdGaz#379]

THISTLE OF GLASGOW, Alexander Marquis, fr. GK to Boston
in Mar. 1769, [E504.15.16]

THISTLE OF GREENOCK, to Boston and NY in 1769; John
Hunter, fr. GK to NY in Nov. 1770. [E504.15.18] [CM#7257]

THOMAS OF GREENOCK, 60 ton brigantine, William Watt,
arr. in Port Roanoke, NC, on 4 May 1738; fr. Glasgow to
Carolina in 1741; fr. GK to Carolina 2 July 1743.
[NCSA.S8.112][GJ#4][CM:7.7.1743]

THOMAS, John Robertson, fr. Port Glasgow to VA in Mar. 1773;
fr. Port Glasgow to the James River, VA, in Sept. 1773; fr. Port
Glasgow to VA in Oct. 1774; James Ramsay, fr Port Glasgow
to Halifax/NY Apr.1777.. [E504.28.21/22/23/28]

THOMAS OF GLASGOW, Robert Lindsay, fr. GK to NY in Apr.
1784; fr. GK to Charleston, SC, in Apr. 1785. [E504.15.39/41]

THOMAS, 362 tons, Capt. Macy, fr. GK *with passengers* to NY on
7 Apr. 1802. [GkAd#25]

THOMAS OF GREENOCK, 270 tons, John McBride, fr. GK to
N.O. in Dec. 1805. [E504.15.75]

THOMAS AND BETTY OF MONTROSE, Robert Mudie, fr. Montrose to VA in July 1748. [E504.24.1]

THOMAS AND HANNA, Capt. Butler, fr. Scotland to VA in 1745, captured by the French and taken to Cape Breton. [SM#8.249]

THOMAS MARTIN OF ANTIGUA, 194 tons, Joseph Sanderson, fr. GK to St Johns, NB., 23 Sept.1814. [E504.15.105]

THOMSON'S PACKET, 201 ton brig, fr. the Carse of Dumfries *with 108 passengers* to St John, NB, on 17 Apr. 1820; Capt. Lookup, fr. Glencaple, Dumfries-shire, *with 80 passengers* to America in 1821. [Times#10916][DCr: 30.1.1821]

THORNTON OF GLASGOW, 260 tons, William Holmes, fr Port Glasgow to NO 8 Sep.1818; fr. GK to NO 20 Nov.1820; fr GK to NO 4 Sep.1821. [E504.28.102;E504.15.133/137]

THREE BROTHERS OF HULL, 357 tons, Josiah Maddison, fr. Stornaway *with 148 passengers* to Pictou, NS, on 28 Aug. 1815; fr Leith and Stornaway *with 148 passengers* to Pictou 9 Aug.1816. [E504.33.3; E504.22.74]

THREE FRIENDS OF BOSTON, Mark Ferran, fr. GK to Boston in Oct. 1771 [E504.15.20]

THREE SISTERS, Robert Gordon, fr. GK to VA in May 1761; fr. GK to VA in May 1763; Robert Brown, fr Port Glasgow to halifax Mar.1778; Capt. Reeve, fr. the Clyde to NY on 26 May 1780; Capt. Stewart, fr. the Clyde to NB in Aug. 1792. [GM#III/174] [GCr#152][E504.15.10/11; 28/28

THREE SISTERS OF WISCASSET, 212 tons, Timothy Wood, fr. GK *with 70 passengers* to NY in Apr. 1795; fr. GK *with 100 passengers* to NY in Sept. 1795; fr. GK *with 20 passengers* to NY in Oct. 1796. [E504.15.69/72/73]

THREE SISTERS OF GLASGOW, 330 tons, John Baird, fr. GK to Boston 7 Sep.1815. [E504.15.109]

THREE SISTERS OF GREENOCK, 329 tons, James Bell, fr GK to Savannah 17 Oct.1820; fr GK to Savannah 29 Mar.1821; fr GK to Savannah 6 Sep.1821; fr GK to Savannah 12 Mar.1822. [E504.15.132/135/137/139]

TIBBY, a brigantine, John Paterson, fr. GK to VA in Mar. 1757; Thomas Archdeacon, fr. GK to VA in Aug. 1758; William Morrison, fr. GK to Boston in Feb. 1763 [E504.15.8/11][GJ#811]

TIBBIE OF VIRGINIA, James Moody, fr. GK to VA in Jan. 1771; Robert Boyd, fr. GK to VA in July 1771[E504.15.18/20]

TIVERTON OF MONTROSE, 60 tons, Patrick Ogilvie, in Charleston, SC, in Apr. 1737, [PRO.CO5.509]

TOBAGO, Alexander McKinlay, fr. GK to Boston in Sept. 1771 [E504.15.20]

TOBAGO, a brigantine, fr. Port Glasgow via the western Highlands to NY, Philadelphia and the Carolinas, in June 1774. [CM#8201]

TODS OF PERTH, a 109 ton brig, William McPherson, fr.Perth via Dundee *with 42 passengers* to Quebec in May 1817, arr. there on 22 July 1817. [MG][E504.11.20; 27.14]

TOM OF NEW YORK, 134 tons, Isaac Hand, fr. GK *with passengers* to NY on 31 Mar. 1789. [E504.15.50][GM#XII.578.32/110]

TOM, Thomas Emery, arr. NY 2 July 1827 *with passengers* fr. GK. [USNA.M237]

TORBAY, Capt. Kerr, fr. the Clyde to NFD on 20 Aug. 1786. [GM#IX.450/270]

TORTULA, a brig, Capt. Douglas, fr. Port Glasgow *with passengers* to the James River, VA, 24 Feb. 1786; fr. the Clyde to Charleston on 23 Oct. 1786. [GM#IX.420.33; 426.70; 460.342]

TRADER OF MONTREAL, 227 tons, Mark Dyett, fr. GK *with 32 passengers* to Montreal, 30 Mar. 1811, [E504.15.91]

TRADER OF GREENOCK, 227 tons, Hector McLean, fr. GK to NB. 8 July 1815; fr. GK to NFD 26 Sept, 1816; William Gammel, fr. GK to NS 8 Aug.1817; fr. GK to Halifax 3 Aug.1818. [E504.15.109/113/117/122]

TRAFALGAR OF LONDON, a brig, T. Mitchell, fr. Leith *with 150 passengers* to Montreal 3 June 1817, arr. Quebec 31 July 1817; James Henderson, arr. NY 22 June 1821 *with passengers* fr. Leith; arr. NY 4 June 1822 *with passengers* fr. Leith. [E504.22.77] [USNA.M237][MG]

TRAVELLER OF GREENOCK, 113 tons, Thomas McNidder, fr. GK to NFD 7 Sep.1815. [E504.15.109]

TRAVELLER OF KIRKCALDY, Thomas Bell, fr Leith *with 64 passengers* to NY 3 July 1816. [E504.22.73]

TRAVELLER OF LEITH, J. Bishop, fr Leith *with 30 passengers* to Halifax 25 Apr.1817. [E504.22.77]

TRAVELLER OF ABERDEEN, 193 tons, James Goldie, fr.
Tobermory *with 143 passengers* to Quebec on 12 Feb. 1819; fr
Aberdeen to Savannah 25 Sep.1821; fr Aberdeen to Savannah
26 Mar.1822; fr Dundee *with passengers* to Savannah 30
Sep.1822; fr Dundee to Savannah Mar.1823; fr Dundee to
Savannah Aug.1823; fr Dundee to Savannah Aug.1824.
[E504.35.2; E504.11.22/23; E504.1.29][CE70.1.17]

TRENT, Benjamin P Foster, arr. NY 10 July 1827 *with passengers*
fr. GK. [USNA.M237]

TREPALSEY OF GREENOCK, 152 tons, Alexander Morris, fr.
GK to NFD in Jan. 1806. [E504.15.77]

TRIAL, Hugh Brown, fr. GK to VA in Aug. 1739; arr. in
Hampton, VA, in Oct. 1739 fr. Glasgow. [CM#3022][VG#171]

TRYAL OF LEITH, 120 tons, fr. Leith to Charleston, SC, 22 Oct.
1763. [E504.22.11]

TRYALL, a 125 ton brigantine, Wade Mims, fr. GK *with 10
passengers* bound to Savannah, Georgia, or Charleston, SC, in
Aug. 1796. [E504.15.73]

TRIDENT, Curtis Blakeman, fr. GK *with passengers* to NY in
Oct. 1810, [E504.15.90]

TRIDENT OF NEW YORK, 422 tons, W W Foreman, fr. GK
with 66 passengers to NY 14 May 1811. [E504.15.92]

TRIM OF GREENOCK, 128 tons, William Robertson, fr. GK to
NFD 2 Sept.1815. [E504.15.109]

TRITON OF GLASGOW, a 180 ton snow, John McCunn, fr. Port
Glasgow to VA in Apr. 1744; Robert Duthie, fr. GK and Port
Glasgow *with passengers* to the Rappahannock River, VA, in
June 1767, *'any tradesmen, well recommended and willing to
indent for 5 years will meet with encouragement'*; fr. Glasgow
to America in 1781 when captured and taken to Morlaix; Capt.
Ewing, fr. the Clyde to MD on 3 Aug.
1790.[GJ#2613][E504.15.14;E504.28.1][GC#19] [SM#43.165]

TRITON OF NEW YORK, 314 tons, G. M. Natvig, fr. GK *with
46 passengers* to NY 16 Aug.1815. [E504.15.109]

TRYALL OF SALTCOATS, Robert Steel, fr. GK to VA in Mar.
1743; fr. GK to VA in Aug. 1745; fr. GK to VA in Mar. 1746;
fr. GK to Boston in June 1748; Robert Crawford, fr. Port
Glasgow *with passengers* to Boston in Sept. 1759. [E504.28.1;
E504.15.1/2][GJ#936]

TRYON, Capt. Duthie, fr. the Clyde to VA 18 Dec. 1767. [GC#46]

TRUE BRITON OF IRVINE, 208 tons, James Reid, fr GK to
Montreal 6 Mar.1820; fr GK to Montreal 8 Mar.1821.
[E504.15.128/135]

TRUSTY OF INVERKEITHING, David Miller, fr Leith to NY 13
Apr.1819. [E504.22.86]

TURNER OF HALIFAX, a 150 ton snow, James Elmslie, fr. GK
with 30 passengers to Halifax, NS, 17 Feb. 1791; Robert
Young, fr. GK *with passengers* to Halifax in Feb. 1792.
[GCr#61/65] [E504.15.58]

TWO BROTHERS OF BOSTON, 40 tons, arr. in the Clyde fr. NE
during 1690. [RPCS#XV.307]

TWO BROTHERS, Peter Bogle, arr. in Charleston, SC, on 29 Jan.
1763 fr. Glasgow. [SCGaz#1489]

TWO BROTHERS OF JOHNSHAVEN, 40 tons, Alexander
Blews, fr. Aberdeen to St John's, NFD, in May 1774; fr.
Aberdeen to St John's, NFD, in Mar. 1777. [E504.1.13]

TWO MARYS OF NEW YORK, 240 tons, Elisha King, fr. GK
with 38 passengers to NY 16 July 1817; fr. GK to NY 30 May
1818. [E504.15.117/120]

TWO SISTERS, Capt. How, to NC in Feb. 1773. [GJ:4.2.1773]

TWO SISTERS, fr GK *with passengers* to Cape Breton July 1828.
[E504.15.165]

UGIE OF PETERHEAD, 168 tons, George Anderson, fr.
Aberdeen to Quebec, 12 Mar. 1817. [E504.1.26]

ULYSSES OF GREENOCK, 217 tons, James Wilson, fr. GK to
Wilmington on the Cape Fear River, NC, *with 111 passengers*
on 10 Aug. 1774, arr. in Port Brunswick, NC, on 18 Oct. 1774;
James Wilson, fr. GK *with passengers* to Wilmington on the
Cape Fear River, NC, 1 May 1775; George Jamieson, fr. GK to
NY in Jan. 1777; George Jamieson, fr. GK to NY and St
Aug.ine Aug. 1777; fr. GK to St Augustine, Fla., in Nov. 1779;
fr. the Clyde to NY captured on 7 Feb. 1780 by the French and
taken to L'Orient; John Burn, fr. GK to Wilmington in Apr.
1787; John Burr, fr. GK to NC on 21 Dec. 1787, arr. in Port
Brunswick, NC, on 29 May
1787.[GJ:30.6.1774][CM#8215/8339, 15.4.1775] [SM#42.332]
[GM#III/117] [E504.15.24/27/28/31/32/44/46][NCSA.S8.112]
"For Wilmington, Cape Fear River, NC, the ship Ulysses,
now lying in the harbour of Greenock, will be ready to take
on board goods by the 20th July and will certainly be clear to

sail by the 10th Aug.. For freight of passage apply to James
Gammel and Company in Greenock. NB the Ulysses is a fine
ship and has good accommodation for passengers. "
[Source: The Caledonian Mercury #8215, 29 June 1774]

UNION, D. Ferguson, fr. GK to Savannah, GA, in Feb. 1802; fr.
    GK to Charleston, SC, in Dec. 1802. [GkAd#4/91]

UNION OF GREENOCK, 257 tons, Matthew Henry, fr. GK *with*
    15 passengers to Quebec 20 July 1815; fr. GK to New Orleans
    14 Feb.1816; fr GK to Quebec 13 Mar.1820; fr GK to Quebec
    8 Aug.1820; fr GK to Quebec 22 Mar.1821; James Scott fr GK
    to Pictou 29 Mar.1822. [E504.15.109/111/128/131/135/139]

UNION OF GLASGOW, 173 tons, Cap.Scott, fr GK to Pictou 18
    Apr.1820. [E504.15.129]

UNION OF QUEBEC, 333 tons, Alexander McColl, fr GK to
    Quebec 14 Aug.1820. [E504.15.131]

UNION OF BOSTON, 219 tons, Paul Post, fr. GK *with 49*
    passengers to NY 10 July 1817; Victor Blair, fr, GK to NY 9
    Apr.1818. [E504.15.117/120]

UNION, a brig, James Craigie, fr. Alloa via Leith *with passengers*
    to NY 10 Mar.1824, arr. NY 6 May 1824 *with passengers* fr.
    Alloa. [USNA.M237][EC#17577]

UNITED STATES OF CHARLESTON, 207 tons, H. C. Vincent,
    fr. GK to Charleston 23 Dec.1817. [E504.15.114]

UNITY OF ABERDEEN, Capt. Thomson, to Halifax when taken
    by the French in 1761. [SM#23.53]

UNITY OF GREENOCK, 219 tons, Capt. Guillis, fr. the Clyde to
    NFD in Mar. 1792; William Service, fr. GK *with passengers*
    to Quebec in Apr. 1793; Robert Millar, fr. GK to Quebec in
    Apr. 1795; Capt. Morrison, fr. GK *with passengers* to Quebec
    in July 1802. [GCr#90/238] [GkAd#46] [E504.15.68]

UNITY OF PORT GLASGOW, 193 tons, Andrew Wallace, fr.
    GK to NB 8 March 1816; Malcolm Watson, fr. GK to
    Miramachi 20 Aug.1816; fr. GK to St Peter's, NB., 26
    Aug.1817; John McVicar, fr port Glasgow to NBr. 4
    Apr.1818; fr Port Glasgow to New Richmond 8 Sep.1818; fr.
    Port Glasgow to New Richmond in Apr. 1820.
    [E504.28.100/102/109/111/113/117]

URANIA OF LEITH, W. Newton, fr Leith to Quebec/Montreal 6
    Mar.1820. [E504.22.91]

URANIA, William Mearns, arr. NY 17 May 1828 *with passengers* fr. Dundee. [USNA.M237]

VANCOUVER OF PHILADELPHIA, 231 tons, Henry Hutchison, fr. GK *with 36 passengers* to Philadelphia 7 June 1817. [E504.15.116]

VENERABLE, Cap. Caithness, fr Dundee to Pictou 1 Apr.1819. [E504.11.21]

VENUS, John McDonald, fr Port Glasgow to St Augustine/NY Nov.1778; fr. Glasgow via Cork *with passengers* to Savannah, GA, in May 1780 when captured by a French privateer and taken to L'Orient. [SM#42.388] [GM#III/143,182,214][E504.28.30]

VENUS OF GREENOCK, 49 tons, John Wilson, fr. Port Glasgow to VA in July 1772; fr. Port Glasgow to VA in July 1774; John Ewing, fr. GK to Wilmington, NC, in Jan. 1787; Robert Cross, fr. GK to NFD in Mar. 1788; fr. GK to NFD on 11 Apr. 1789 [GM#XII.590.126] [E504.15.44/46/47/51; E504.28.21/23]

VENUS OF GLASGOW, 146 tons, Alexander McGill, fr. GK *with 4 passengers* to NFD, 7 June 1814; fr. GK *with 3 passengers* to NFD 3 Apr.1815; fr. GK *with 2 passengers* to NFD 28 Mar.1816; Hugh Ramsay, fr. GK to NFD 7 Mar.1817; fr. GK to NFD 16 June 1818. [E504.15.104/107/111/115/120]

VENUS OF THOMASTON, Colman Sanders, fr. GK to NY 8 June 1818. [E504.15.120]

VERNON OF GLASGOW, John Brown, fr. GK to VA in Feb. 1744, fr. Port Glasgow and GK to VA in Oct. 1744, fr. GK to VA in Apr. 1745; fr. Glasgow to VA in 1745, captured by the French and taken to Brest. [E504.15.1/2; E504.28.1] [SM#8.249]

VICTORY OF GREENOCK, Robert Orr, fr GK to St Augustine May 1779. [E504.15.31]

VINE OF PETERHEAD, fr. Thurso *with 82 passengers* bound for Pictou, NS, on 12 June 1816. [IC,28.6.1816]

VIRGINIA, Alexander Thomson, fr. GK to VA in Nov. 1764; Alexander Thomson, fr. Port Glasgow to the James River, VA, in Aug. 1773; fr. Port Glasgow to VA in Mar. 1774 [E504.28.22/23] [E504.15.12]

VIRGINIA MERCHANT OF ABERDEEN, (formerly the JOANNA), Alexander Inglis, fr. Aberdeen to VA before Aug. 1711.[AC7/17/352-362]

VIRGINIA MERCHANT, Capt. Lockhart, fr. Dumfries to VA in 1747, captured by the French and taken to Carpoon, NFD. [SM#9.503]

VIRGINIA, Alexander Thomson, fr. Port Glasgow *with passengers* to the James River June 1768. [GC#67]

VIRGINIA OF LONDON, 134 tons, Thomas Crawford, fr. GK to Charleston 17 Nov. 1788; James McCunn, fr. GK to VA 2 June 1791, [E504.15.49/59]

VIRGINIA OF NEW BEDFORD, Moors Rogers, fr. GK to NY 16 Oct.1818 [E504.15.122]

VIRGINIA PACKET OF NEW YORK, 30 tons, William Lowther, fr. GK to NY on 9 May 1788, [E504.15.48]

VITTORIA OF GLASGOW, 222 tons, Hugh Ramsay, fr. GK to NFD 8 March 1814; fr. GK to NFD 26 Sept.1814; John Hutchison, fr. GK to NFD 15 May 1815; fr. GK to NFD 26 Jan.1816; Alexander McGill, fr. GK *with 3 passengers* to NY 22 Apr. 1816; fr. GK *with 2 passengers* to NFD 31 Aug.1816; James Paterson, fr. GK to Boston 1 Sep.1818; fr GK to NFD May 1828.
[E504.15.103/105/108/111/112/113/121/164]

VOLANT OF CHARLESTON, 176 tons, William Hill, fr. GK to Charleston in Jan. 1806. [E504.15.77]

VOLUNTEER, 350 tons, David Munro, fr. the Clyde *with passengers* to Charleston, SC, and Wilmington, NC, 10 Sept. 1795. [GC:18.8.1795]

WALLACE, Hugh Moody, fr. GK via Jamaica to Philadelphia in Aug. 1765, [E504.15.13]

WALLACE OF NEWBURYPORT, 324 tons, Isaac Stone, fr.Gk *with 20 passengers* to Philadelphia 4 July 1815. [E504.15.108]

WALTER OF GREENOCK, 300 tons, William Hastie, fr GK to NY, Halifax, and St Augustine May 1779; fr. GK to NY in Dec. 1779; fr. GK *with passengers* to NY in Nov. 1780; fr. GK to NY on 27 Jan. 1781; John Hamilton, fr. GK to VA 21 Dec. 1790. [E504.15.31/32/33/57][GM#III.352; IV/38]

WARNER OF SALTCOATS, 161 tons, James Steven, fr. GK to Savannah 27 May 1817; Andrew Low, fr. GK to NFD 17 Apr.1818; fr. GK to NFD 19 Apr.1819. [E504.15.116/120/124]

WARRINGTON OF BOSTON, 300 tons, Thomas Hinkley, fr. GK to Savannahh, in Feb. 1806. [E504.15.77]

WARRIOR, Alexander McVicar, arr. NY 16 Mar. 1826 *with passengers* fr. GK. [USNA.M237]

WARRIX, Hugh Wilson, fr. Irvine to MD in Apr. 1774. [E504.18.8]

WARWICK, Andrew McVey, fr. Port Glasgow to the James River, VA, in Oct. 1773; fr. Port Glasgow to VA in Oct. 1774. [E504.28.22/24]

WASHINGTON, Capt. Noyes, fr. Port Glasgow to NY on 2 June 1802. [GkAd#3]

WATERS, a brigantine, Charles Dixon, arr. in Charleston, SC, in Mar. 1772 fr. GK. [SCGaz:17.3.1772]

WATSON OF PORTSMOUTH, USA, 206 tons, H. Tibbets, fr. GK *with 25 passengers* to NY 30 March 1816. [E504.15.111]

WELCOME, a snow, Alexander Leith, arr. in Charleston, SC, in June 1745 fr. Glasgow. [SCGaz#586]

WELLINGTON OF CHEPSTOW, 157 tons, John Farish, fr. GK to Miramachi 14 Apr.1817. [E504.15.116]

WHYDAH OF GREENOCK, 260 tons, Robert Balfour, fr. GK to Savannah, GA, in Nov. 1802; wrecked off SC on 6 Jan. 1803. [GkAd#89][ChCr#12]

WILKINSON OF WHITEHAVEN, 217 tons, Joseph Patterson, fr. GK to Halifax and St John 18 Aug.1815. [E504.15.109]

WILLIAM OF IRVINE, 100 tons, John McLean, fr. GK to VA in Oct. 1750; fr. GK to VA in Mar. 1754 [E504.15.5/6]

WILLIAM, Capt. McLeish, fr. VA to the Clyde, captured by the French and taken to Bayonne in 1760. [SM#22.610]

WILLIAM OF GLASGOW, William Noble, fr. GK to Philadelphia in Apr. 1759; fr. GK to SC in Jan. 1761; arr. in Charleston, SC, in Apr. 1761 fr. Glasgow; John Cathcart, fr. GK to VA in Sept. 1762; fr. GK to VA in June 1763; arr. in Charleston on 1 Feb. 1765 fr. Glasgow; fr. GK to VA in Feb. 1766; fr. GK to VA in Oct. 1766; James Cuthbert, fr. GK to NC in Aug. 1770. [GJ#922] [E504.15.10/11/13/14/18] [SCGaz#1394/1569]

WILLIAM, John Cathcart, fr. GK to SC in Nov. 1764, arr. in Charleston in Jan. 1765. [E504.15.12][SCGaz.2.2.1765]

WILLIAM OF NEW YORK, brigantine, John Waddell, fr Orkney to NY 22 Nov.1764. [E504.26.4]

WILLIAMS, William Fulton, fr. GK to VA in Mar. 1766. [E504.15.13]

WILLIAM OF PORT GLASGOW, to Boston in 1769.
[CM#7257]

WILLIAM, Capt. Smith, fr. the Clyde to NFD on 10 July 1780.
[GM#III.222]

WILLIAM, Capt. Leggat, fr. the Clyde to MD in Dec. 1791.
[GCr#48]

WILLIAM OF GREENOCK, 160 tons, George Harrison, fr. GK
to NFD in Oct. 1805. [E504.15.75]

WILLIAM OF ABERDEEN, 172 tons, James Laird, fr. Aberdeen
with 6 passengers to Halifax, NS, 20 Mar. 1816. [E504.1.26]

WILLIAM OF GLASGOW, 213 tons, David Wallace, fr. GK
with 1 passenger for NO on 17 Jan.1817. [E504.15.115]

WILLIAM OF NEWPORT, 266 tons, John Burroughs, fr. GK
with 9 passengers to NY 1 May 1817. [E504.15.116]

WILLIAM OF ST ANDREWS, NB, 328 tons, Thomas Simpson,
fr. GK to St Andrews, NB., 2 July 1817. [E504.15.116]

WILLIAM OF CHARLESTON, 238 tons, E. Purrinton, fr. GK to
Charleston 22 July 1819. [E504.15.125]

WILLIAM OF ABERDEEN, 172 tons, James Laird, fr Aberdeen
to Pictou 7 May 1821. [E504.1.29]

WILLIAM OF NEW YORK, 238 tons, Ezekial Parinton, fr. GK
with 25 passengers to NY 29 Aug.1817; Cap. Noyes, fr GK to
NY 20 Dec.1821. [E504.15.117/138]

WILLIAM, Charles W. Noyes, arr. NY 18 Mar. 1828 *with
passengers* fr. GK. [USNA.M237]

WILLIAM AND EZRA OF RICHMOND, R.Luck, fr Leith to
Richmond 15 Sep.1820. [E504.22.91]

WILLIAM AND JAMES OF MARYPORT, 170 tons, Joseph
Carr, fr. GK *with 6 passengers* to Montreal 18 Apr. 1815.
[E504.15.108]

WILLIAM AND JOAN OF BELFAST, [renamed the St
Lennard], David Hepburn, fr. GK via Dublin *with passengers
and servants including 2 fr. Edinburgh* to Accomack, VA,
and return to the Clyde in Aug. 1679. [RD3.48.513]

WILLIAM AND JOHN OF GLASGOW, fr. the Clyde to VA
before 1733. [AC9.1248]

WILLIAM AND MARGARET, 300 tons, Jonathan Reynolds, fr.
Glasgow *with passengers* to NY on 11 Mar. 1802. [GkAd#6]

WILLIAM AND MARY, a brig, Capt. Dodd, fr. Port Glasgow *with passengers* to the Potomac River, VA and MD on 4 June 1786. [GM#IX.435.143/182]

WILLIAM FELL OF WORKINGTON, 256 tons, John Boan, fr. GK *with 221 passengers* to Cape Breton and Pictou 5 May 1817. [E504.15.116]

WILLIAM WILBERFORCE OF CUMBERLAND, NOVA SCOTIA, 167 tons, Thomas Balfour, fr. GK to Halifax 26 Aug.1817. [E504.15.117]

WILMINGTON, James Harvie (later William Alexander), fr. GK *"passengers - wanted house and ship carpenters, blockmakers, blacksmiths, coopers, bricklayers and tailors willing to indent will meet with good encouragement."* to Charleston, SC, and Wilmington, NC, 25 June 1784; Sylvester Child, fr. the Clyde to Wilmington on 25 July 1789, arr. at Port Brunswick, NC, on 28 Sept. 1789. [CM:24.4.1784; 5.6.1784] [GM#XII.605.246][E504.15.39][NCSA.S8.112]

WILSON OF GLASGOW, James Robertson, fr. GK to VA in May 1760; John Heastie, fr. Port Glasgow to Port South Potomac, VA, in Sept. 1773; fr. GK to Halifax in Aug. 1756; John Heastie, fr Port Glasgow to Halifax Aug.1776; John Johnston, fr. GK to Halifax in June 1777 [E504.15.9/23/26/27; E504.28.22/26]

WILSON, fr GK to St Andrews, NBr, Apr.1828. [E504.15.164]

WINFIELD, Capt. Allgood, fr. the Clyde to NC in 1764. [GJ:15.3.1764]

WISCASSET, a US ship, Capt. Holbrook, fr. GK *with passengers* to Boston or the Sheepscut River in Mar. 1793. [GCr#239]

WOLF, Alexander Auld, fr. GK to Boston in Oct. 1760 [E504.15.10]

WOLFE OF BOSTON, a brigantine, William Hayes, fr Orkney to Boston 3 Sept.1762; fr Orkney to Boston 8 Aug.1763, arr. in Boston on 21 Oct. 1763 *with 1 passenger* fr. Kirkwall, Orkney; Capt. Richard Hambleton, fr. Orkney to Boston, arr. there on 29 Dec. 1765 *with 1 passenger;* John Bryant, fr. Orkney to Boston in July 1768. [PAB][E504.26.3/4/5]

WOODS OF IRVINE, John McKelvie, fr. GK to NFD 26 Aug.1818. [E504.15.122]

WOOLWICH, a schooner, D. G. Scott, arr. in Boston *with passengers* fr. Scotland in 1820. [pa]

XENOPHON OF NEW YORK, 369 tons, B. Lord, fr. GK *with 40 passengers* to NY 29 June 1815. [E504.15.108]

YAMACRAW OF NEW YORK, 243 tons, Andrew Bates, fr GK to NY 13 feb.1821, arr. NY 10 May 1821 *with passengers* fr. GK. [E504.15.135] [USNA.M237]

YORK OF NEW YORK, William Mercer, fr Orkney to NY 9 Aug.1757; P.Berton, fr Orkney to NY 1 Sep.1761;fr orkney to NY 17 Aug.1762; fr Orkney to NY; 22 Sep.1763. [E504.26.3/4]

YORKSHIRE GRAY OF NEW YORK, Joseph Morris, fr Orkney to NY 26 Sep.1757. [E504.26.3]

YOUNG, a 75 ton brig, Capt. Wyllie, arr. in NC fr. the Clyde in 1786; John Miller, arr. at Beaufort, NC, on 2 Feb. 1787 fr. Glasgow; Capt. Maxwell fr. the Clyde to NC 9 Sept. 1791. [GM:6.12.1786][GCr#5] [NCSA/S8/112]

YOUNG MOWAT OF QUEBEC, Stephen Tuck, fr GK to Quebec 11 Mar.1820. [E504.15.128]

YTHAN OF ABERDEEN, 264 tons, A. Craigie, fr. Aberdeen *with 17 passengers* to Miramachi, NB, 21 Mar. 1816; fr. Aberdeen *with 6 passengers* to Miramachi, 26 Feb. 1817. [E504.1.26]

ZAMOA, F. Johnson, arr. NY 5 Nov. 1823 *with passengers* fr. GK. [USNA.M237]

..........., Capt. Thompson, arr. in Patowmack, MD, in Nov. 1759 fr. Glasgow. [MdGaz#758]

1759: 134, 135, 136, 138,
139, 146, 148,
154, 159, 164,
167
1760: 3, 11, 14, 15, 16,
17, 20, 24, 26,
27, 31, 32, 42,
45, 54, 56, 57,
58, 61, 63, 76,
78, 79, 86, 89,
94, 104, 107,
116, 117, 118,
123, 127, 128,
129, 133, 134,
135, 142, 143,
146, 150, 164,
166
1761: 7, 11, 14, 16, 19,
20, 21, 26, 27,
31, 32, 35, 41,
44, 48, 52, 54,
56, 61, 63, 66,
72, 86, 87, 89,
94, 96, 100,
104, 112, 117,
118, 121, 123,
129, 134, 136,
138, 142, 150,
153, 157, 161,
164, 167
1762: 1, 5, 9, 15, 16, 17,
19, 20, 26, 27,
29, 30, 31, 32,
40, 41, 42, 44,
46, 51, 53, 54,
63, 66, 69, 86,
91, 99, 103, 112,
113, 117, 118,
123, 129, 136,
139, 142, 144,
146, 147, 148,
150, 164, 166,
167
1763: 5, 12, 16, 19, 20,
21, 22, 25, 26,
31, 33, 34, 42,
43, 44, 46, 51,
52, 53, 54, 56,
60, 61, 63, 66,
82, 86, 88, 89,
92, 95, 99, 100,
102, 113, 116,
118, 123, 128,
129, 134, 135,
140, 142, 147,
150, 153, 157,
159, 160, 164,
166, 167
1764: 4, 9, 11, 14, 16, 17,
19, 21, 22, 30,
41, 42, 43, 44,
46, 50, 51, 52,
53, 56, 58, 61,

1764: 61, 63, 64,69,
76, 86, 88,
93, 96, 97,
99, 102, 107,
114, 121,
128, 133, 134
135, 142, 162,
164, 166
1765: 5, 11, 14, 16, 25,
26, 30, 31, 34,
44, 50, 51, 53,
56, 60, 63, 67,
69, 75, 82, 84,
86, 96, 97, 98,
99, 102, 107,
108, 114, 116,
117, 118, 121,
129, 133, 136,
141, 142, 147,
149, 163, 164,
166
1766: 19, 25, 26, 30, 31,
32, 44, 50, 54,
56, 63, 64, 78,
81, 82, 86, 88,
91, 94, 97, 99,
101, 102, 107,
111, 117, 118,
121, 122, 126,
129, 134, 135,
136, 137, 141,
153, 156, 164
1767: 5, 6, 13, 14, 16,
19, 20, 23, 25,
26, 31, 32, 37,
42, 44, 50, 51,
52, 56, 63, 65,
66, 81, 86, 91,
94, 97, 98, 99,
100, 102, 103,
108, 111, 112,
118, 119, 121,
126, 129, 130,
134, 135, 136,
139, 148, 153,
159
1768: 5, 12, 13, 15, 17,
19, 21, 23, 26,
31, 42, 43, 44,
45, 50, 51, 56,
61, 63, 65, 70,
71, 74, 76, 81,
82, 84, 86, 87,
88, 93, 94, 96,
97, 98, 99, 100,
102, 114, 118,
119, 121, 122,
126, 130, 134,
135, 136, 141,
152, 155, 163,
166
1769: 6, 13, 14, 18, 19,
23, 26, 29, 31,

1769: 33, 34, 39, 40, 43,
44, 45, 48, 50,
51, 52, 55, 61,
63, 64, 65, 71,
73, 75, 81, 82,
84, 86, 88, 92,
93, 94, 96, 97,
99, 103, 104, 108,
111, 112, 116, 119,
126, 128, 130, 131,
135, 136, 141, 147,
148, 156, 165
1770: 6, 11, 12, 13, 14, 15,
22, 25, 26, 29, 31,
33, 34, 45, 47, 48,
50, 52, 55, 61, 63,
64, 65, 68, 74, 81,
86, 88, 92, 93, 95,
96, 97, 102, 103,
114, 121, 122, 126,
127, 129, 130, 145,
146, 150, 151, 156,
164
1771: 6, 12, 19, 26, 29, 31,
34, 35, 37, 39, 41,
44, 45, 46, 47, 48,
50, 51, 55, 61, 62,
63, 64, 65, 68, 70,
73, 75, 79, 81, 82,
84, 86, 88, 93, 94,
96, 97, 102, 103,
114, 121, 122, 126,
130, 136, 138, 141,
144, 145, 146, 147,
151, 157, 158
1772: 1, 3, 4, 7, 9, 13, 14,
15, 20, 21, 22, 23,
26, 32, 37, 43, 44,
46, 51, 52, 55, 58,
61, 63, 64, 65, 73,
74, 81, 82, 86, 88,
93, 96, 97, 103,
113, 114, 122, 123,
125, 126, 127, 128,
130, 131, 133, 134,
136, 142, 146, 151,
162, 164
1773: 1, 4, 6. 7. 9, 11, 15,
19, 20, 21, 22, 23,
26, 31, 32, 35, 36,
37, 40, 41, 42, 44,
49, 51, 55, 56, 58,
62, 64, 65, 68, 69,
70, 71, 76, 81, 82,
83, 86, 88, 89, 91,
93, 95, 96, 97, 102,
103, 105, 111, 112,
113, 114, 117, 121,
123, 125, 127, 128,
129, 130, 131, 132,
134, 138, 140, 141,
146, 147, 152, 156,
160, 162, 164, 166

170

1774: 2, 3, 6, 9, 14, 15,
17, 19, 21, 22,
23, 26, 29, 31,
34, 35, 36, 37,
39, 40, 41, 42,
44, 46, 49, 51,
56, 58, 62, 64,
65, 67, 68, 69,
70, 73, 76, 80,
81, 84, 85, 86,
87, 88, 89, 91,
93, 96, 97, 98,
103, 104, 105,
112, 114, 116,
121, 122, 125,
127, 128, 130,
131, 132, 134,
138, 140, 141,
142, 146, 147,
150, 151, 155,
156, 158, 160
1775: 2, 3, 14, 15, 17,
18, 34, 36, 37,
39, 42, 44, 51,
57, 61, 62, 64,
65, 66, 67, 73,
89, 93, 95, 96,
99, 114, 116,
130, 131, 132,
138, 140, 160
1776: 15, 19, 23, 26, 34,
43, 46, 56, 61,
62, 67, 69, 76,
85, 87, 88, 89,
93, 97, 98, 104,
114, 116, 121,
122, 138, 150
1777: 9, 11, 16, 17, 25,
26, 31, 32, 34,
38, 49, 51, 55,
61, 62, 73, 85,
89, 94, 95, 97,
98, 100, 101,
113, 121, 126,
128, 130, 131,
133, 142, 147,
151, 156, 160,
166
1778: 2, 4, 17, 19, 25,
32, 3, 49, 51,
66, 69, 79, 83,
92, 94, 96, 98,
101, 103, 122,
123, 126, 127,
128, 131, 132,
143, 147, 151,
157, 162
1779: 2, 13, 15, 17, 19,
25, 30, 32, 34,
35, 37, 38, 44,
45, 47, 50, 53,
70, 73, 75, 80,
85, 93, 94, 95,

1779: 98, 107, 112, 114,
118, 119, 121,
122, 126, 127,
130, 141, 147,
151, 160, 162,
163
1780: 1, 2,3, 4, 6, 9, 11,
14, 17, 31, 32,
33, 38, 54, 56,
60, 64, 70, 73,
75, 80, 83, 87,
95, 98, 99, 100,
102, 105, 107,
114, 119, 124,
128, 129, 131,
133, 138, 141,
143, 145, 154,
157, 160, 162,
163, 165
1781: 1, 2, 3, 4, 12, 13,
17, 31, 36, 38,
43, 53, 55, 63,
70, 72, 73, 80,
83, 85, 86, 87,
88, 92, 98, 99,
104, 108, 129,
130, 131, 134,
138, 141, 144,
145, 154, 159,
163
1782: 3, 9, 11, 15, 23,
25, 40, 53, 62,
104, 118, 129,
141, 145, 146,
155
1783: 9, 10, 15, 17, 25,
40, 66, 69, 79,
83, 93, 101, 109,
110, 112, 124,
125, 129, 131,
133, 134, 137,
151, 154
1784: 1, 6, 7, 9, 15, 17,
19, 20, 21, 32,
34, 40, 47, 62,
66, 73, 76, 79,
82, 83, 84, 85,
86, 87, 89, 93,
96, 101, 104,
108, 109, 114,
118, 119, 122,
124, 133, 139,
142, 147, 150,
151, 152, 153,
154, 155, 156,
166
1785: 1, 4, 6, 9, 18, 20,
27, 43, 45, 47,
57, 61, 62, 71,
76, 78, 83, 84,
89, 93, 94, 97,
98, 99, 101, 102,
104, 105, 108,

1785: 109, 116, 119, 120,
121, 124, 130
131, 132, 133,
138, 139, 143,
147, 151, 154,
156
1786: 3, 4, 7, 9, 16, 17, 18,
20, 21, 22, 25, 27,
29, 34, 35, 36, 39,
40, 47, 49, 56, 58,
63, 70, 73, 75, 76,
80, 82, 84, 85, 86,
89, 90, 93, 98,
101, 105, 108, 109,
110, 111, 112, 114,
119, 122, 123, 124,
125, 127, 130, 132,
145, 147, 148, 151,
152, 154, 155, 158,
166, 167
1787: 1, 3, 4, 7, 8, 9, 14, 17,
20, 24, 29, 32, 35,
36, 37, 39, 40, 42,
43, 49, 51, 56, 57,
58, 62, 63, 75, 76,
78, 80, 82, 86, 87,
88, 90, 99, 105,
108, 110, 119, 121,
122, 130, 131, 132,
134, 145, 146, 148,
160, 162
1788: 3, 8, 19, 24, 29, 32,
36, 40, 42, 43, 51,
54, 55, 56, 58, 63,
68, 75, 76, 78, 84,
86, 88, 89, 91, 93,
95, 100, 101, 105,
108, 119, 122, 130,
131, 138, 139, 145,
147, 148, 151, 162,
163
1789: 3, 7, 8, 9, 17, 20, 24,
25, 29, 32, 34, 36,
38, 39, 47, 49, 51,
52, 54, 55, 57, 58,
59, 63, 68, 75, 76,
77, 79, 80, 82, 84,
85, 86, 89, 90, 100,
101, 104, 108, 110,
114, 119, 120, 122,
130, 138, 139, 145,
151, 158, 162
1790: 4, 15, 18, 23, 24, 32,
37, 52, 55, 59, 66,
78, 82, 89, 101,
104, 105, 108, 109,
119, 122, 128, 130,
138, 148, 155, 159,
163
1791: 1, 3, 4, 6, 8, 10, 12,
17, 23, 26, 30, 37,
39, 42, 51, 52, 55,
56, 58, 59, 63, 67,

171

172

1820: 110, 115, 116, 124,
126, 128, 132,
133, 135, 137,
140, 141, 143,
146, 147, 149,
150, 151, 152,
154, 156, 157,
160, 161, 165,
166, 167
1821: 4, 5, 6, 10, 13, 15,
20, 28, 34, 35,
36, 38, 40, 42,
46, 47, 48, 49,
50, 52, 60, 67,
71, 72, 74, 76,
77, 83, 85, 90,
93, 94, 100,
101, 105, 107,
111, 115, 116,
120, 126, 127,
133, 135, 137,
140, 141, 143,
144, 146, 153,
154, 156, 157,
158, 159, 160,
161, 165, 167
1822: 2, 8, 10, 12, 13,
28, 32, 34, 35,
36, 40, 46, 50,
52, 54, 60, 64,
65, 67, 71, 72,
77, 79, 90, 91,
93, 101, 103,
105, 106, 115,
117, 120, 123,
133, 137, 138,
140, 141, 143,
144, 145, 147,
149, 151, 157,
158, 159, 161
1823: 10, 12, 16, 24, 28,
36, 37, 40, 45,
50, 53, 57, 60,
69, 71, 72, 76,
77, 81, 90, 106,
125, 153, 159,
167
1824: 28, 50, 60, 68, 71,
72, 91, 92, 106,
111, 113, 115,
124, 133, 139,
140, 143, 144,
159, 161
1825: 10, 28, 31, 47, 52,
60, 71, 73, 81,
99, 124, 148,
154
1826: 21, 26, 28, 31, 32,
40, 45, 54, 58,
59, 60, 72, 79,
81, 109, 159, 164
1827: 1, 12, 24, 26, 28, 36,
39, 41, 49, 50, 53

1827: 60, 62, 76, 79, 81,
85, 92, 93, 101,
115, 116, 120,
126, 142, 144,
148, 153,158,
159
1829: 4, 12, 25, 40, 85,
92, 103, 143

173